LEGENDARY LOCALS

OF

LANSING

ILLINOIS

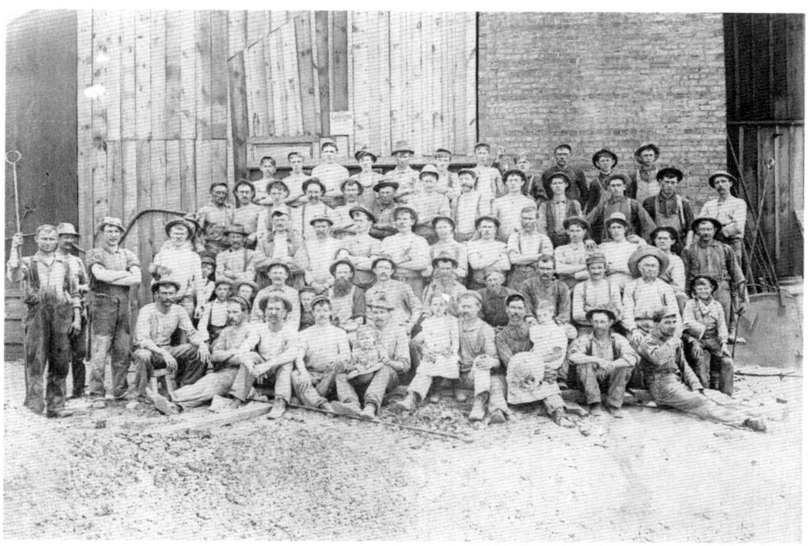

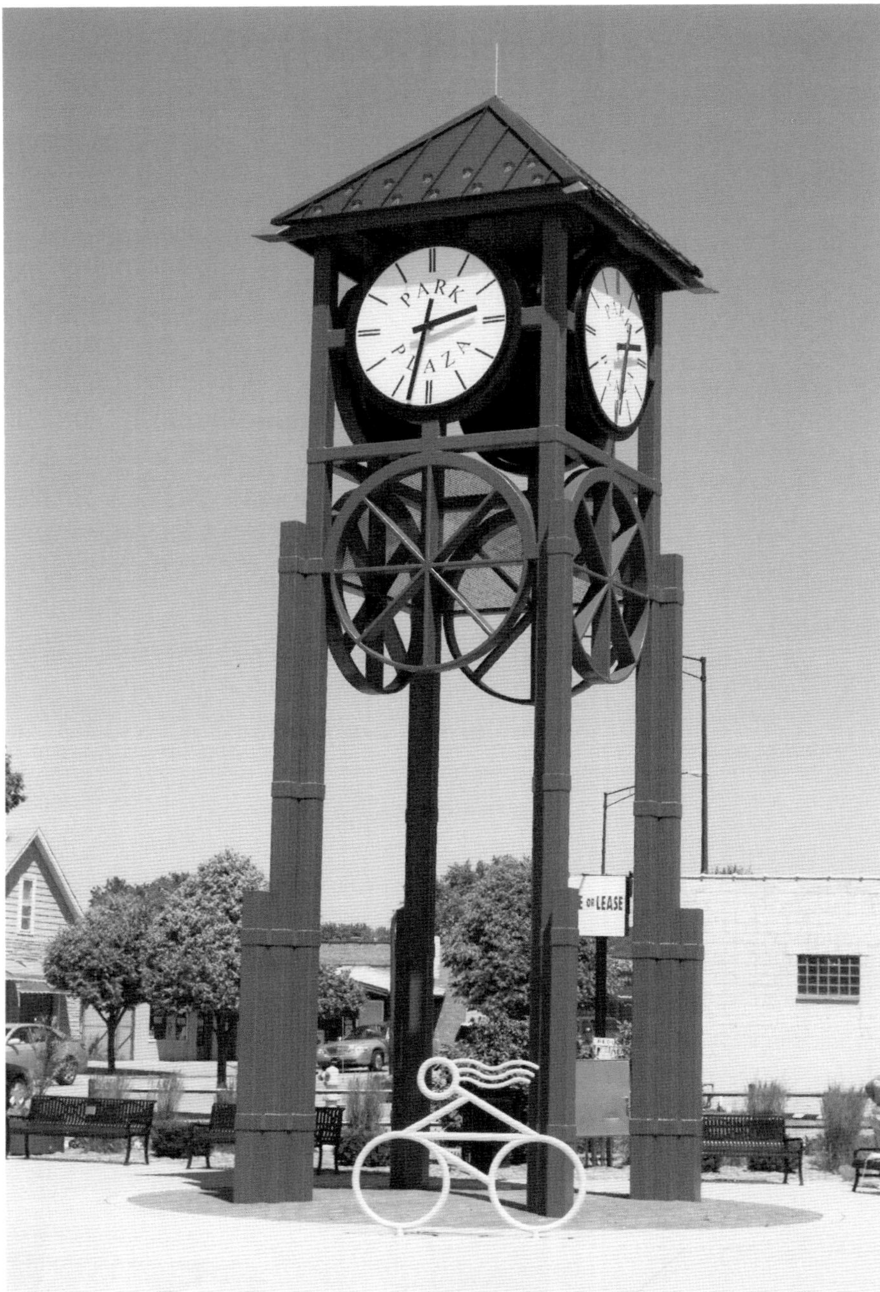

Park Plaza

Park Plaza has become the central focus of the downtown area in recent years. With the addition of the clock tower (pictured) and benches on Ridge Road at Grant Street, it has become a gathering place for locals during summer cruise nights, the farmers market, and the Christmas tree lighting. (Author's collection.)

Page 1: See page 70 for more information.

LEGENDARY LOCALS

OF

LANSING

ILLINOIS

CARRIE STEINWEG

LEGENDARY LOCALS

ISBN 978-1-4671-0031-1

Legendary Locals is an imprint of Arcadia Publishing
Charleston, South Carolina

Printed in the United States of America

Library of Congress Control Number: 2012936161

For all general information, please contact Arcadia Publishing:
Telephone 843-853-2070
Fax 843-853-0044
E-mail sales@arcadiapublishing.com
For customer service and orders:
Toll-Free 1-888-313-2665

Visit us on the Internet at www.arcadiapublishing.com

Dedication
To Don Olsen, Paul Schultz, and Herb Krumm
for their contagious love and enthusiasm for this wonderful place we call home.

On the Cover: From left to right:
(TOP ROW) Jim Kijewski, teacher and coach (Courtesy of JoAnn Kijewski, see pages 46–47); Paul Schultz, historian (Courtesy of Carol Schultz, see page 98); Patty Eidam, village clerk (Courtesy of Patty Eidam, see page 23); Hal Gronewold, teacher and principal (Courtesy of Eileen Gronewold, see page 49); Don Schultz, business owner (Courtesy of Terri Marsee, see page 92).
(MIDDLE ROW) Philip Martini, Marine (Courtesy of Laura Martini, see pages 16–17); Joyce (Siegfried) Dykhuis, volunteer (Courtesy of Lori Siegfried, see page 102); Alfred Van Steenberg, mayor (Lansing Historical Society Collection, see page 30); Toni DeLaurentis, teacher (Carrie Steinweg, see page 51); Kenneth Novak Jr., police officer (Courtesy of Pat Novak, see pages 14 and 15).
(BOTTOM ROW) August Olsen Jr., US Army (Courtesy of Don Olsen, see pages 10–11); Durward Schuetz, school principal (Courtesy of Durward Schuetz, see page 48); Ruth Hale Canaga, high school history teacher (Lansing Historical Society Collection, see pages 44 and 45), Rear Admiral Ralph Hedges, US Army (Lansing Historical Society Collection, see page 20); Curtis Granderson, Major League Baseball player (Carrie Steinweg, see pages 120–121).

CONTENTS

ACKNOWLEDGMENTS

Members of the Lansing Historical Society, which was founded in 1976, have worked hard throughout the years to preserve the history of three villages that became one (Lansing, Bernice, and Oak Glen). Without the diligence of such eager volunteers, glancing into our village's past would not be so easy. In archiving photographs and artifacts, the past comes to life inside the Lansing Historical Museum. I thank all those who have played a part in preserving Lansing's history for future generations. I am also grateful to individuals, both in town and far away, who were willing to share photographs and memories to make this book possible.

Special thanks go to the following for their insight and assistance: Herb Krumm, Don Olsen, Millie Ogborn, Norm Abbott, Patty Eidam, Chris Mahoney, June Cole, Barb Dust, Debbie Albrecht, and Paul Schultz.

And many thanks to my husband, Paul, and my boys, Brad, Chandler, Carter, Brandon, and Ian, for your love and patience with my writing projects. I hope you will value this collection in the years to come as you recall your days growing up in Lansing.

INTRODUCTION

As the centuries passed, the waters of Lake Michigan that covered present-day Lansing receded to become prairies inhabited by Indian tribes. By the mid-1800s, Cook County was created and townships designated. Lansing's first family, the Hildebrandts, arrived in 1843 to build a log cabin and begin farming.

Early families raised their own food and soon built businesses and homes near Ridge Road. The arrival of the Lansing brothers in 1846 proved a pivotal time for the area. Henry, John, and George Lansing moved to the area from New York, with a fourth brother, Peter, arriving in 1865.

Henry served in the Mexican-American War, settling in California as a miner. He later returned to the area in 1864 and opened the first general store. In 1865, he became Lansing's first postmaster and the community became known by the name of Lansing. His brother John laid out the town plat early that year and died soon after.

Growth in Lansing continued as the railroad expanded and brickmaking became the main industry in town. With men immigrating from as far away as Quebec to become workers in one of the good-paying laborer jobs in the brickyards, the community of Bernice came to be with a rail station built for transporting brick and with homes and boarding houses built to accommodate the employees.

Oak Glen existed in what is now the southwest portions of the village, with its own rail station on the Grand Trunk Railroad. First known as Cummings Corner, after a minister named Kris Cummings settled in the area with the intention of starting a college, the area around Torrence and Indiana Avenues became Oak Glen, with a post office, several businesses, and farms.

In 1893, the three communities combined and were incorporated into Lansing. However, the Oak Glen neighborhood continued to be referred to by that name and a separate post office continued to operate on Torrence Avenue into the 1950s. At the time of the incorporation, Lansing had a population of around 250; today, it is around 30,000.

It was the early families that set us on the road we are on today, pioneering families like the Hildrebrandts, Lansings, Schultzes, Winterhoffs, Eeningenburgs, Krumms, Busacks, and Bocks. They built homes from the ground up and set businesses in motion that would service the community for years, and in some cases, decades to come.

Before the incorporation of those three communities and in the years since, countless individuals have helped shape the direction of the village, and by helping their neighbors and reaching out, each has touched others and left a mark on this place they called home. In the schools, places of worship, and other gathering places, friendships have been made and lives have been changed.

As we moved into the 20th century, families grew, businesses grew, and soon an airport was created and many service organizations and social groups were born. Such groups as the Lansing Lions Club and the Lansing Junior Woman's Club organized service projects. Groups like the American Legion and Veterans of Foreign Wars were formed to bring together those within the community with the common bond of military service. Girl Scout and Boy Scout troops were initiated to offer education, instill values, and create fun and memorable events for local youths. Community bands, baseball teams, and dramatic groups became forms of entertainment and recreation for adults as well as children in the community. Within each group, there were leaders who stood out and who touched others.

That is the purpose of this book, to gather photographs and stories of many of those who had an impact on others, whether it was through leading the village, leading a Girl Scout troop, leading a family business, or leading a group of soldiers in battle or through more subtle methods of influence. No matter what time in its history, our village has grown and progressed and improved because of such people.

As the population boomed after World War II, the landscape of the village, as well as the country, changed. New homes were built to accommodate returning soldiers, and in the years that followed, school enrollment reached its peak. Roller skating and taking in a movie at the Lans Theatre were forms of entertainment. The Lan-Oak Park District was formed, designating Lansing's first park, Lan-Oak, on 30 acres donated by brothers Walter and George Schultz and Gus Bock, with several smaller parks to follow. A community swimming pool opened in 1961, providing summer fun for generations of Lansing residents.

Today, most of the farm fields have disappeared and been built upon. The deep holes where bricks were once produced have been filled in. Much has changed since the days of dirt roads and horse-drawn wagons, when life was in many ways harder and in many ways simpler. But pieces of the locals who made Lansing remain.

CHAPTER ONE

Hometown Heroes

Hundreds of heroes have lived, been educated, and worked in our community with the goal of protecting others. Back in the earliest days, a county constable and town marshal took charge of keeping the peace. The department eventually grew to a large full-time staffed department with K-9 units, a community policing department, drug enforcement officers, a fleet of squads and equipment, and a shooting range. One of those heroes died doing what he most loved. The fire department, which originated 90 years ago as a volunteer department, has evolved into a full-time department operating out of three fire stations with a fire prevention unit, arson investigation unit, dive unit, and four ambulances. The tradition of serving and protecting residents in all emergencies continues. Countless individuals from our village have served their country in the military, some in peacetime and some in times of war. They have left as young boys and girls and returned, altered by their experiences, more wise and confident adults. Several paid the ultimate price for their country, sacrificing their lives as they served. It is they who hold the highest honor, their names inscribed in a marble wall in the Lansing Veterans Memorial at the Lansing Airport. Let their names, their courage, and their sacrifice never be forgotten.

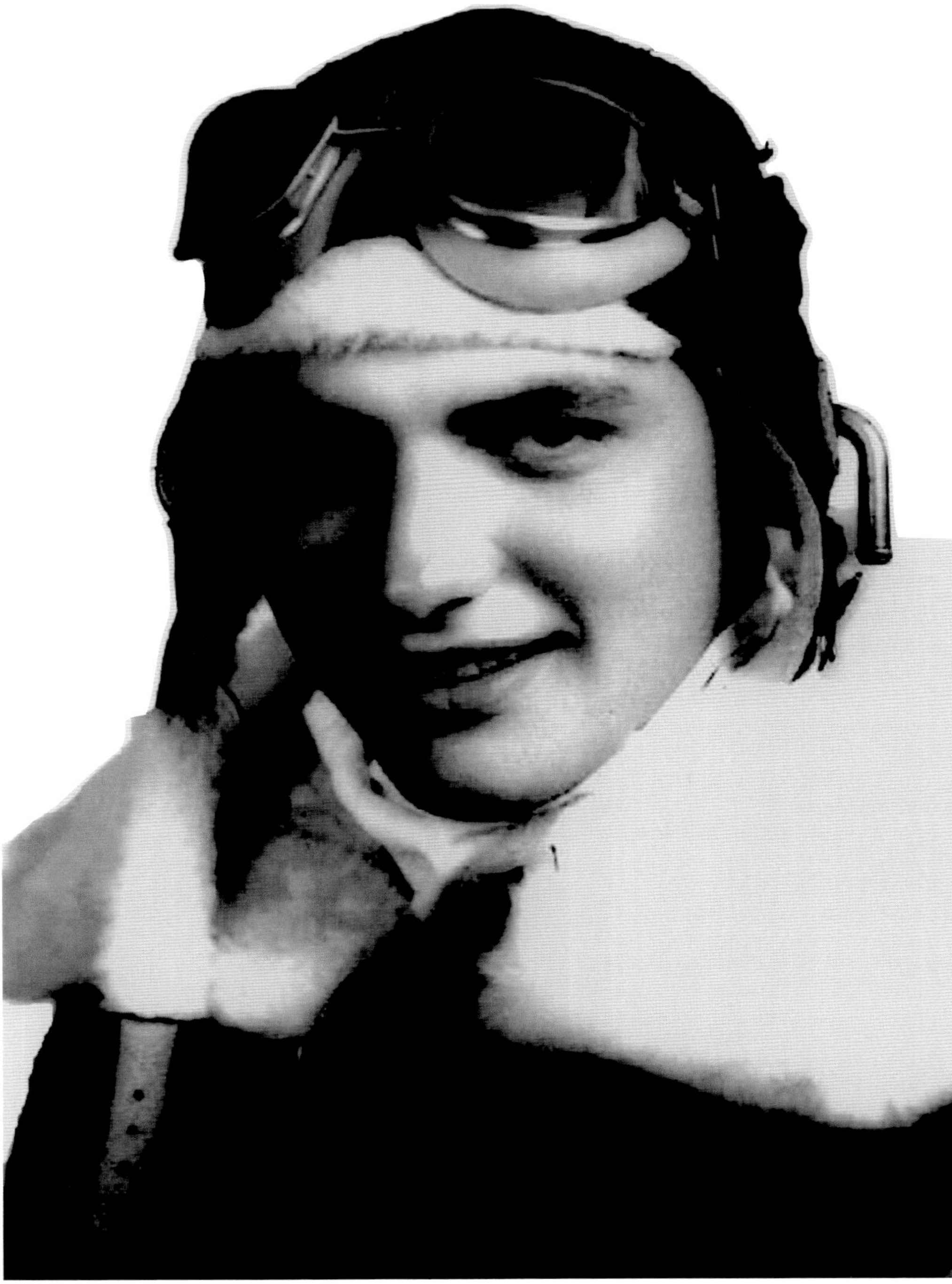

August "Juny" Olsen Jr.

The oldest of seven siblings, August Olsen Jr. (who went by the nickname "Juny") was born on February 5, 1919, and graduated from Trinity Lutheran School in 1932, a year earlier than his classmates. He attended Thornton Fractional High School in Calumet City, earning membership in the National Honor Society and participating in the drama department. After high school, he worked at Hammond Brass Works and met his future wife while bowling at the 20th Century Bowling Alley. In early 1941, he enlisted in the Army, and in June he married Marcella Crist. Juny later transferred to the US Army Air Corps and shortly after, nearly his entire former division was killed in North Africa. Juny enjoyed baseball and was an active member of the church baseball team that played in the Walther League. The below photograph was taken on April 7, 1941, at spring training in El Paso, Texas. Olsen is pictured with pitcher Jerome "Dizzy" Dean, who played the last year of his career that year for the Chicago Cubs. While doing Army training in Texas, Olsen had the opportunity to meet several professional baseball players. After attending radio school, he was part of the 487th Bombardment Group sent to fly over France on June 7, 1944. Of 88 B-24s, only one was shot down, and it was the one Juny was on. He died at the age of 25 and is buried at the Brittany American Cemetery in St. James, France. In 2011, part of the plane was recovered and a memorial service, attended by several of Juny's family, took place on June 9, 2012. (Both, courtesy of Don Olsen.)

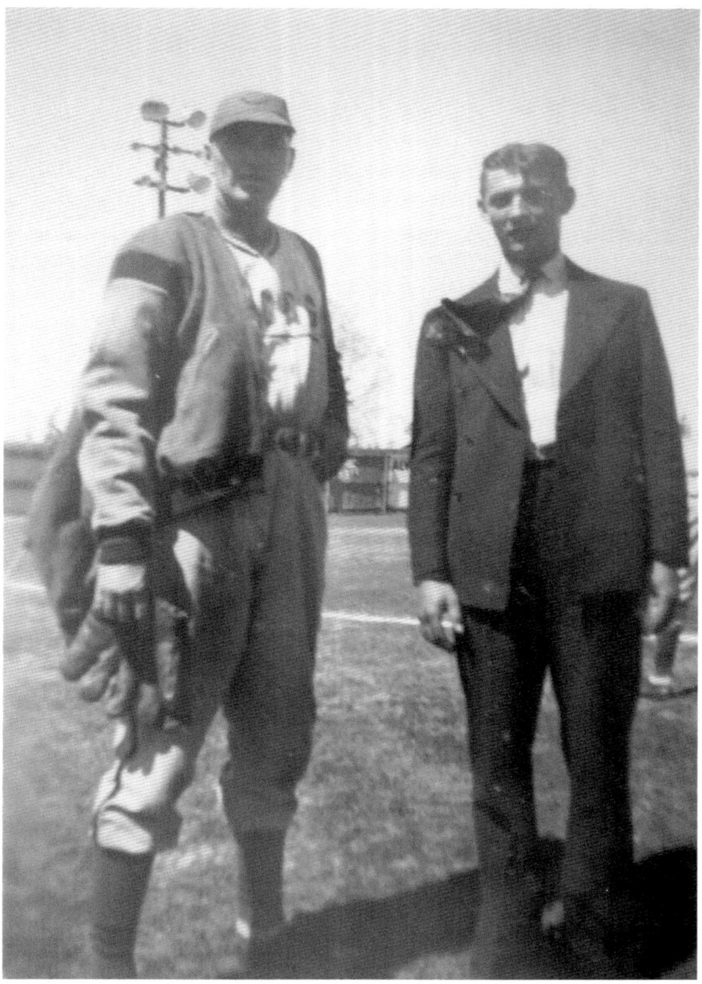

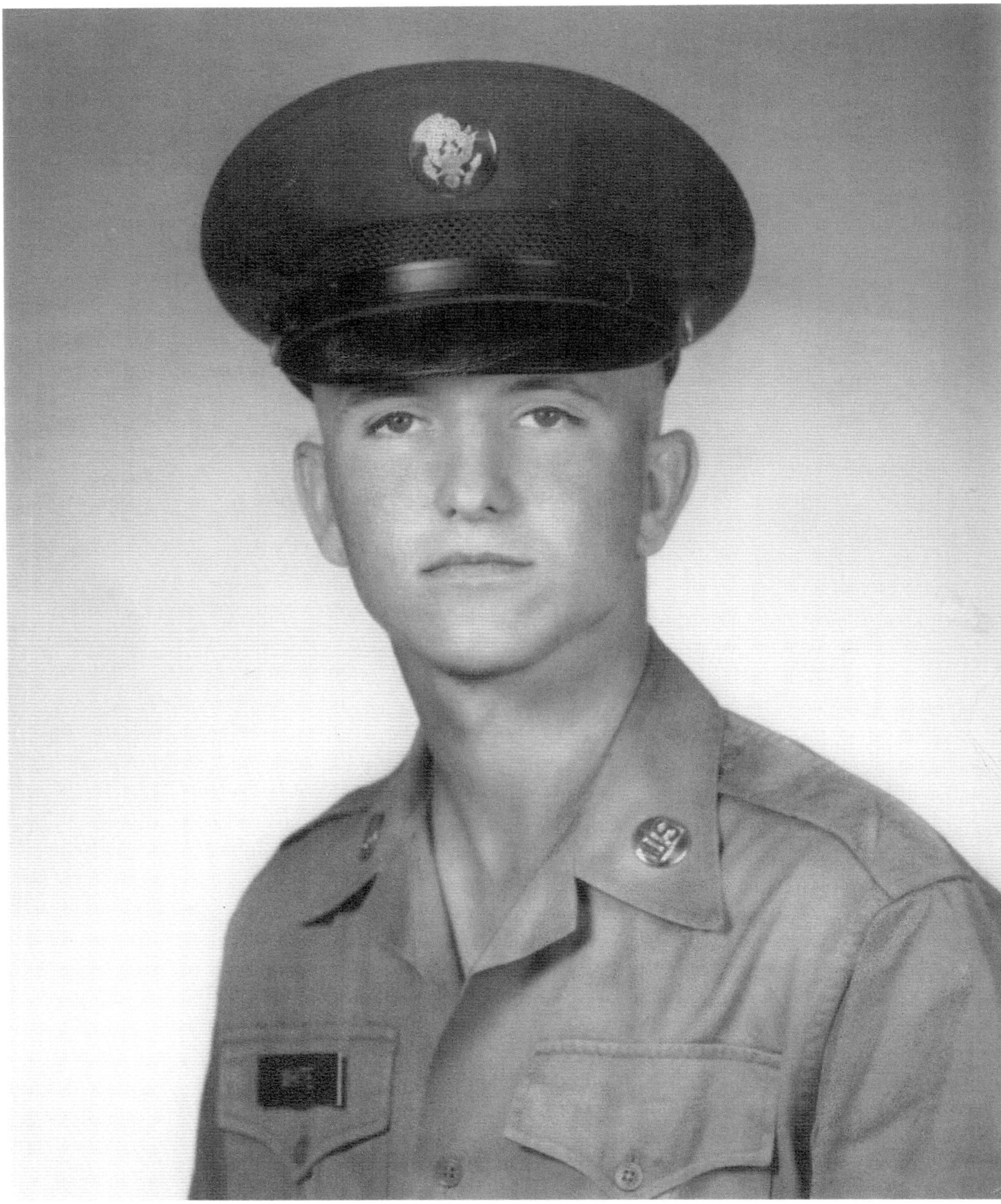

Gene Lewis White

Gene White was born in Hammond, Indiana, on September 13, 1946, to Selma and George White. He had two siblings, Daniel and Gail. After attending Coolidge School and Memorial Junior High School, Gene went to Thornton Fractional South High School, where he received letters in three sports: football, basketball, and track. Following high school, he married his high school sweetheart, Jennie Courtney, and was drafted into the US Army. He served in Vietnam and was killed in action on April 3, 1969. His graduating class from Thornton Fractional South High School donated a plaque in his honor. Each year the name of a "most improved" athlete is added to the plaque. (Courtesy of Selma White.)

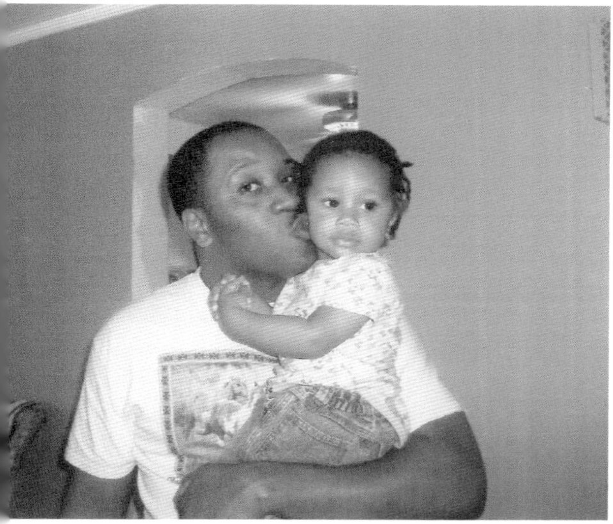

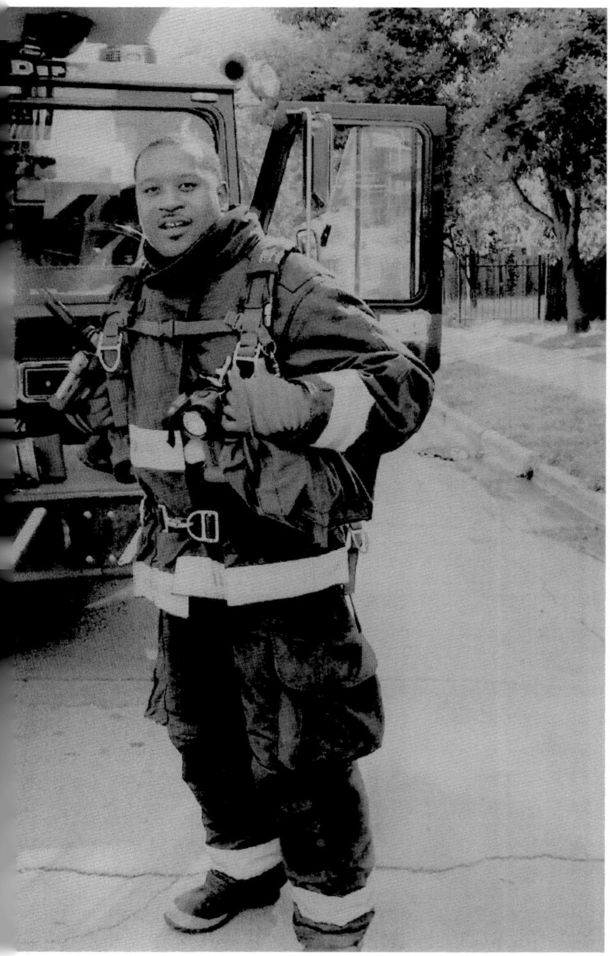

Corey D. Ankum
Firefighter and EMT Corey Ankum first worked with the Chicago Police Department before joining the Chicago Fire Department. A 1994 graduate of Thornton Fractional South High School, Corey enjoyed playing basketball and went on to Kishwaukee College, where he earned an associate's degree in business. He earned a bachelor's degree in business from Kendall College in Evanston. He became the director of Jack and Jill Day Care, where he met Demeka Wade. The two were married in 2008. In November 2008, he graduated from the Chicago Police Academy. He then decided to pursue a career in the fire service and graduated from the Chicago Fire Academy on April 1, 2010. Corey was a sports fanatic who followed the San Antonio Spurs and New England Patriots. He was a proud father of two girls, Demia and Baylee, and a son, Torey. On December 22, 2010, a roof and wall collapse during a fire in a vacant building took the lives of Corey, age 34, and firefighter Edward J. Stringer Sr. and injured 17 other firefighters. Corey's older brother Gerald Glover, also a firefighter, worked at the same firehouse but on a different shift. Corey's wife, Dameka, was the personal secretary of Mayor Richard M. Daley. (Both, courtesy of Demeka Wade Corey.)

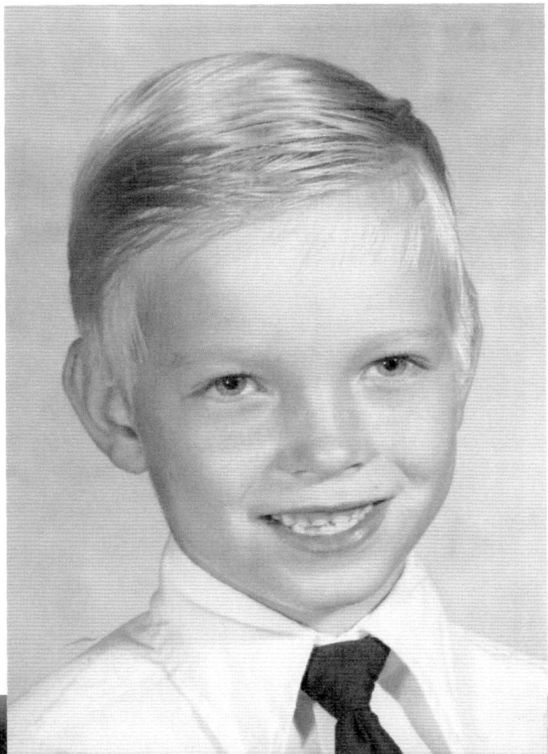

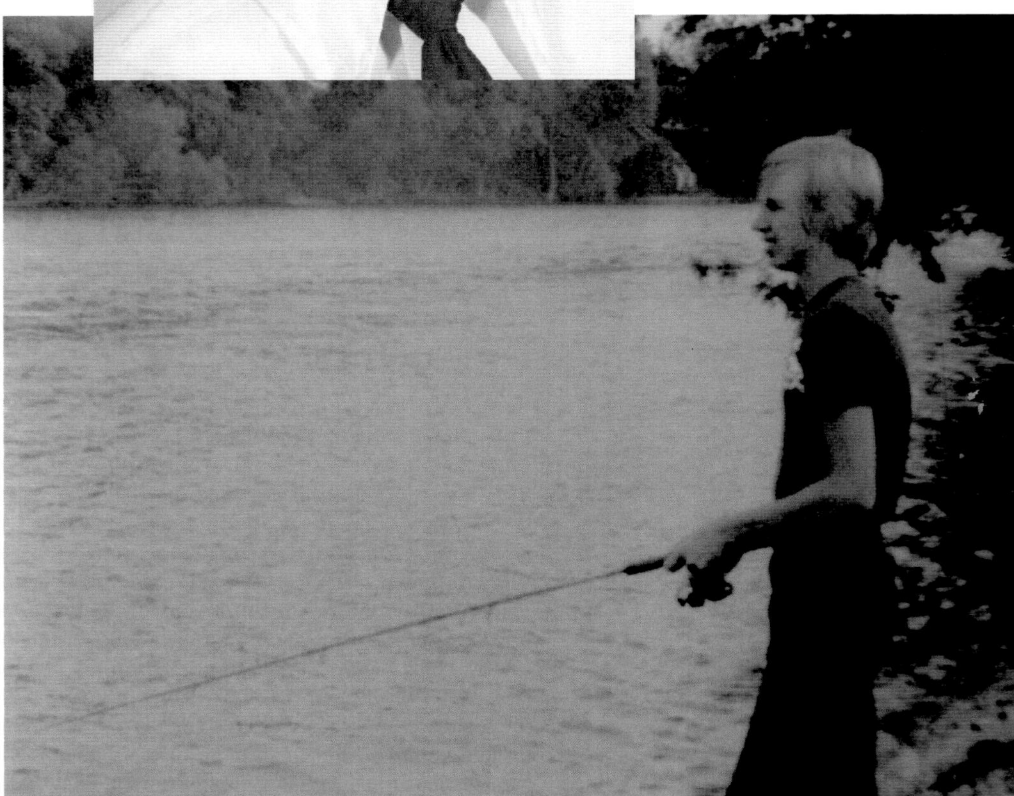

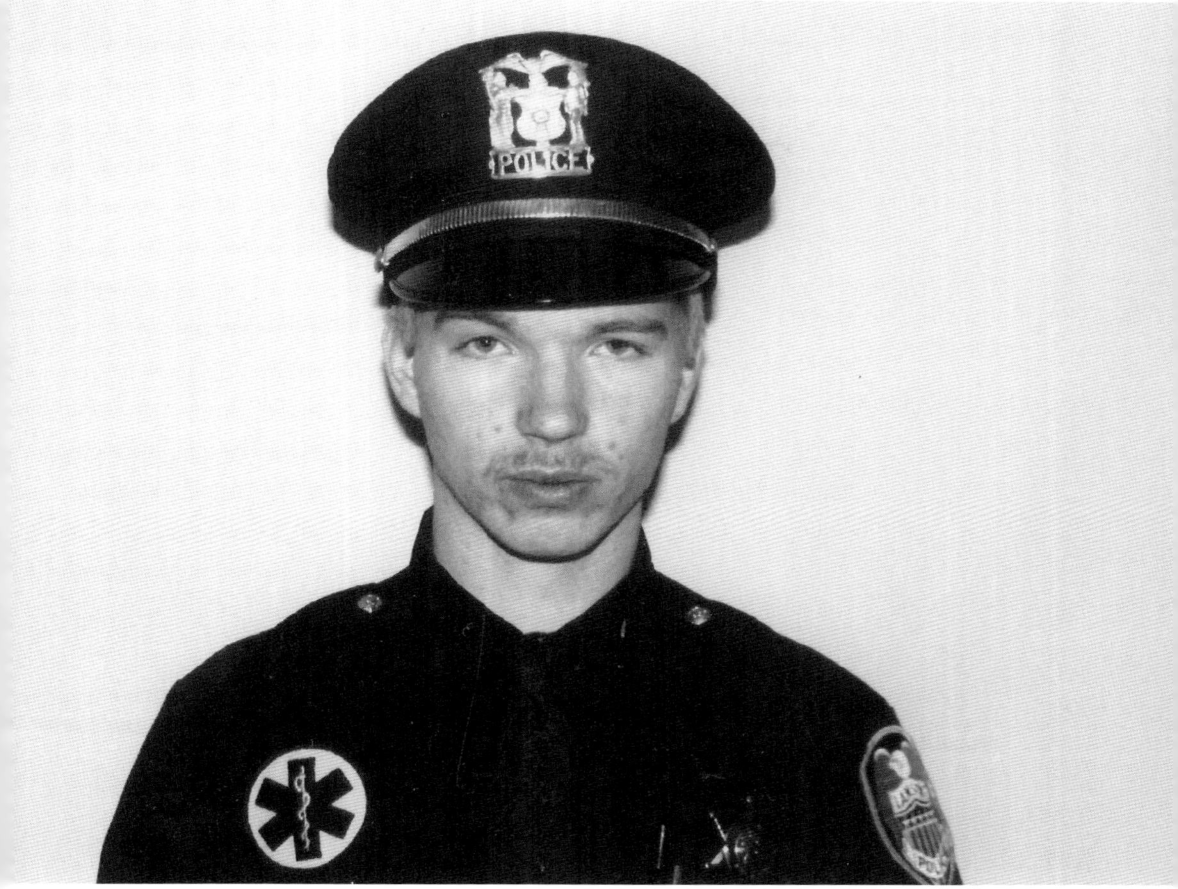

Kenneth R. Novak Jr.

As a young child, Ken Novak was always playing police officer. According to his mother, Pat, he would add siren sounds while riding his bike and stop his peers to give them tickets for speeding. As a teen, he joined the Lansing Cadet Program. He graduated from Thornton Fractional South High School and Thornton Community College (now South Suburban College.) Ken became a part-time police officer and paramedic and a full-time dispatcher. Known for his dedication to the department, he often offered to work holiday shifts so that the officers with children could spend time with their families. Among Ken Novak's interests were fishing, playing guitar, and trains. He enjoyed watching trains and had a large model train set. On April 8, 1992, while stopping to assist a vehicle that appeared to be disabled, Ken was shot and died from his wounds. He was 27 years old. He is the only Lansing police officer to be killed in the line of duty. The street along the police station has been renamed Kenneth R. Novak Jr. Drive. (All, courtesy of Pat Novak.)

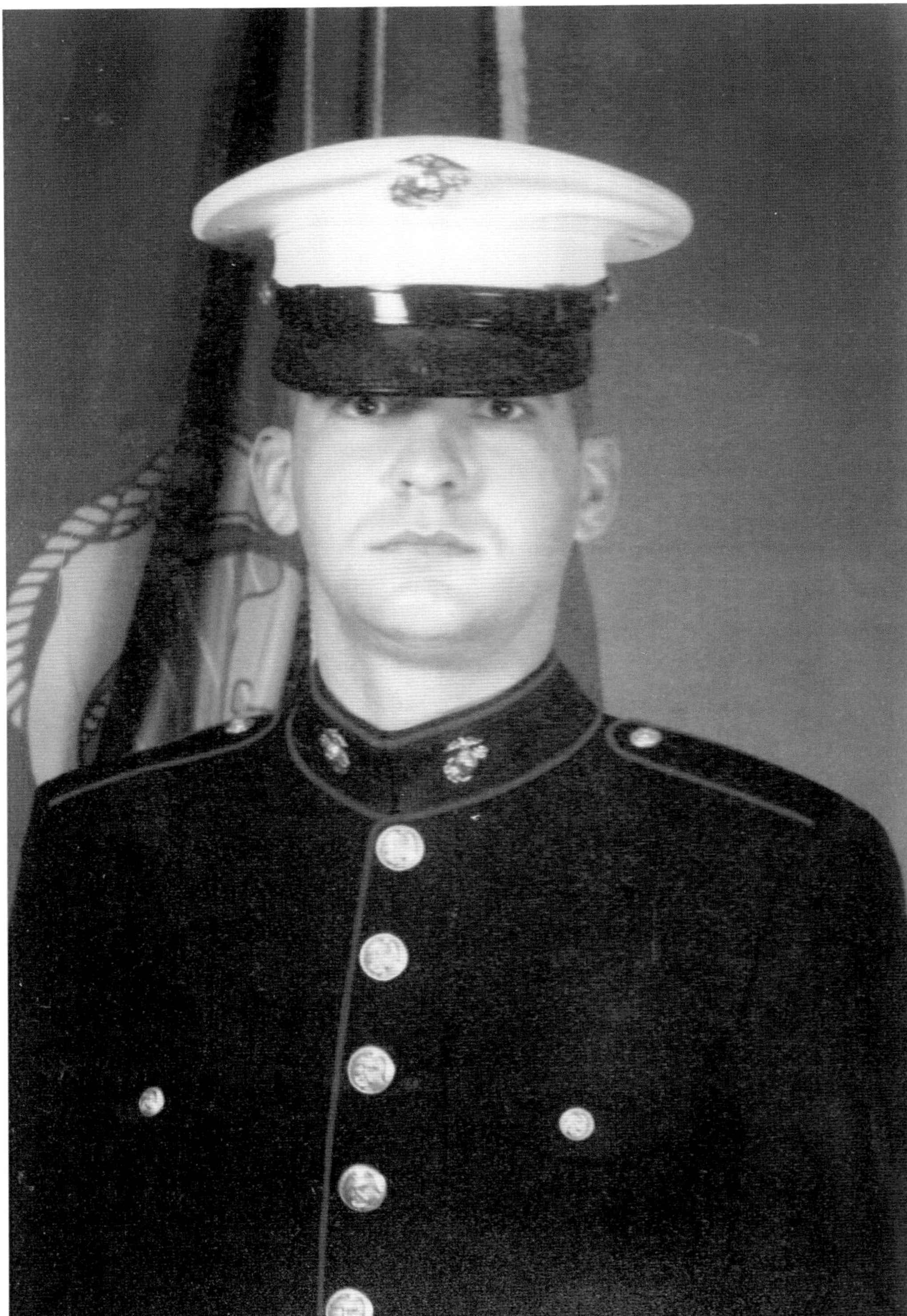

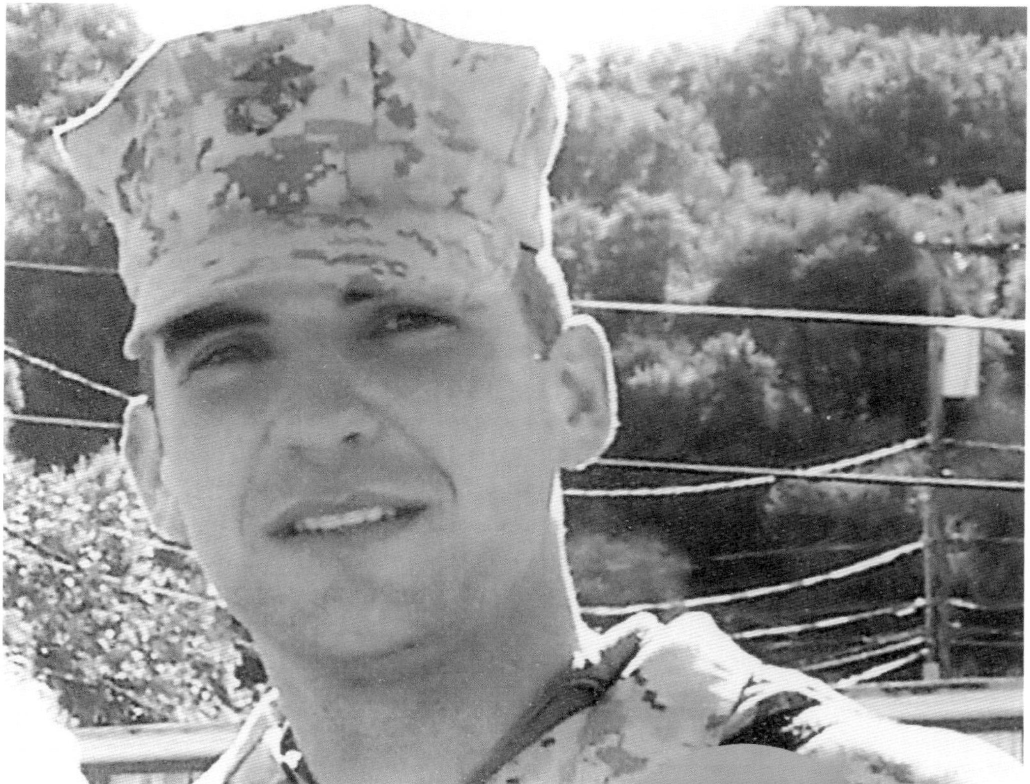

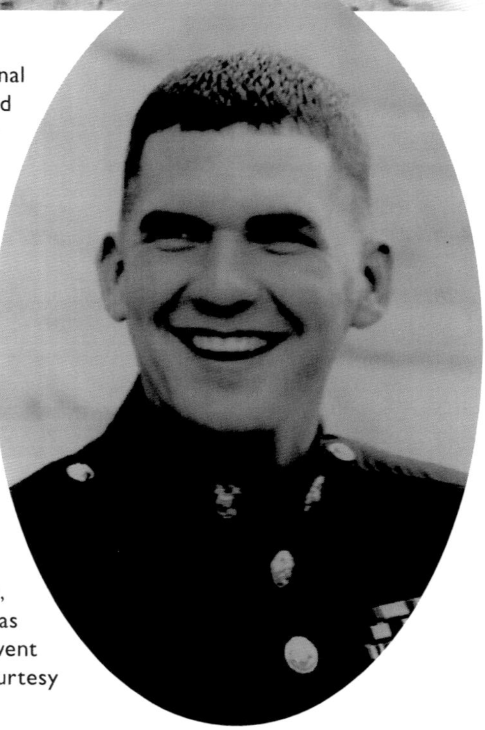

L.Cpl. Philip J. Martini

Phil Martini was a well liked guy at Thornton Fractional South High School, where he graduated in 2000, and was the youngest of three boys. Three years after graduation, he and two friends, John Aylmer and Ryan Hensley, decided to join the US Marine Corps. Martini was a little older than his two friends, and once he enlisted, he found himself in the big brother role to younger recruits. It was November 2003 when the trio joined the Marines, and all three were soon deployed to Iraq. Before serving his first deployment, Phil Martini spent time on a tsunami-relief assignment in Southeast Asia. In January 2006, he was deployed for a second tour and was killed by sniper fire in Al Anbar Province. A tree was planted in Winterhoff Park with a plaque in his memory. In 2011, to celebrate Phil's life on the fifth anniversary of his death, his brothers and friends organized a fundraiser with proceeds going to the Semper Fi Fund. In 2012, the L.Cpl. Philip J. Martini Memorial Foundation was formed with plans to hold an annual fundraising event to benefit various Marine-related charities. (All, courtesy of Laura Martini.)

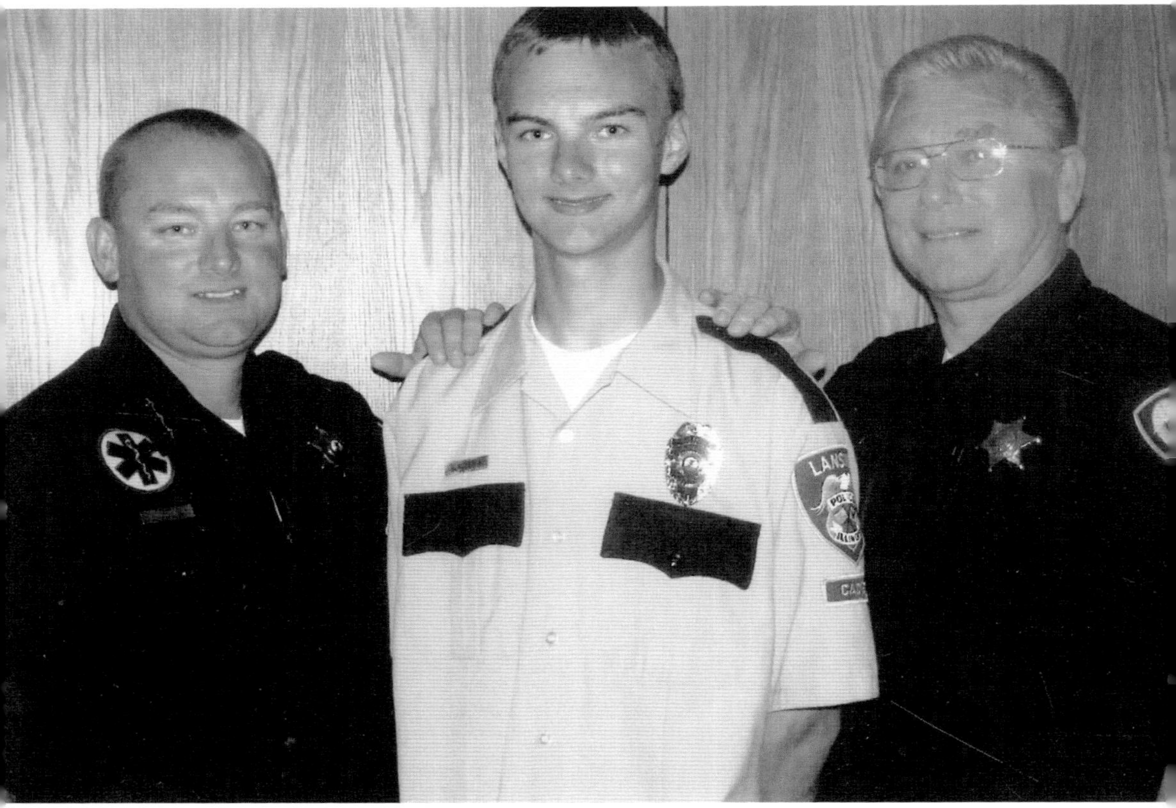

The Murrin Family

Pictured from left to right are Dennis Murrin Jr, Dennis Murrin III, and Dennis Murrin Sr. Dennis Murrin Sr. was a Thornton Fractional South High School graduate and served in the US Army from 1968 to 1970, deployed to Korea. He joined the police department as a reserve office in 1970 and became a full-time officer in 1974. He earned a bachelor of arts degree in police management from Calumet College in 1990 and a master of science degree in criminal social justice from Lewis University in 1994. He retired at the rank of lieutenant in 1998 and remains an active reserve officer. Since retirement, he has taught law enforcement classes at South Suburban College. He has been married to his wife, Shirley (Gretencord), for 43 years, and they have three children: Dennis Jr., Kelly, and Katie. Dennis Murrin Jr. was involved in the cadet program as a teen, earning the ranks of lieutenant and captain. He worked as a part-time radio operator, full-time dispatcher, and reserve officer before becoming a full-time officer and paramedic in 1991. He was appointed chief of police in May 2009 and continues to serve in that role. He has been married to his wife, Carrie (Witvoet), for 17 years, and they have four children: Dennis III, Ashley, Alyssa, and Allison. Dennis Murrin III is currently in the police cadet program and was awarded the Robert Henriech Award for outstanding academy dedication and academic excellence. He attends Illiana Christian High School. (Courtesy of Dennis Murrin.)

The Murrin Family

Dennis Murrin Sr. is pictured with his father, Gale F. Murrin Jr. Gale served in the US Coast Guard from 1942 to 1946 and served on the SF-278. After his military service, he was employed as a crane operator while serving in the police reserve program. He joined the police department in 1950 as a reserve officer, and in 1957 he became a full-time officer. He retired in 1978 as a captain. He was a member of the Lansing Lions Club and the Edward Schultz American Legion Post. He was post commander of the VFW from 1951 to 1952. He married Agnes (Follmar) Murrin in 1946, and they had four children: Gale Murrin III, Dennis, Martin, and Michelle. Gale died in 1995 and was preceded in death by his son, Martin, who was a Joliet, Illinois, police officer killed in the line of duty in 1984. (Courtesy of Dennis Murrin.)

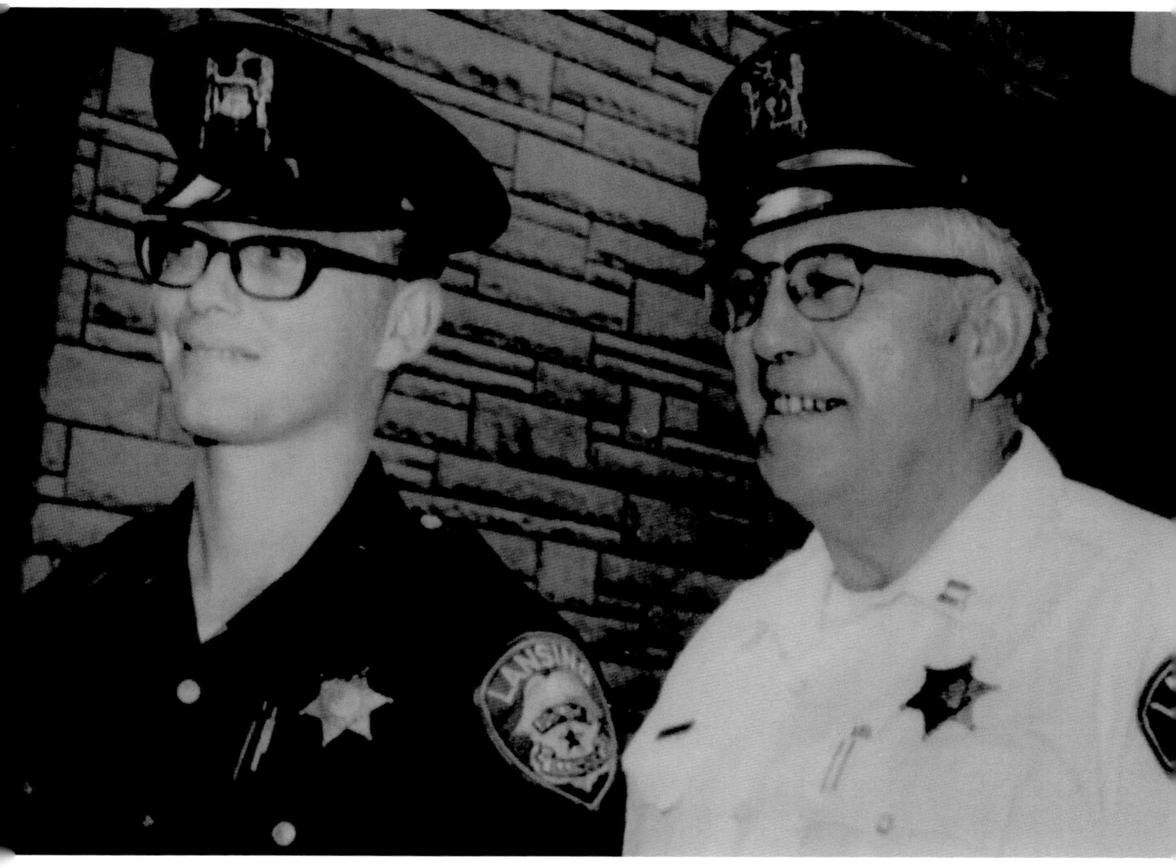

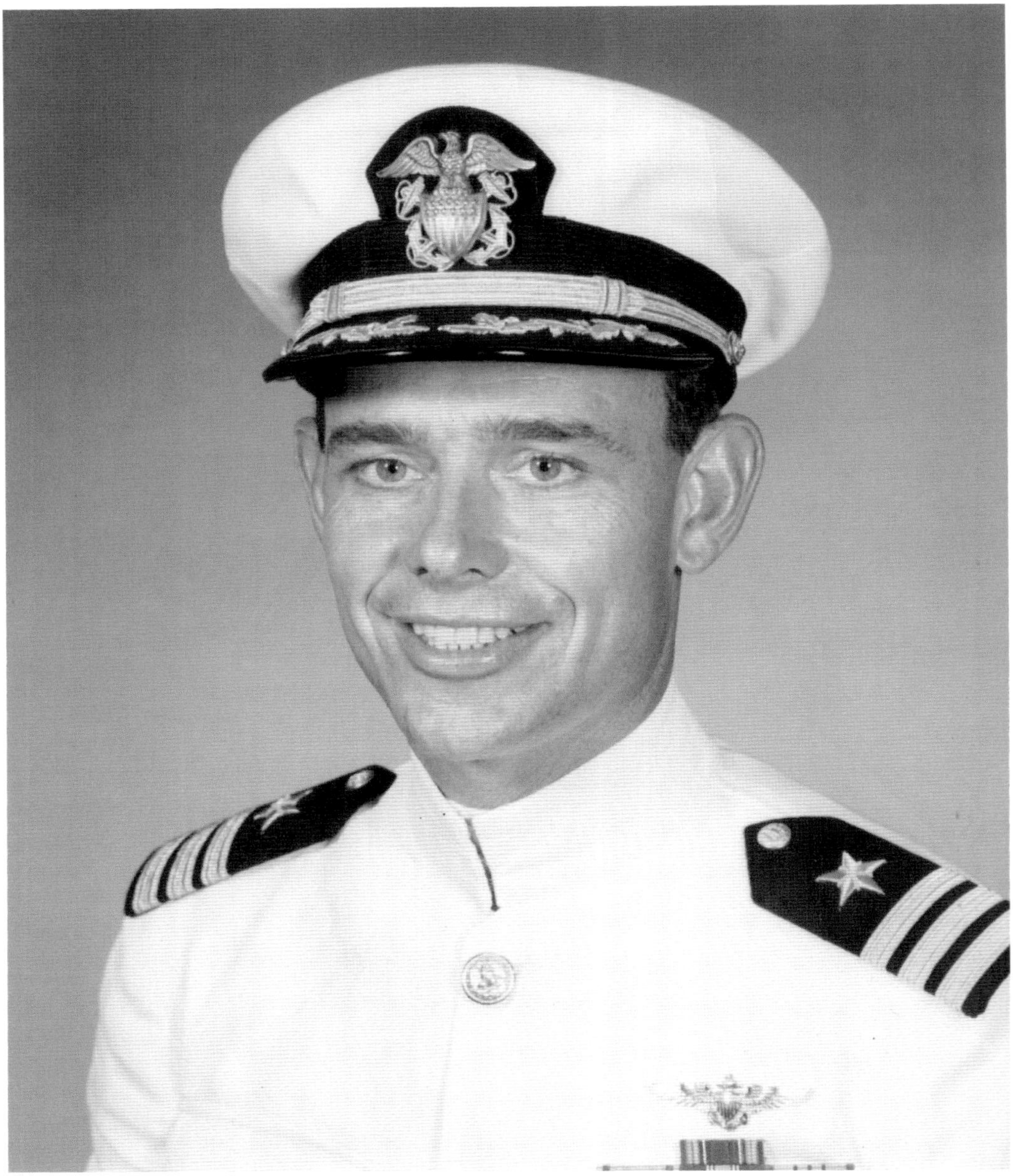

Rear Adm. Ralph Hedges

Ralph "Dick" Hedges was born in Chicago on October 26, 1927, and his family moved to Lansing in 1941. One of three boys, Dick attended Thornton Fractional High School, where he graduated as salutatorian. He was one of the first Eagle Scouts in Lansing. He enlisted in the US Navy in 1945 and entered the US Naval Academy in Annapolis, Maryland, in 1948. In 1976, he was promoted to the rank of rear admiral. He earned a degree in aeronautical engineering from the Naval Postgraduate School and a master's degree in nuclear engineering from Iowa State. He met his wife, Phillis Bacon, of Hammond, through her brother, who was also in the naval academy. The couple had two children, son Scott, who now resides in Washington and daughter Jen Tebbetts of California. Dick retired in 1985 as commander of US Naval Forces in Japan and now resides in San Diego, California. (Courtesy of the Lansing Historical Society.)

Edward Schultz
In this photograph, Chuck Schultz, the grandson of Edward Schultz, holds a portrait that hangs at the Edward Schultz Post 697 American Legion, which was dedicated in his honor in 1950. The grandchildren visited Lansing in 2010 after coming across an online article written by Lansing Historical Society member Paul Schulz (no relation). Paul set out to find information on Edward when a new headstone was requested at Oak Glen Cemetery by post service officer Ron Haney. Edward, born on January 30, 1896, signed up for the draft in 1917 at age 21. At the time, he was working as a laborer at the Illinois Brick Company in Lansing. He served during World War I with the US Army, 132nd Infantry, 53rd Division. He was the last of the Lansing men to return home in 1920, likely because he had been recovering from wounds. He died in 1925 from chronic myocarditis due to his war service. The tradition of military service continued through the Schultz family, with son Kenneth serving in World War II, grandson Chuck serving in Vietnam, and a great-great-grandson who served a recent deployment to Afghanistan. (Author's collection.)

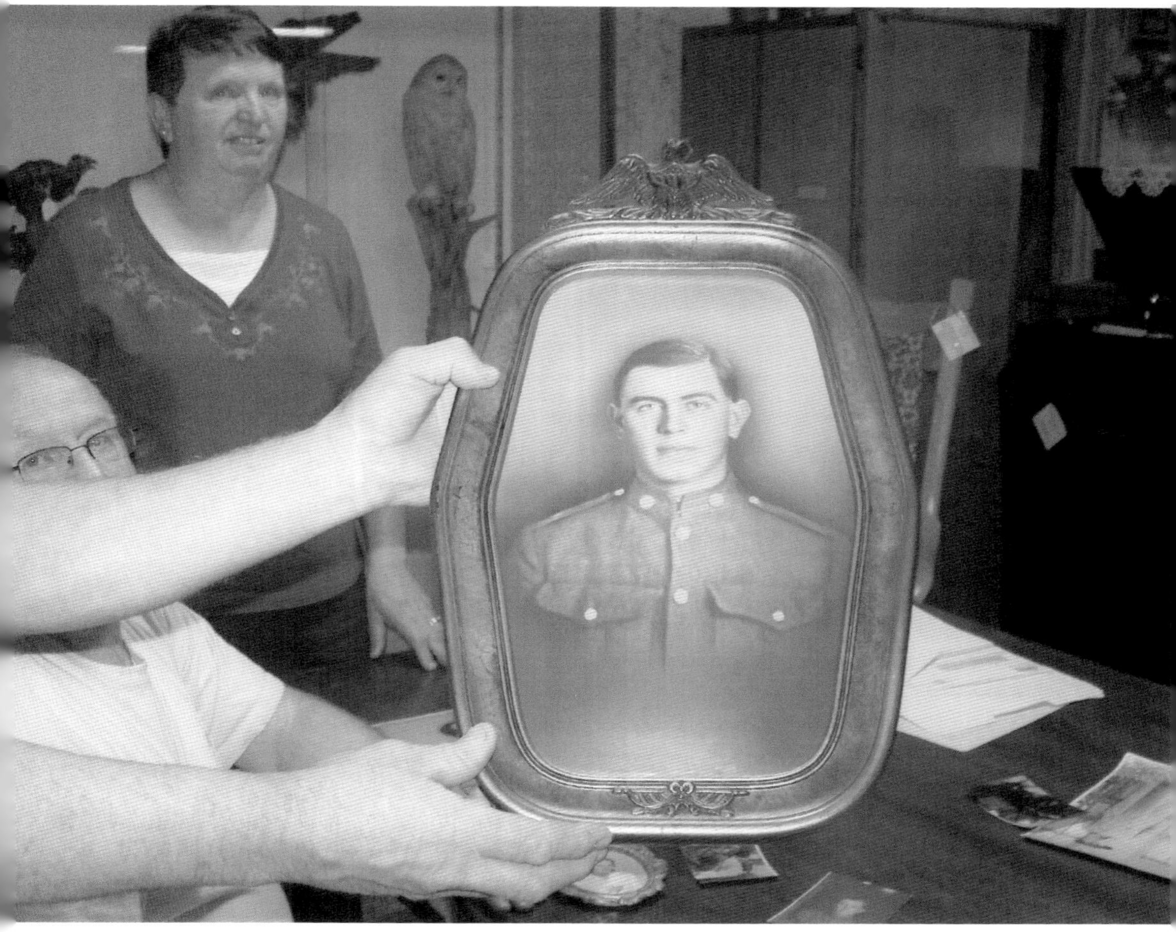

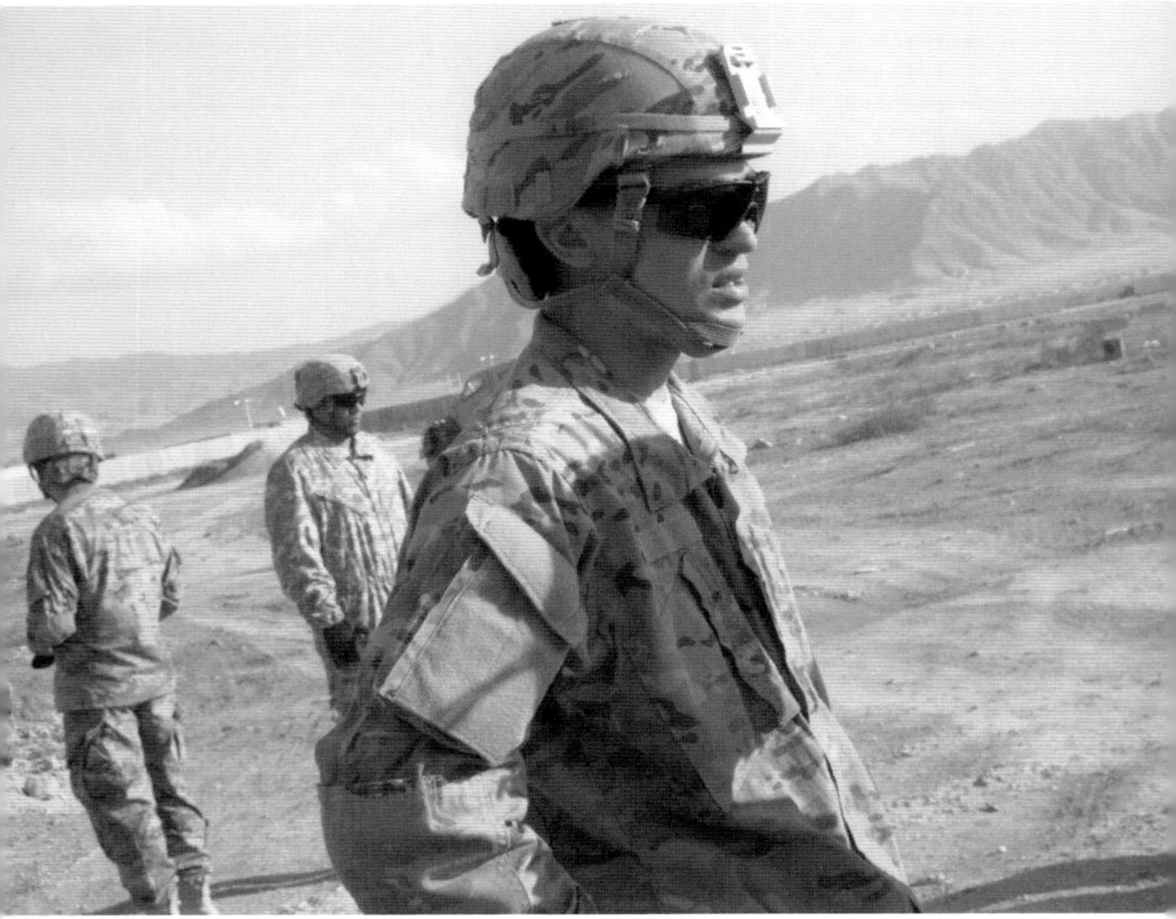

Sgt. Jim Dorsch
Jim Dorsch moved to Lansing during grade school, attending Trinity Lutheran School and Thornton Fractional South High School and graduating in 2000. He played Little League baseball, youth basketball, and ran cross-country and track in high school. He enlisted in the US Army in 2002 and served three tours in Iraq and recently finished serving a tour in Afghanistan. (Courtesy of Patti Dorsch.)

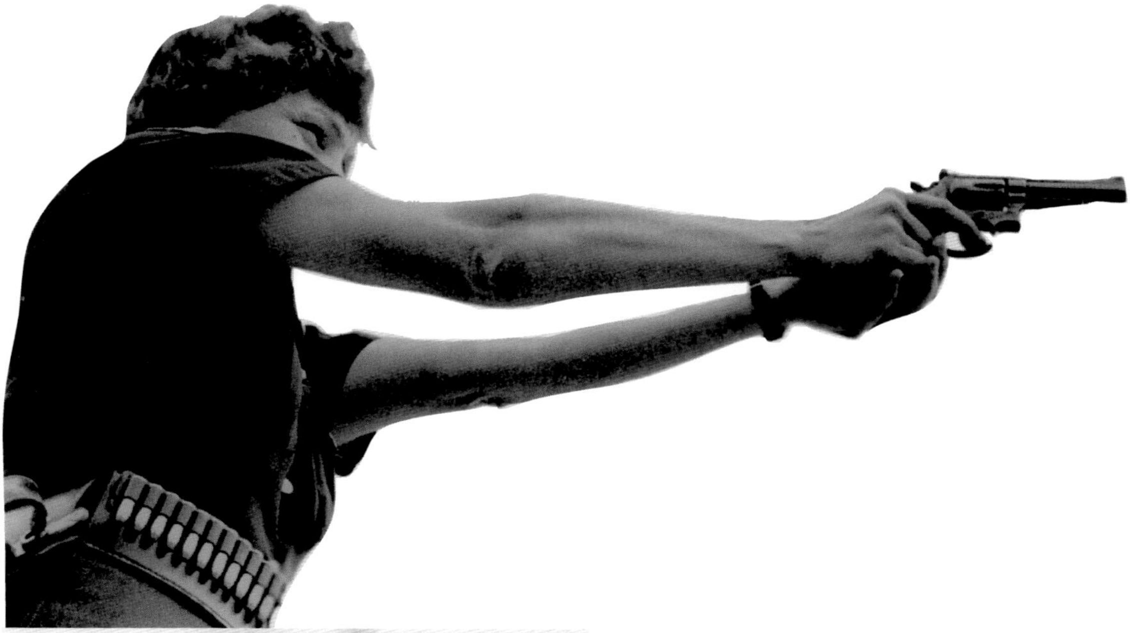

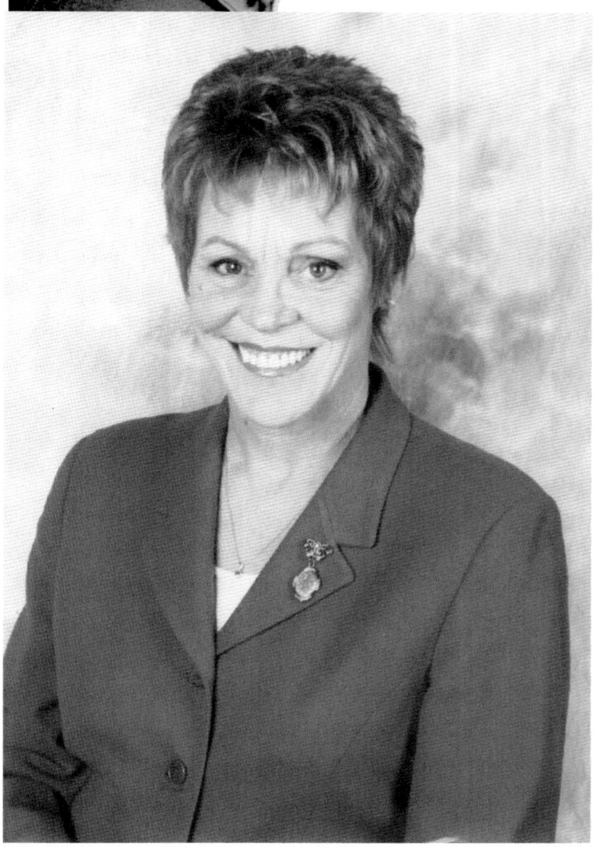

Patty Eidam
Born in Sault St. Marie, Michigan, Patty relocated to Lansing and became the village's first female police officer in June 1979. A US Army veteran, wife to Bud, and mother of four, she served as a village trustee from 2001 to 2009. She has served as village clerk since 2009. Patty served as president, vice president, and advisor of the Lansing Historical Society and spearheaded Lansing's first public art project, "Tri Motors In Plane View," which celebrated the 80th anniversary of the Ford Hangar and raised $60,000 for the restoration and preservation of the hangar by bringing decorated trimotor planes to the sidewalks of Lansing. Patty was awarded the ATHENA Award by the Lansing Chamber of Commerce in 2007. (Both, courtesy of Patty Eidam.)

Mike Manno

For several years, Mike Manno was the face of the Lansing Police Department to local kids who encountered him at school as part of the D.A.R.E. Program aimed at keeping kids away from drugs and gangs and encouraging them to make good choices. Manno recently retired from the Lansing Police Department and continues to work part-time for the department. He designed a new program called D.A.N.G.E.R. after funding for the D.A.R.E. Program was no longer available. (Courtesy of Patty Eidam.)

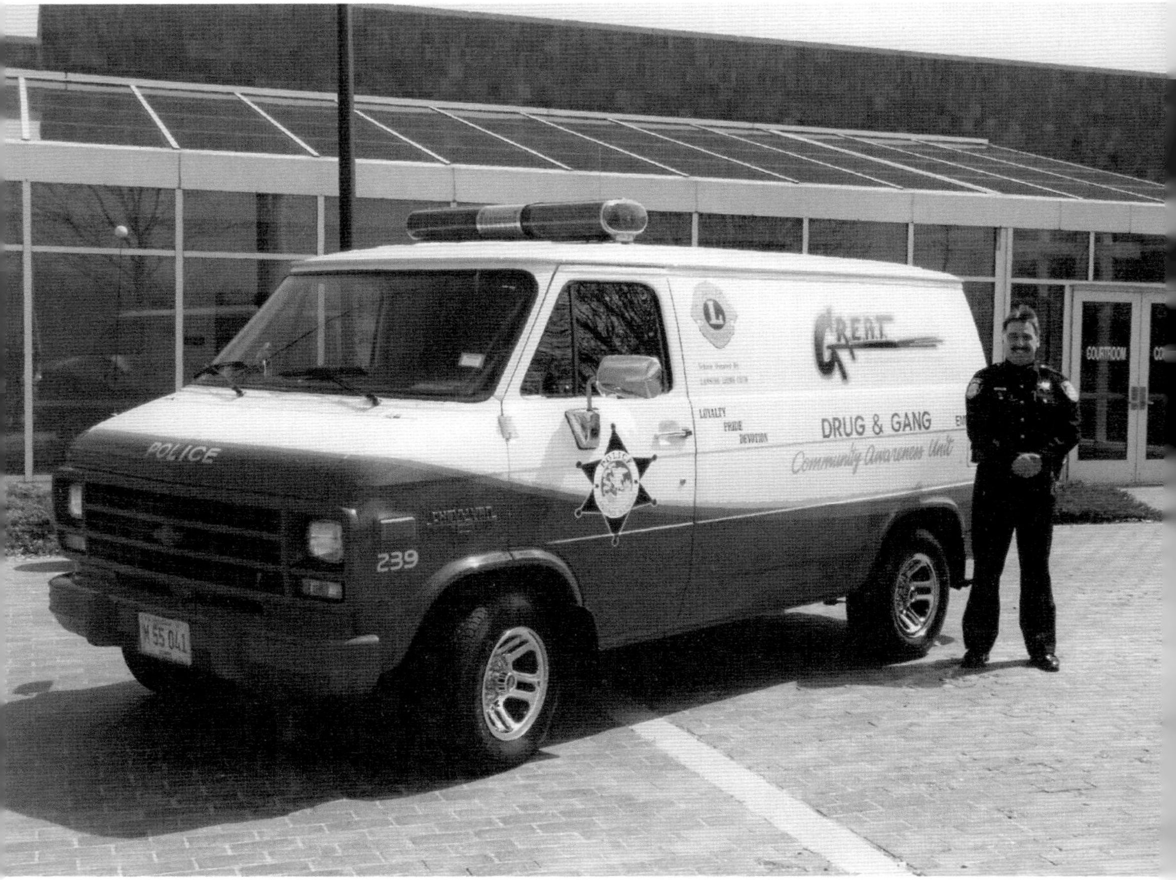

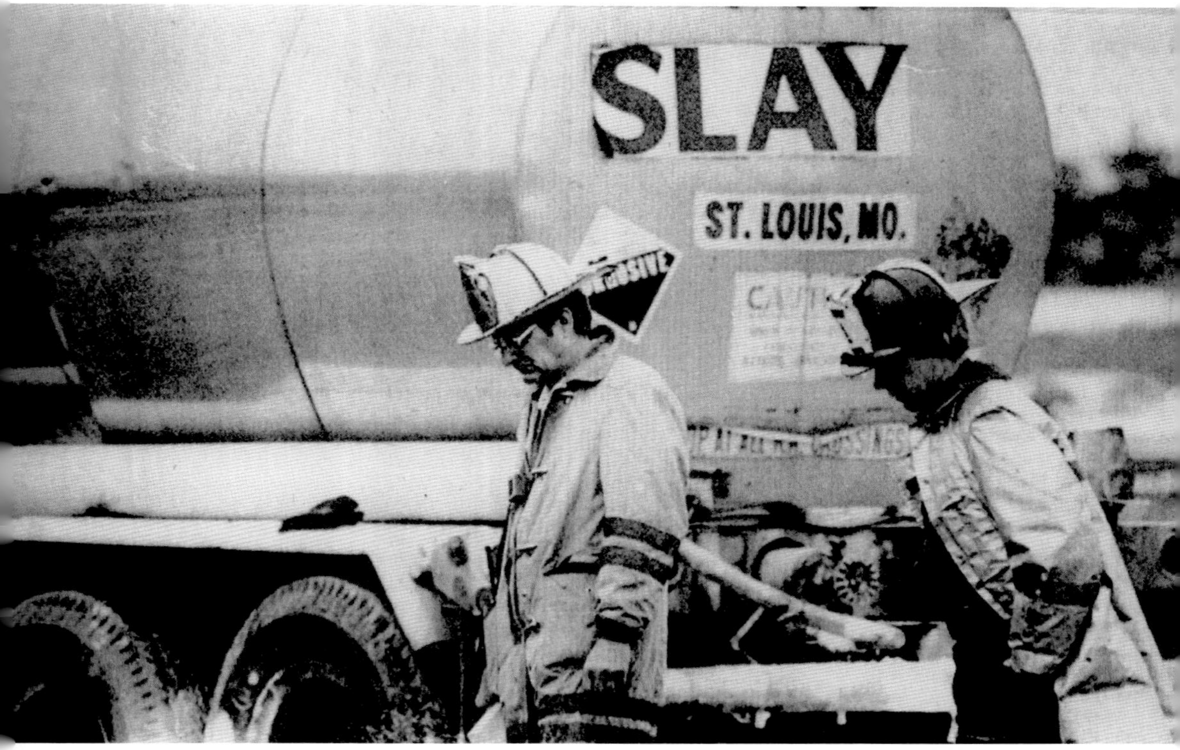

Ralph Schauer

Pictured in this newspaper photograph with firefighter Ken Myers (right), Ralph Schauer is the longest-serving fire chief in the department's history. The son of a Lansing firefighter, Schauer became the village's first full-time firefighter in 1970. With 47 years in the fire department and about 40 of them as a chief, Schauer saw the department grow, resulting in additional fire stations and apparatuses, increased personnel, and one of the first paramedic programs in Illinois as the village jumped from a population of 9,000 to around 30,000 before his retirement in 2001. (Courtesy of Patty Eidam.)

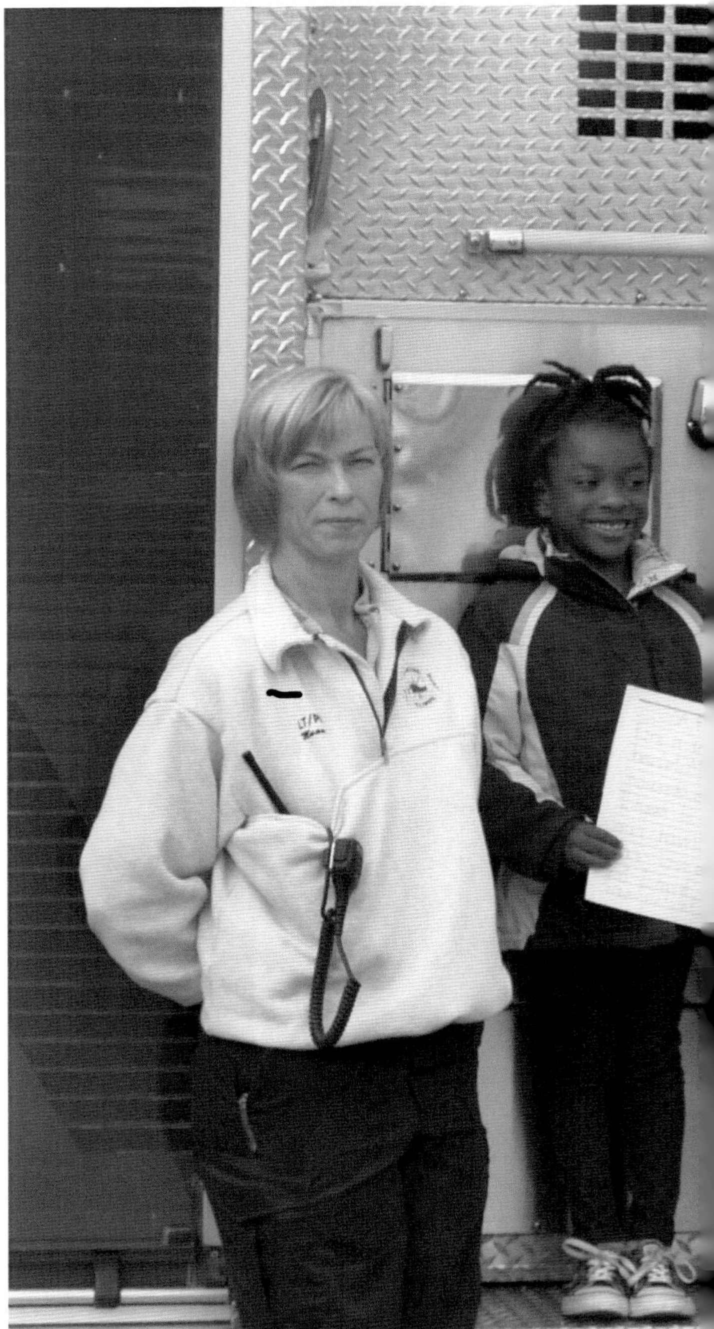

Beth Musser
Beth Musser became the department's first female firefighter and served as a firefighter and paramedic and later the first female lieutenant in the department before her retirement in 2012. A mother of two, Beth is married to retired Lasing police officer Scott Musser. (Author's collection.)

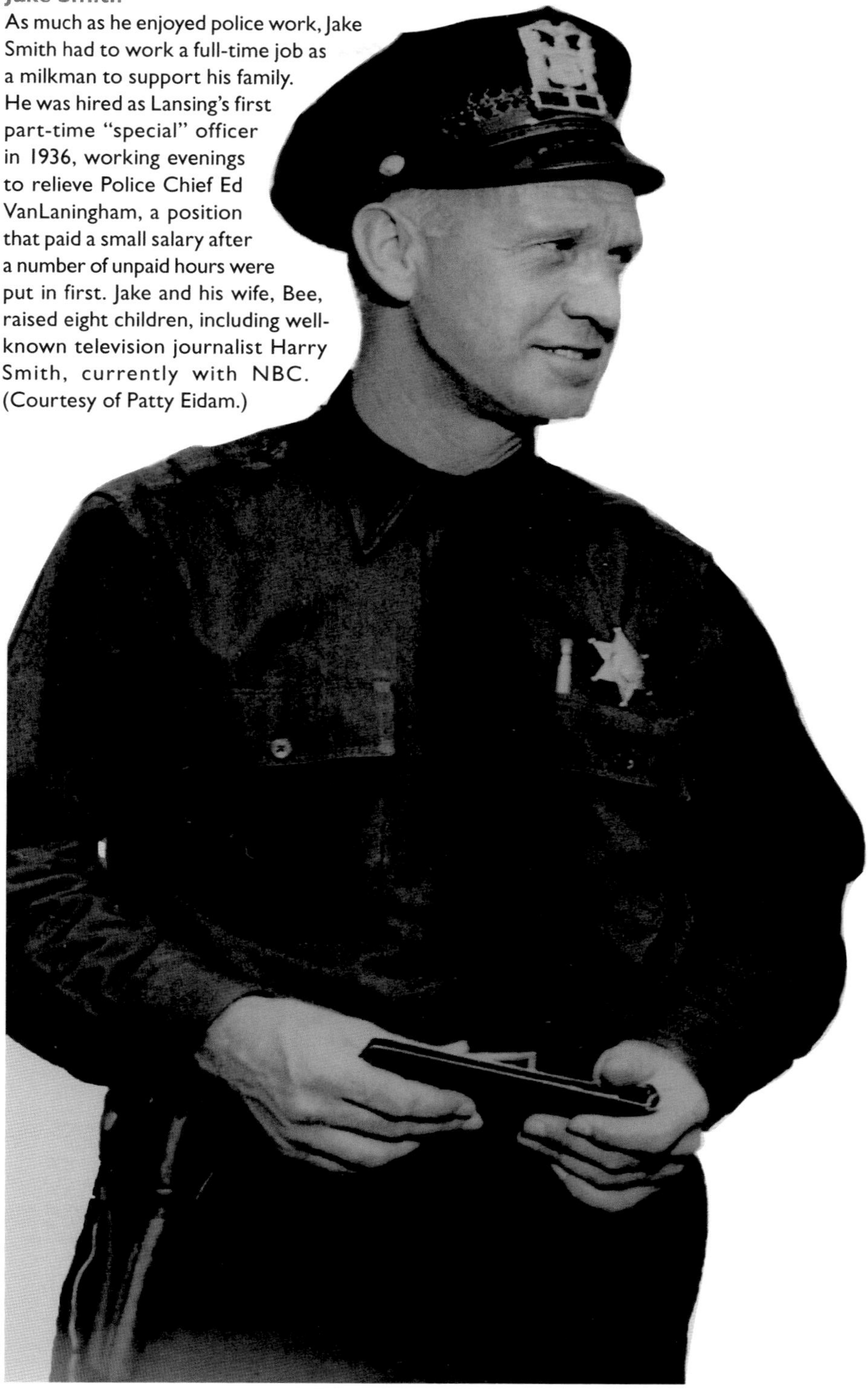

Jake Smith
As much as he enjoyed police work, Jake Smith had to work a full-time job as a milkman to support his family. He was hired as Lansing's first part-time "special" officer in 1936, working evenings to relieve Police Chief Ed VanLaningham, a position that paid a small salary after a number of unpaid hours were put in first. Jake and his wife, Bee, raised eight children, including well-known television journalist Harry Smith, currently with NBC. (Courtesy of Patty Eidam.)

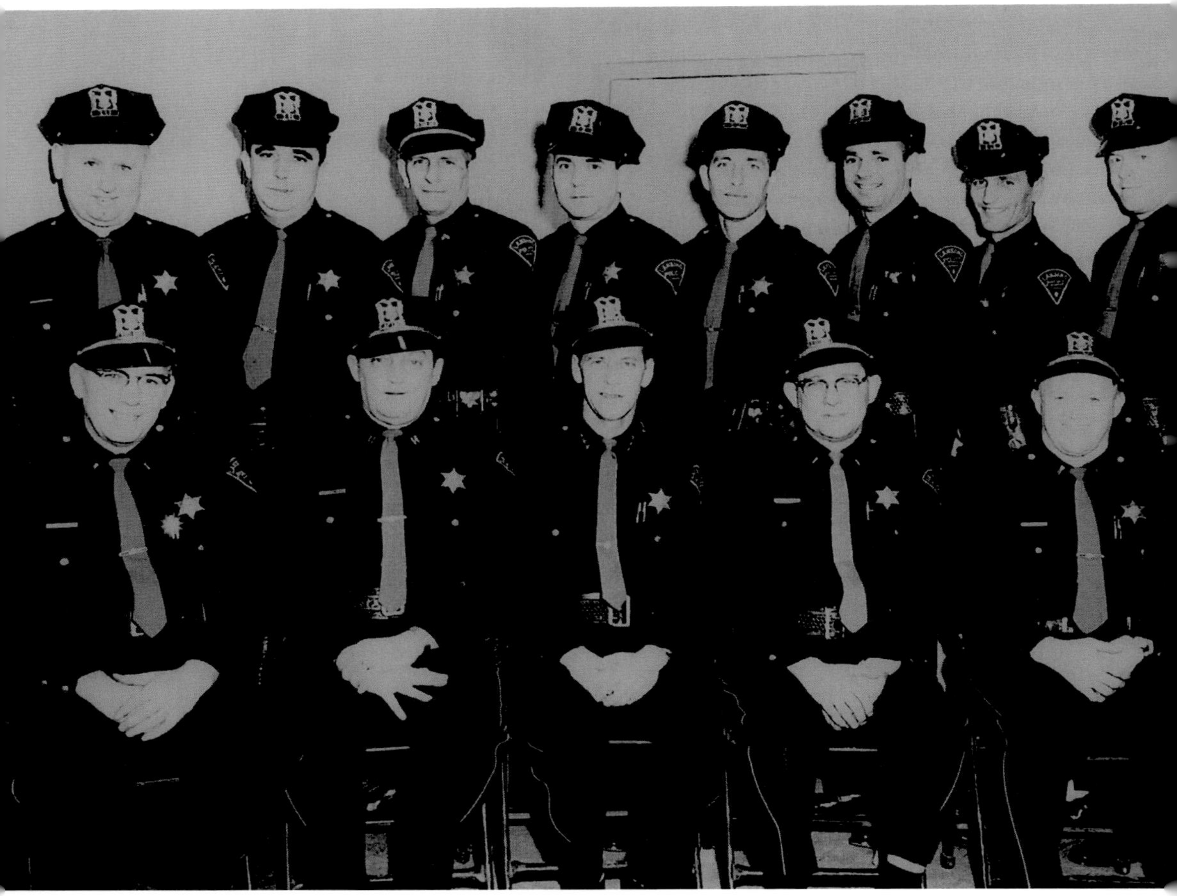

Lansing Police Department Full-Time Officers, 1964

Before there was a title of police chief, William Busack was responsible for keeping the peace in his role as Thornton Township constable. John Eckstein later served as town marshal from 1919 to 1931. After short stints as police chief by Fred Holdt (1927–1930), Charles Zitek (1930–1932), and Thomas Strauss (1932–1935), Edward Van Laningham became police chief and served from 1933 to 1957. His friendly demeanor led some to describe him as the "Andy Taylor" of Lansing. Following Van Laningham, John Braschler served as chief from 1957 to 1974. He is pictured here in this 1964 photograph. From left to right are (seated) Gale Murrin, Henry Szymburski, John Braschler, Robert Turbin, and Kenneth Koppitz; (standing): Gil Helwig, Lorn Larsen, Henry VanDerNoord, George Crossariol, Nelsen Boender, William Hutchison, Leroy Metz, and Ken Nevills. (Courtesy of Bud Eidam.)

CHAPTER TWO

Mayors

Fourteen men have been elected to lead the village of Lansing during its nearly 120-year history. Each individual had a different variety of challenges in running the village. The first mayor, J.B. McDonald, of whom there is no picture available, served during a time when horses and buggies served as transportation on dirt roads, much of the population consisted of farmers and brickyard laborers, and many transplants and transients landed here to work at producing bricks. McDonald himself was employed as a superintendent at the Purington Brick Company. Public service has always gone hand in hand with the office; many mayors have volunteered with different civic organizations over the years, or have served in local government previously, or have been involved in commissions and committees. McDonald also served on the board of education of the Lansing Public School. Mayors have served terms both short (in some cases two years) and long (Alfed Van Steenberg served a total of 34 years.) After a political scandal that resulted in a prison sentence for a former mayor, term limits were imposed that have prevented subsequent mayors from serving more than two terms. Without doubt, each of these men has left a significant impact on the village he presided over.

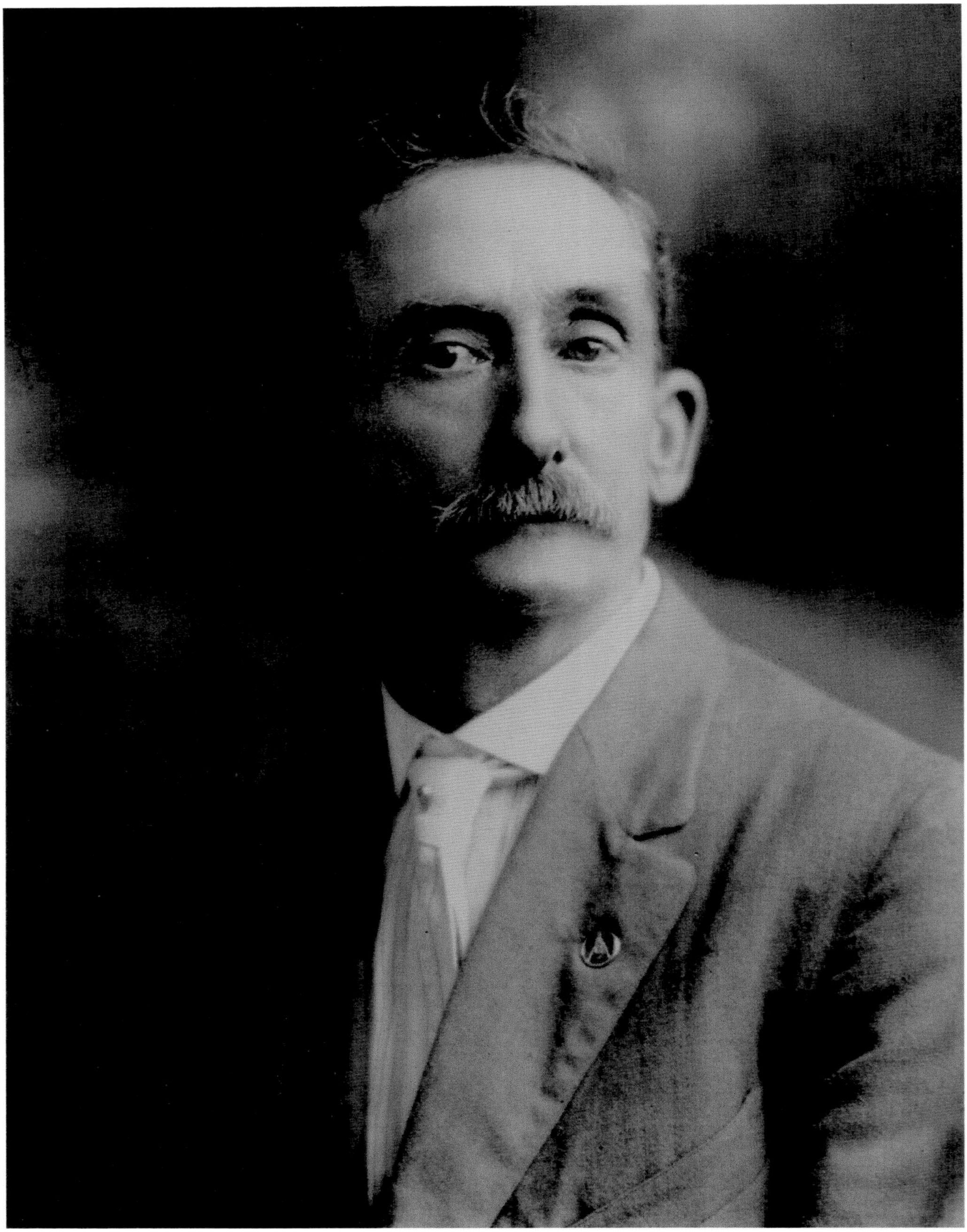

Alfred Van Steenberg
Alfred Van Steenberg is Lansing's longest-serving mayor, holding that title from 1895 to 1919 and then again from 1921 until 1931. Born in 1853 in New York, Alfred's father, Cornelius, relocated to the area and purchased a large parcel of land. His father was credited with establishing the first public school in Lansing. Alfred served as a county commissioner for 14 years, a tax collector for 10 years, and mayor for a total of 34 years. He died in 1933. (Courtesy of the Lansing Historical Society.)

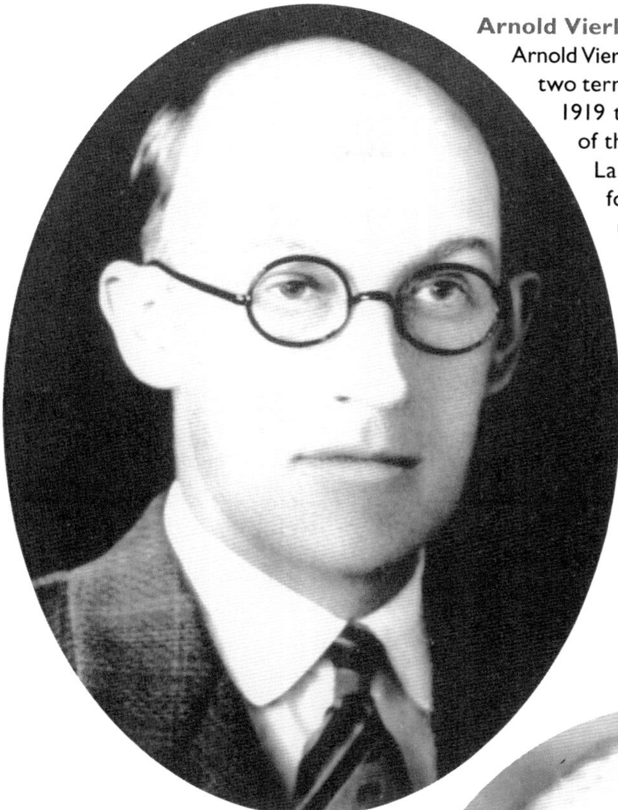

Arnold Vierk

Arnold Vierk served as mayor for three years between two terms served by Alfred Van Steenberg, from 1919 to 1921. His grandparents were some of the early settlers to the area, arriving in Lansing in 1872. His father, Fred, was a founding member of the brickworkers' union and served as a postmaster in Lansing. The family ran a dry goods store. Arnold was the youngest of four children. (Courtesy of the Lansing Historical Society.)

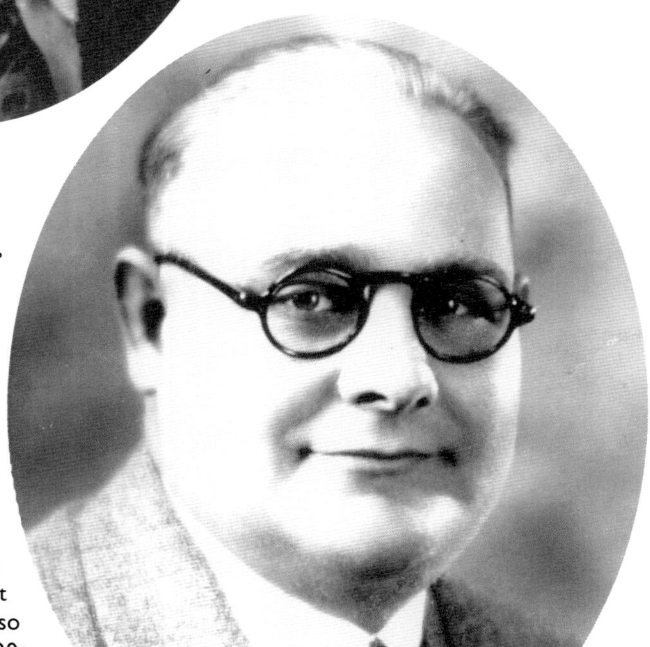

William Winterhoff

Serving as mayor from 1931 to 1935, Winterhoff impacted the village in a variety of ways that can still be seen today. At the age of just 21, Winterhoff organized the Lansing Fire Department and served as its first chief. He owned the Winterhoff Ford dealership and donated a flat-bed truck that became the department's first fire engine. Often called "Big Bill," he organized the first chamber of commerce and served as executive secretary and president. He was the first president of Lansing Lions Club and also served as police magistrate in the 1920s. He later was appointed Thornton Township clerk and was then elected Thornton Township supervisor. He served in the fire department until his death in 1973. (Courtesy of the Lansing Historical Society.)

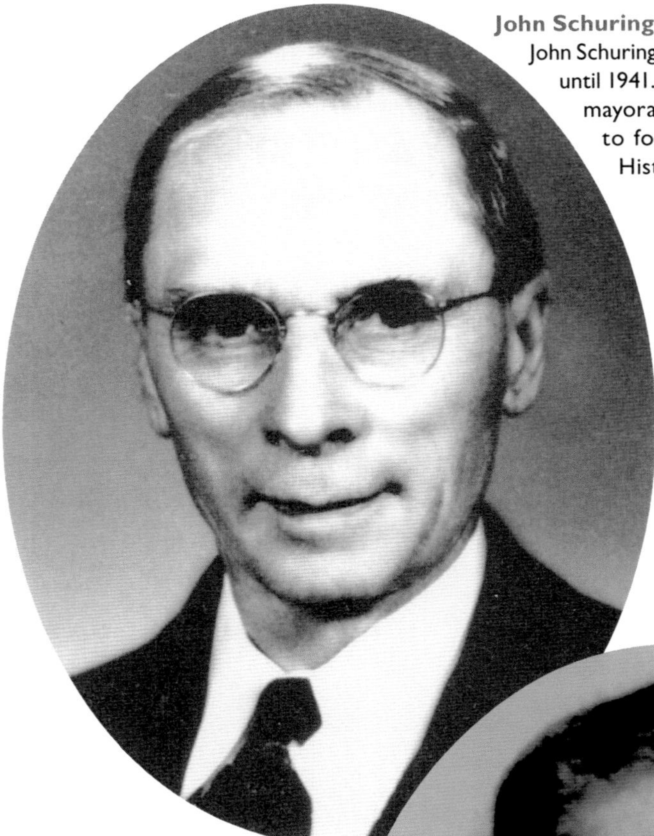

John Schuringa

John Schuringa served as mayor of Lansing from 1935 until 1941. During Schuringa's administration, the mayoral term was extended from two years to four years. (Courtesy of the Lansing Historical Society.)

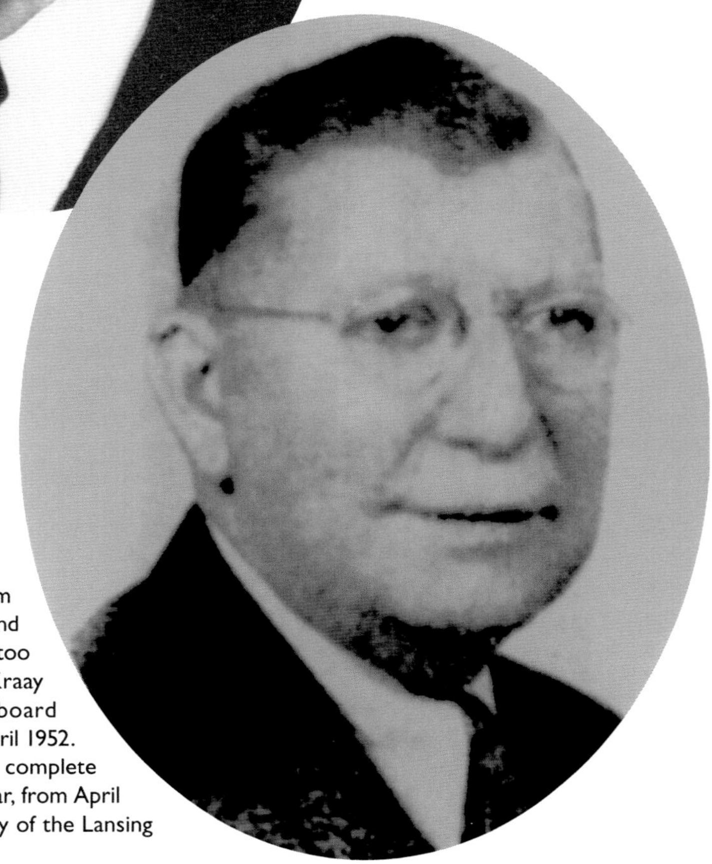

George Jones

George Jones served as mayor from 1941 to 1953. During his third and final term as mayor, Jones was too ill to fulfill his duties. Raphael Kraay was appointed to chair the board meetings from July 1949 until April 1952. Lee Dimmitt was appointed to complete Jones's term in office for one year, from April 1952 until April 1953. (Courtesy of the Lansing Historical Society.)

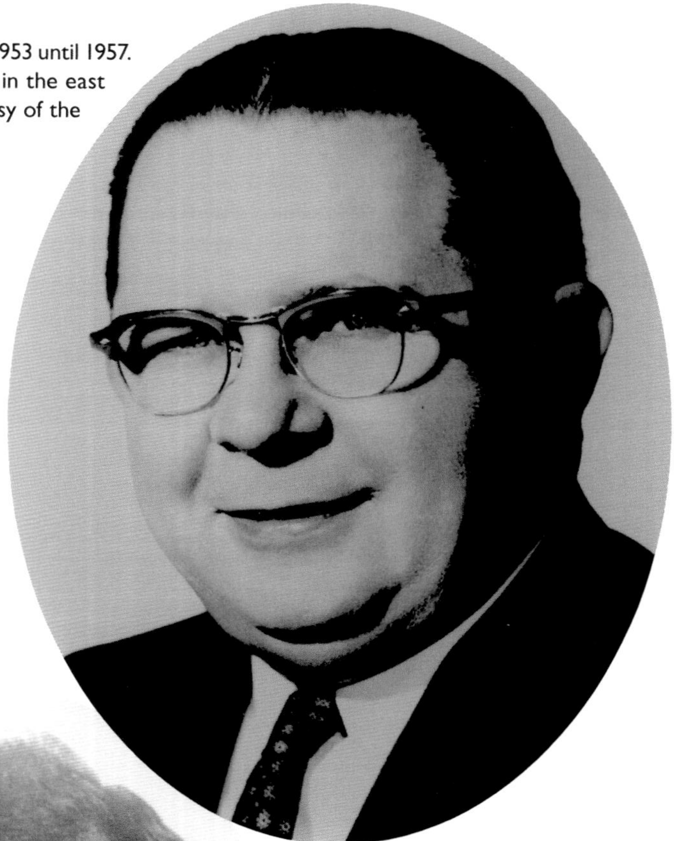

Evert S. Schultz
Evert Schultz served as mayor from 1953 until 1957. Schultz had an upholstery business in the east addition of Kilroy's Tavern. (Courtesy of the Lansing Historical Society.)

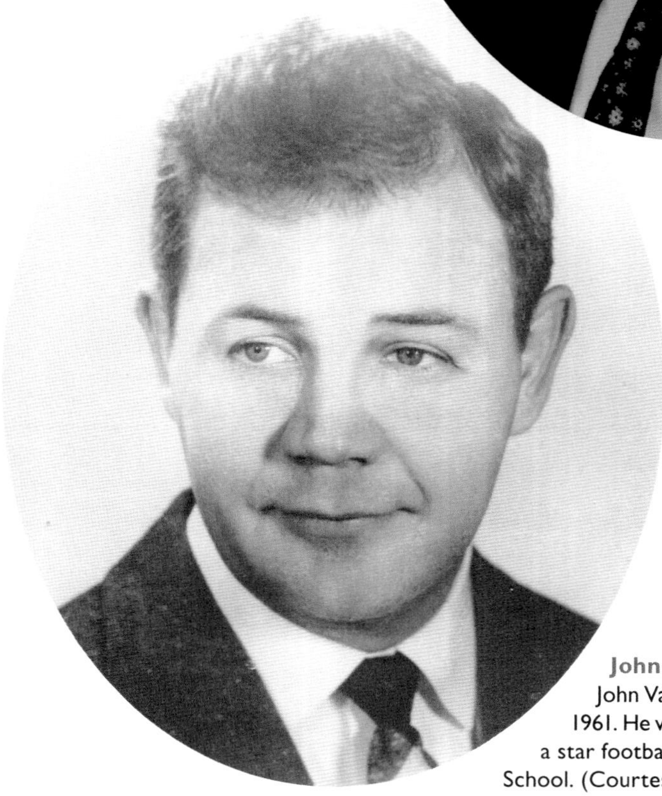

John M. Vanderaa
John Vanderaa served as mayor from 1957 to 1961. He was described as "soft spoken." He was a star football player at Thornton Fractional High School. (Courtesy of the Lansing Historical Society.)

Jack O. McNary

A World War II veteran, Jack McNary served in the US Navy aboard the USS *Hancock* in the South Pacific. He was elected as a village trustee in 1953 and served in that capacity until 1961. He served as mayor of Lansing from 1961 to 1977. In 1978, McNary was convicted in federal court of accepting payoffs in connection with village zoning matters and served 18 months in prison. After his release, he became active in fundraising for a home for troubled youth. He and his wife, Meleda, had two sons and six grandchildren. (Courtesy of the Lansing Historical Society.)

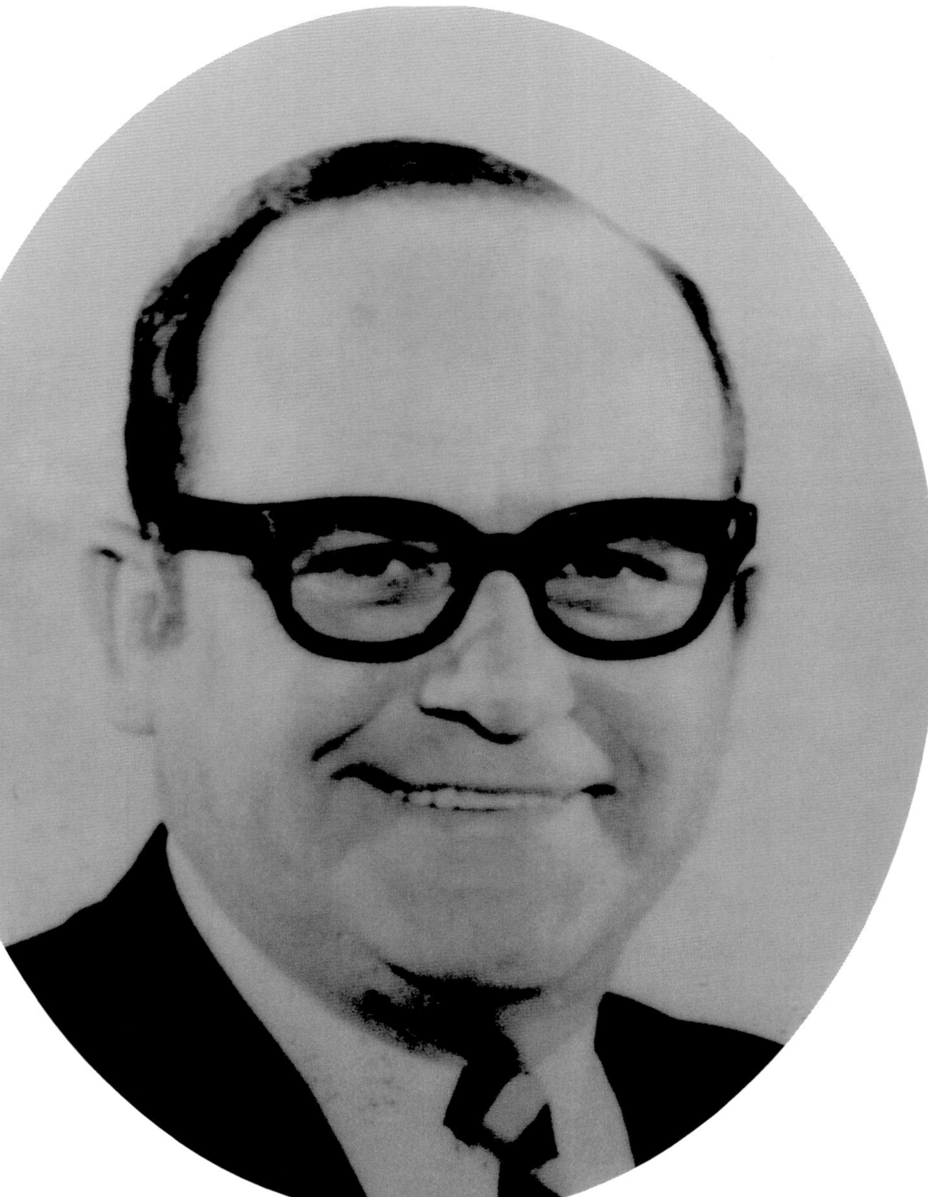

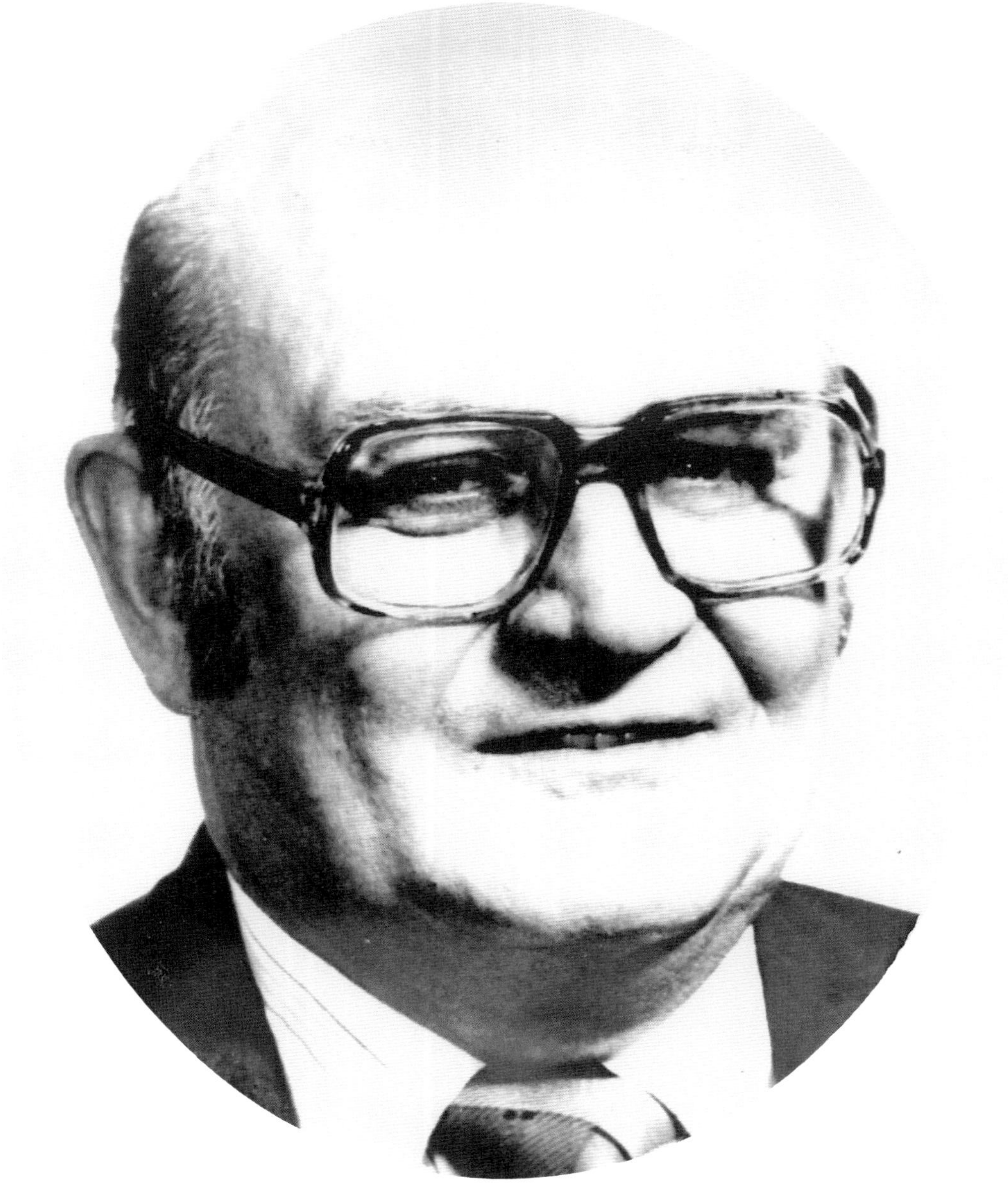

Louis LaMourie
Louis LaMourie served as mayor from 1977 to 1985. LaMourie was a barber and had a barbershop on Burnham Avenue. He was also an active member of the Knights of Columbus. (Courtesy of the Lansing Historical Society.)

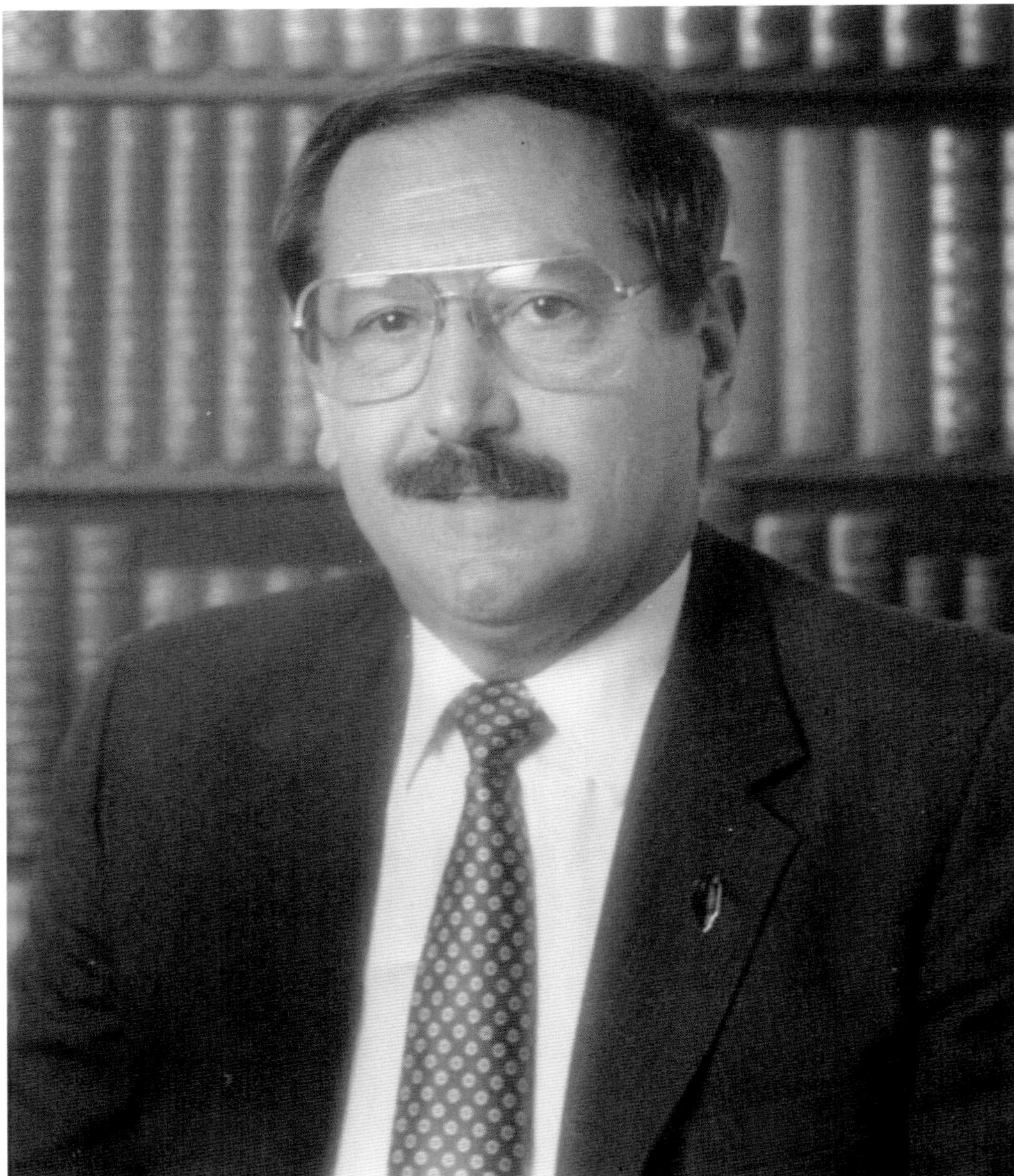

Bill W. Balthis

Serving as mayor of Lansing from 1985 to 1992, Bill Balthis took a seat in the Illinois House of Representatives in a vacancy left by Robert J. Piel in the 79th House District in April 1991. He continued to serve in the Illinois House until 1997 and was appointed to committees on financial institutions, transportation, consumer protection, human service, appropriations, and aging. A veteran of the US Air Force and former owner of an insurance agency, he was president of the South Suburban Mayors and Managers Association. He was also active in the Kiwanis Club and was a president of the Lan-Oak Park District. He and his wife, JoAnn, have five children and eight grandchildren. (Courtesy of the Lansing Historical Society.)

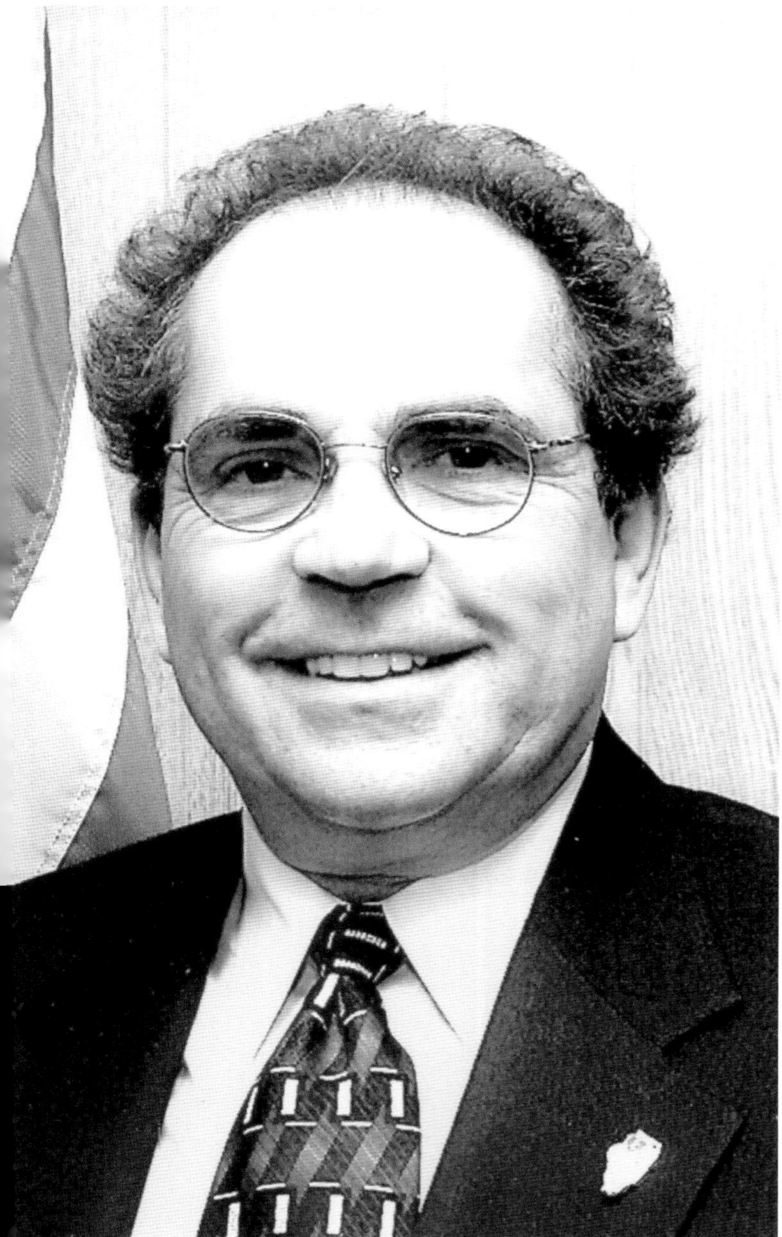

Robert W. West
After serving for 13 years on the village's zoning board and more than five years as a village trustee, Robert West was appointed interim mayor to replace Bill Balthis, who resigned as mayor after winning a run to keep his appointed spot in the Illinois House of Representatives. West, owner of a television sales and repair store, was then elected mayor in the next election and served until 2001. (Courtesy of the Lansing Historical Society.)

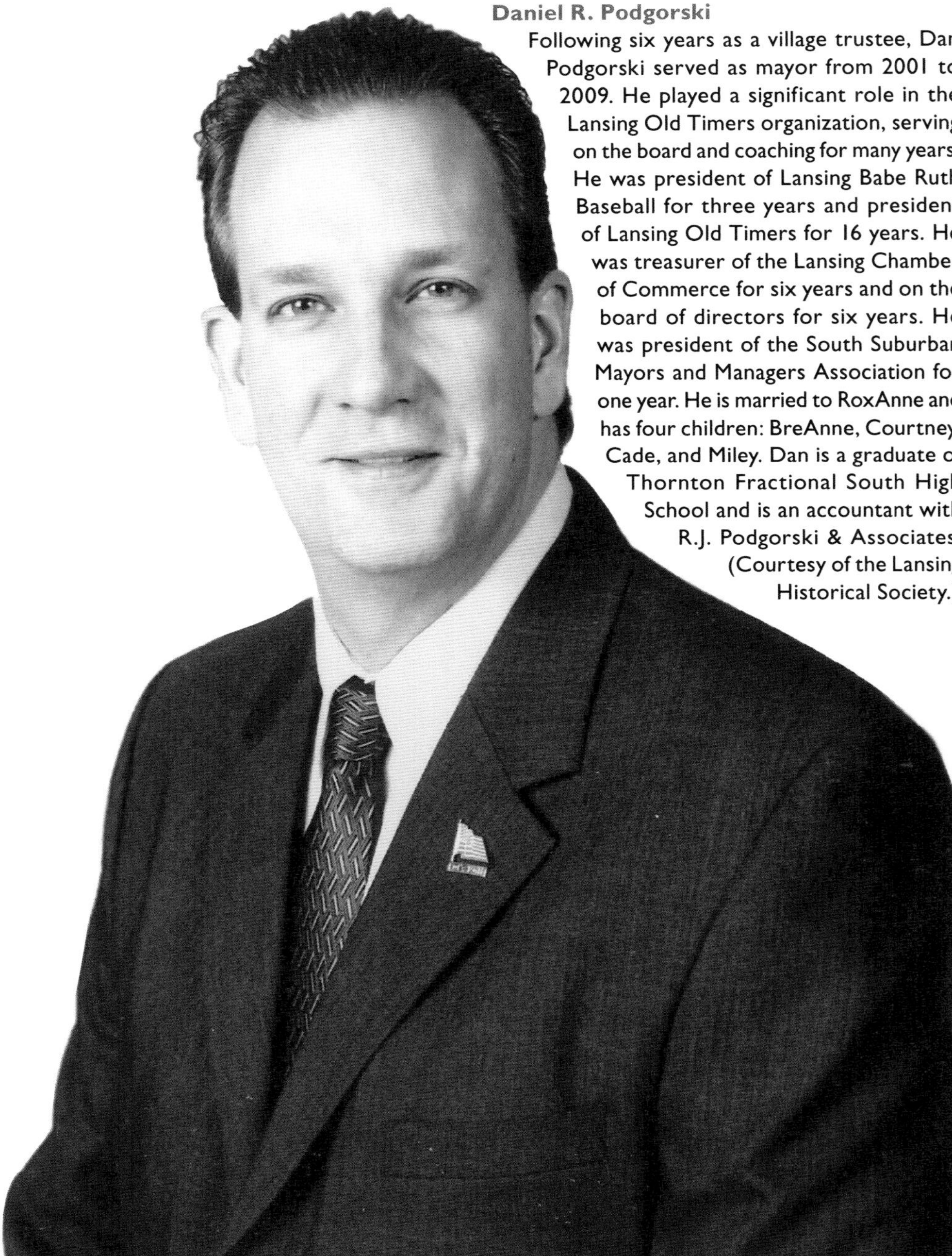

Daniel R. Podgorski

Following six years as a village trustee, Dan Podgorski served as mayor from 2001 to 2009. He played a significant role in the Lansing Old Timers organization, serving on the board and coaching for many years. He was president of Lansing Babe Ruth Baseball for three years and president of Lansing Old Timers for 16 years. He was treasurer of the Lansing Chamber of Commerce for six years and on the board of directors for six years. He was president of the South Suburban Mayors and Managers Association for one year. He is married to RoxAnne and has four children: BreAnne, Courtney, Cade, and Miley. Dan is a graduate of Thornton Fractional South High School and is an accountant with R.J. Podgorski & Associates. (Courtesy of the Lansing Historical Society.)

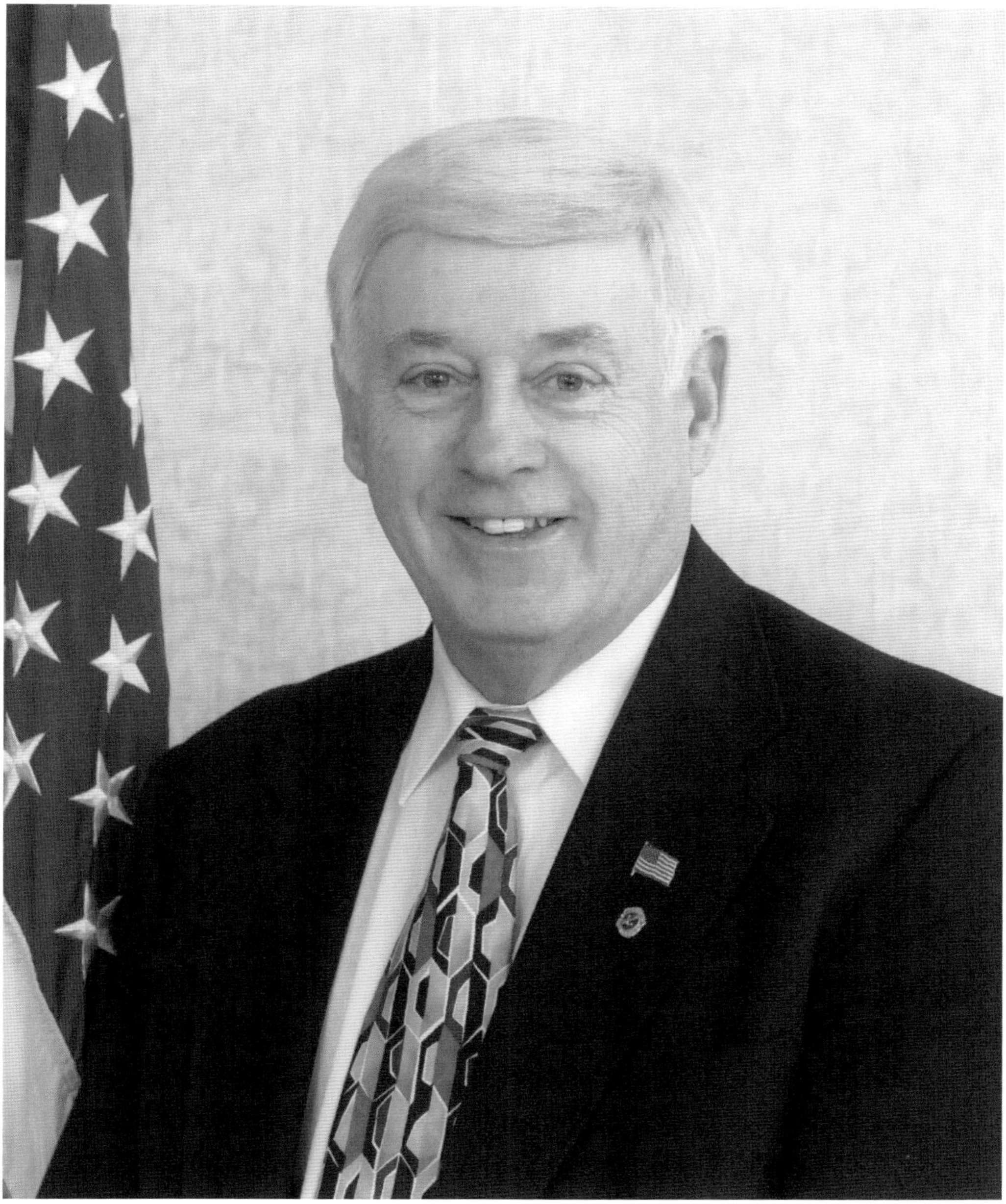

Norman Abbott
Norm Abbott graduated from Thornton Fractional South High School in 1959 and shortly after married his sweetheart, Diane. The two had been together since they were classmates at Memorial Junior High. He served in the Army and later worked at his father-in-law's insurance company, Walter Schultz Insurance (which is still in business and managed by his daughter Cheryl), for 40 years before retiring. He has been a longtime member of the chamber of commerce, has served as a parade chairman, and has been a Lions Club member since 1973, which included two terms as president. He has been an usher at St. Ann Church for more than 35 years. Norm served 13 years on the village planning and zoning board and four years as a village trustee. He has served as mayor since 2009. (Courtesy of the Lansing Historical Society.)

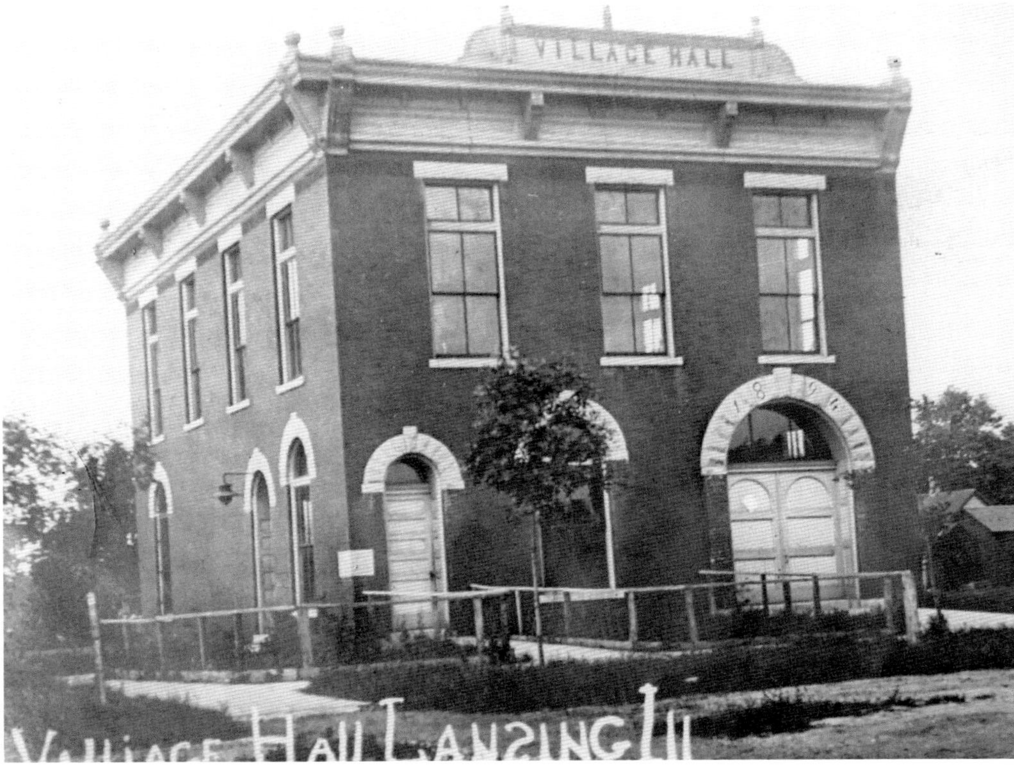

Village Halls

This building, located at the corner of Lake and Henry Streets, was built in 1894 and served as village hall, jail, and courthouse for decades before village offices moved to the southwest corner of Ridge Road and Chicago Avenue and the police station was built on 170th Street. The Lansing Fire Department also used part of the building as a fire station. It now houses the Lansing Chamber of Commerce. The new Village Municipal Center opened in 2010 at 3141 Ridge Road in the former Illinois Bell building. It houses the offices of the mayor, clerk, and building department. (Above, courtesy of the Lansing Historical Society; below, author's collection.)

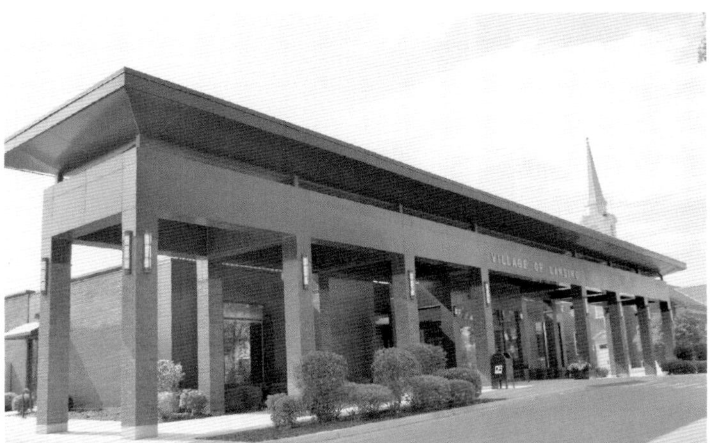

CHAPTER THREE

Education

The educational system in Lansing has come quite a way since the introduction of the first Lansing Public School. Today, school district No. 158 is comprised of five school buildings: Memorial Junior High School, Coolidge School, Reavis School, Oak Glen School, and Lester Crawl School. All of these schools continue to implement state-of-the-art educational services and upgrade facilities to meet the needs of their students. School district No. 171 continues to serve students in the southern part of the village and neighboring Lynwood at Nathan Hale School and Heritage Middle School. Four private schools—St. Ann, Trinity Lutheran, St. John, and Lansing Christian—continue to offer religious education for children in preschool through eighth grade. Three high schools are located within Lansing, educating those in grades nine through 12: Thornton Fractional High School, which opened in 1959; Illiana Christian School, which opened in 1947; and Luther East High School. It is the dedication of teachers like Ruth Canaga, Patti Leach, and William Kraegel that has played a part in the success of many of the students to pass through the classrooms of Lansing schools. The teaching field has changed in countless ways since the first one-room schoolhouses filled with pupils, but the goals and commitment of the profession continue in the present day.

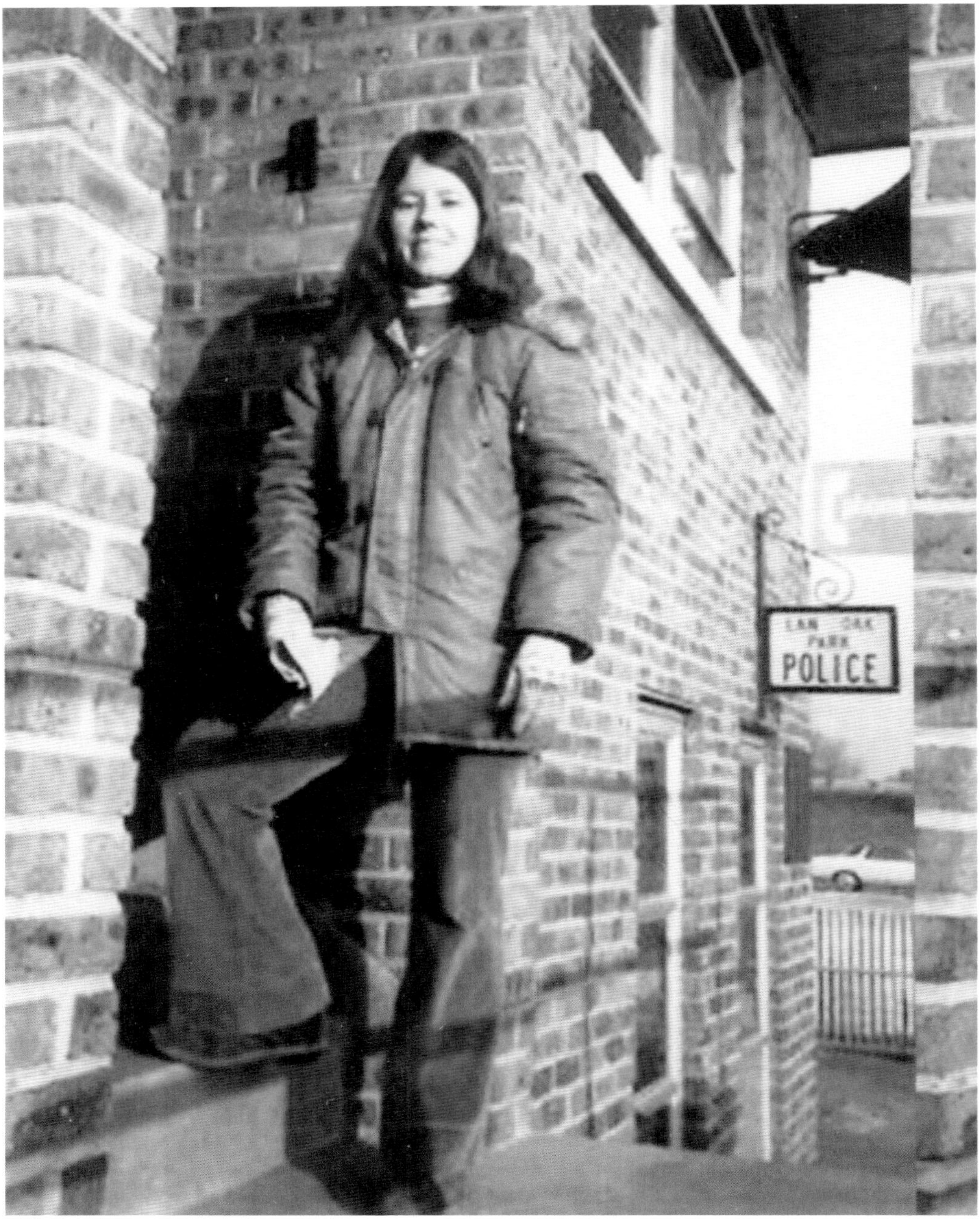

Patti Leach

A physical education teacher in school district No. 158 from 1968 to 2005, most kids who went through the Lansing elementary schools in that time had Patti Leach as a teacher. Leach also served as a coach, Girl Scout leader, and park district board member. She also served as a village trustee. She was instrumental in the creation of the Lansing Youth Center, which opened in 1997. Following her death, a dedication ceremony was held to rename the facility the Patti Leach Youth Center in her honor. (Courtesy of Chris Mahoney.)

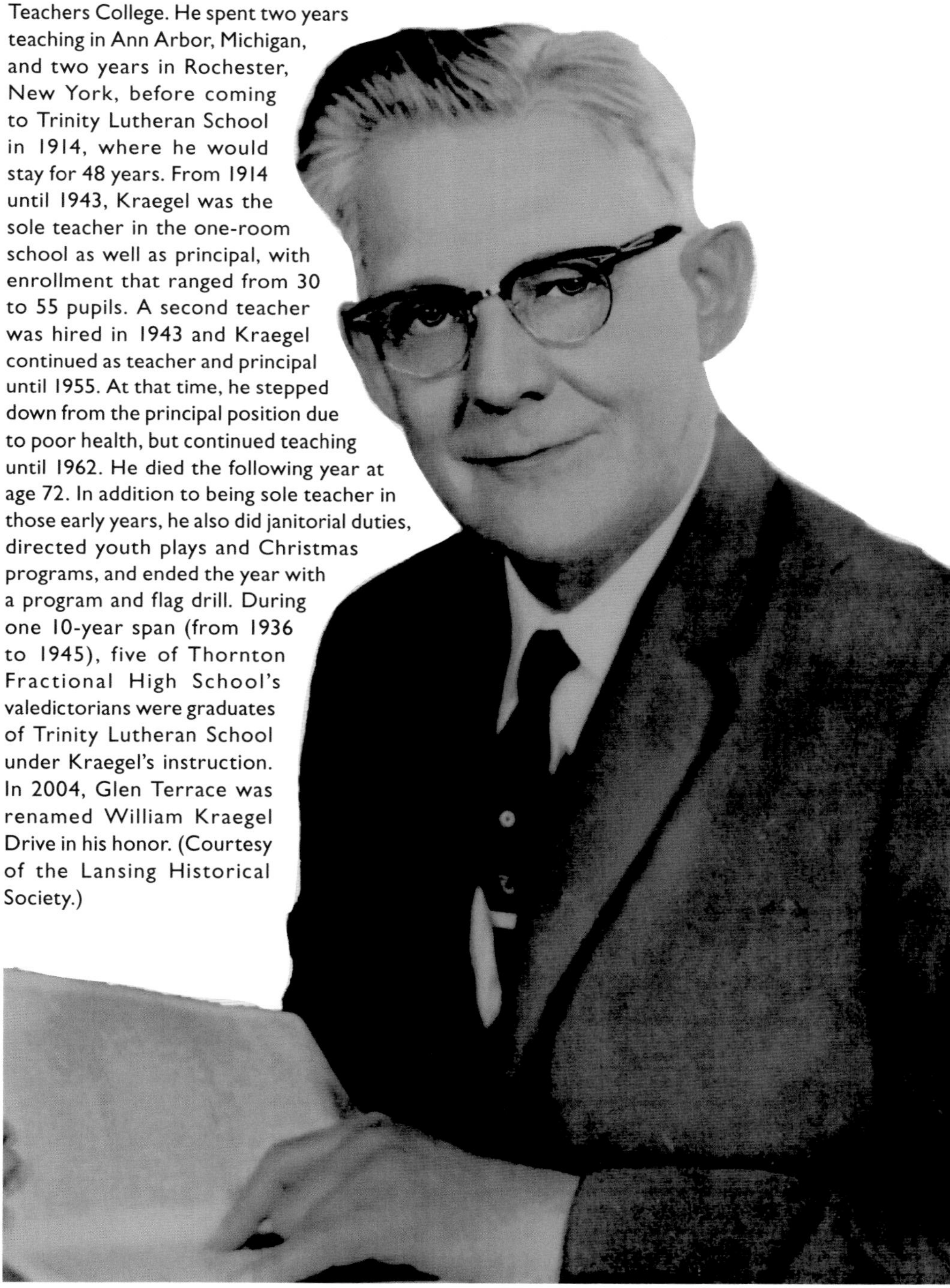

William Kraegel
William Kraegel was born on May 19, 1891, in Addison, Illinois. At a young age, he decided he wanted to become a Lutheran schoolteacher and he enrolled at Concordia Teachers College. He spent two years teaching in Ann Arbor, Michigan, and two years in Rochester, New York, before coming to Trinity Lutheran School in 1914, where he would stay for 48 years. From 1914 until 1943, Kraegel was the sole teacher in the one-room school as well as principal, with enrollment that ranged from 30 to 55 pupils. A second teacher was hired in 1943 and Kraegel continued as teacher and principal until 1955. At that time, he stepped down from the principal position due to poor health, but continued teaching until 1962. He died the following year at age 72. In addition to being sole teacher in those early years, he also did janitorial duties, directed youth plays and Christmas programs, and ended the year with a program and flag drill. During one 10-year span (from 1936 to 1945), five of Thornton Fractional High School's valedictorians were graduates of Trinity Lutheran School under Kraegel's instruction. In 2004, Glen Terrace was renamed William Kraegel Drive in his honor. (Courtesy of the Lansing Historical Society.)

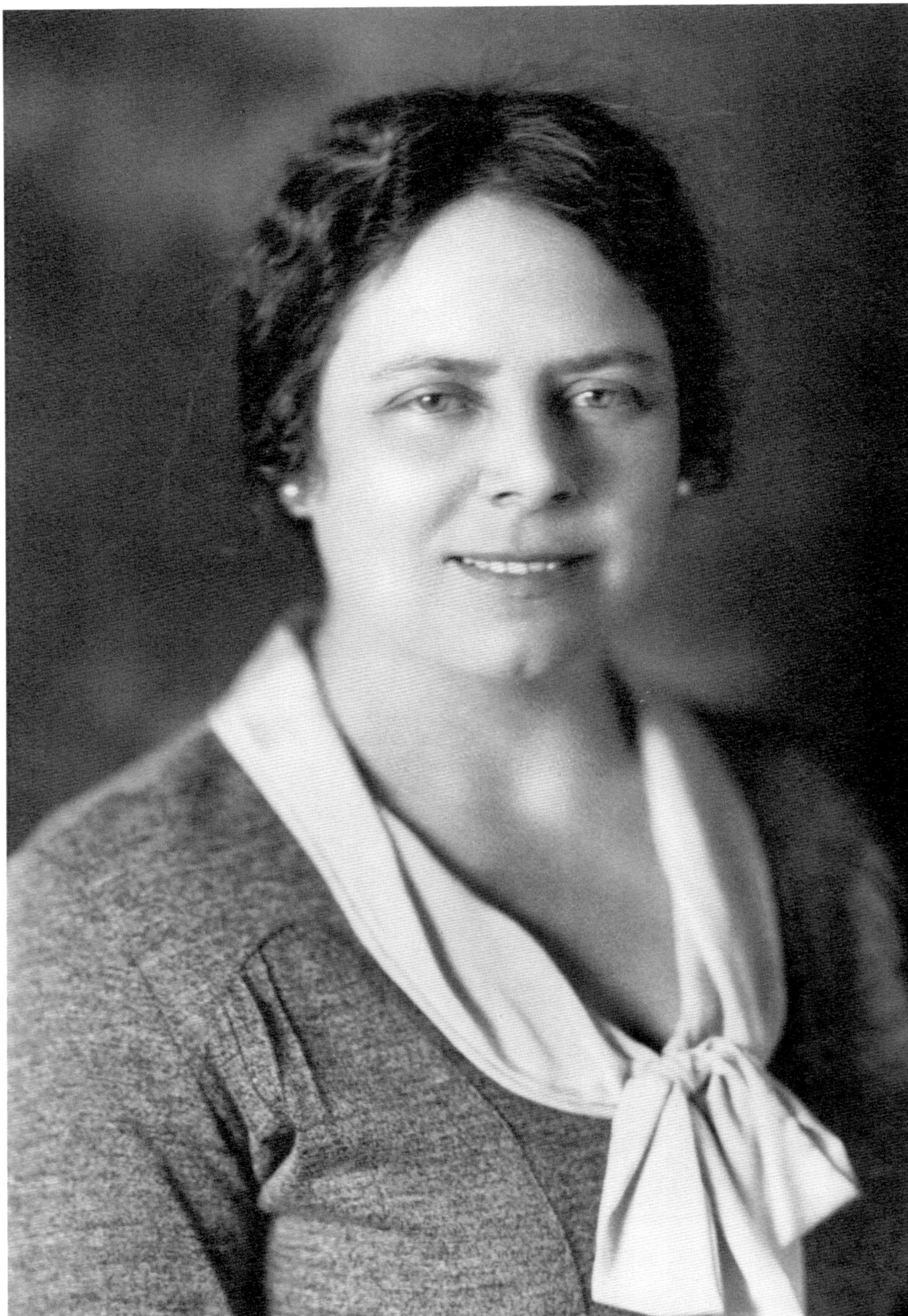

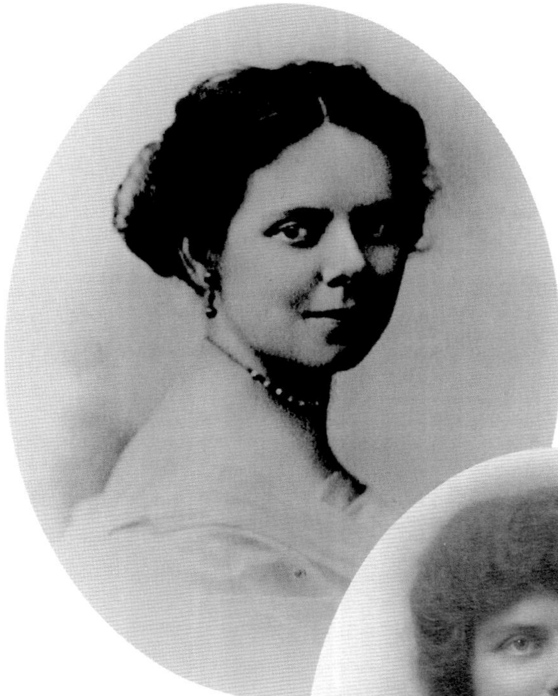

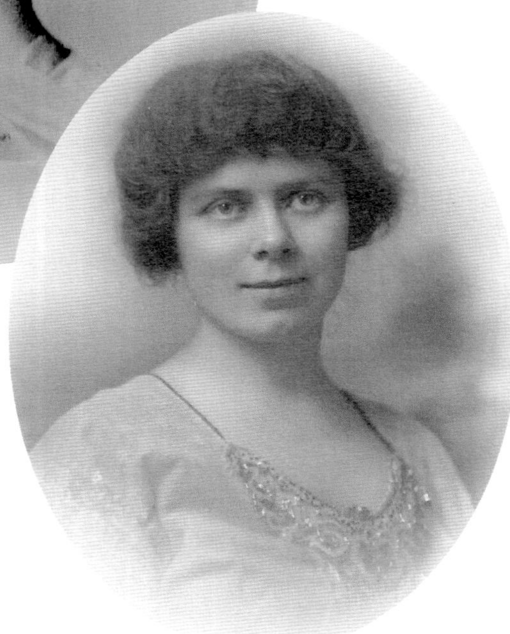

Ruth Hale Canaga
A dedicated teacher at Thornton Fractional High School in Calumet City for many years, Ruth Canaga, though regarded as "tough," "strict," and "uncompromising," loved sharing American history with her students. She attended the University of West Virginia, graduating in 1917. Many former students recalled receiving weekly letters from her during their military service during World War II. She and her husband lived on Ridge Road near Burnham Avenue and built a redbrick building on the property that housed Lansing's first telephone switchboard. It was said that until her husband's death, the couple never missed a Thornton Fractional High School basketball game. Ruth traced her roots to indicate a relation to Capt. Nathan Hale, a soldier of the Revolutionary War. A certificate dated March 29, 1912, is on file in the Lansing Historical Museum that inducted her into the National Society of Daughters of the American Revolution as a descendant of Robert Hale. One of Lansing's elementary schools is named in honor of Nathan Hale. Following Ruth's death, the contents of her home were auctioned off and some items were donated to the Lansing Historical Museum. (All, courtesy of the Lansing Historical Society.)

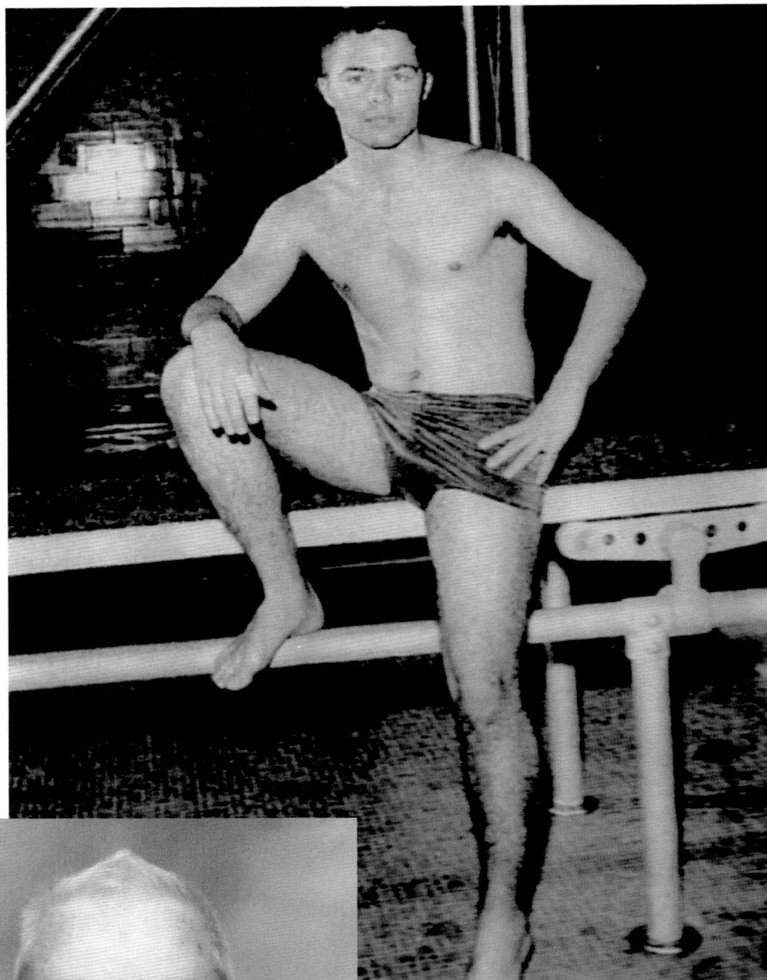

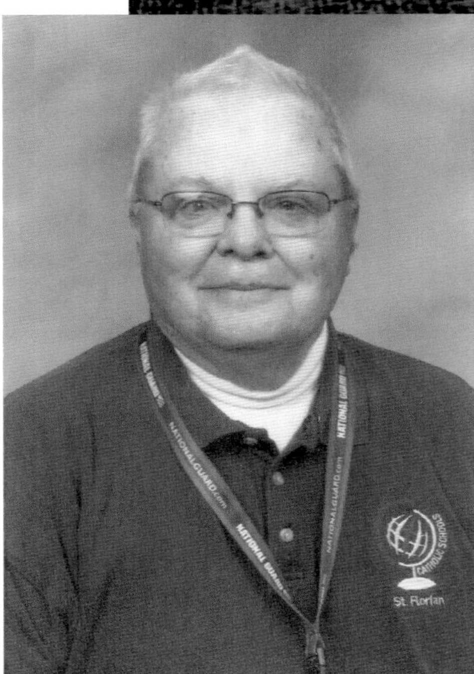

Jim Kijewski

A much-loved history teacher and swimming coach at Thornton Fractional High School, Jim Kijewski is probably best remembered as the manager of the Lan-Oak Pool. Kijewski was there from day one and was the second person to set foot in the pool upon its completion. His teaching schedule allowed him to spend his summers managing the popular summer hangout where local kids went to cool off. Since his retirement from Thornton Fractional South High School, he has worked as the physical education teacher at St. Florian School in Chicago. Kijewski has been active in the community as a member of the Golden Ks and for years has traveled to local schools to read to young students and tutor them. (Both, courtesy of JoAnn Kijewski.)

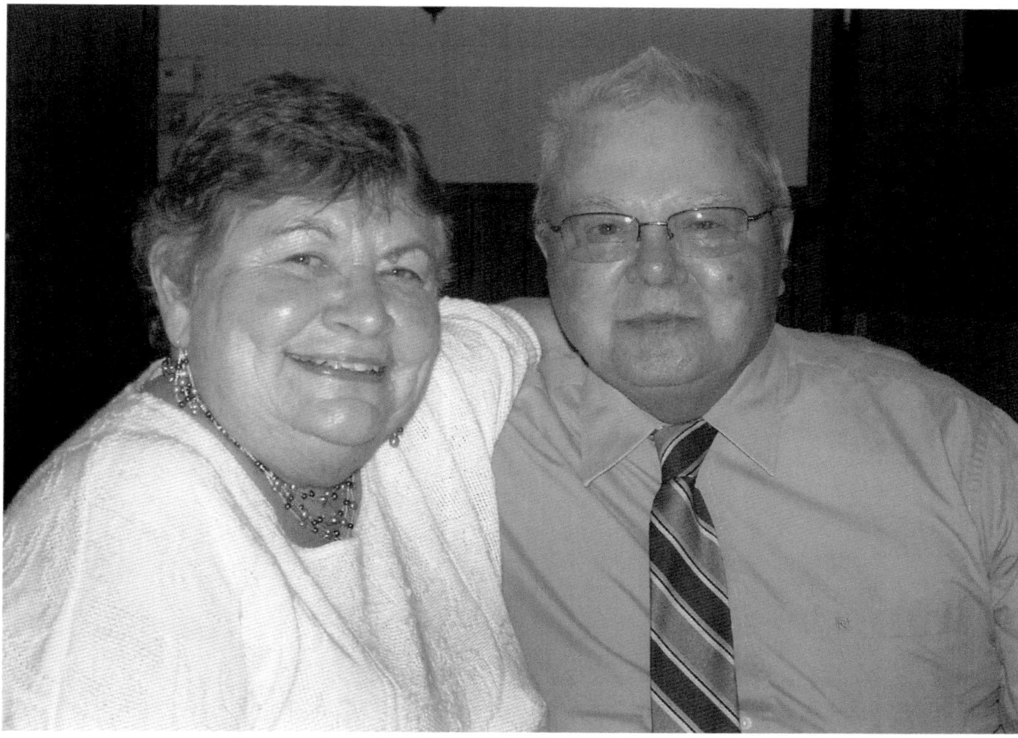

JoAnn Kijewski
Jim Kijewski is pictured with his wife, JoAnn, also a long-time educator as a kindergarten teacher at St. Florian School in Chicago. She has also been an active member of the Lansing Junior Woman's Club for the past 40 years. (Author's collection.)

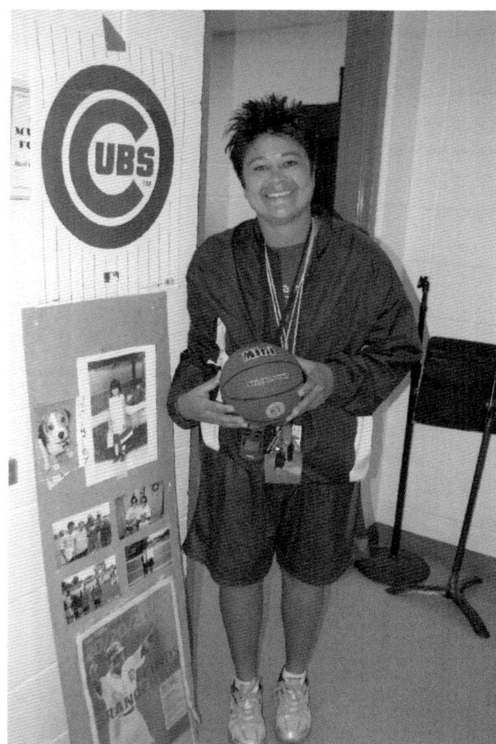

Sally Reynolds
Sally Reynolds worked alongside Patti Leach as a physical education teacher in school district No. 158. She and Rick Seymour have put together the Lansing Roundball Classic, a basketball tournament that includes all the Lansing elementary schools. Her husband, Ken, is a high school teacher and the couple has two children: Cori and Louis. (Author's collection.)

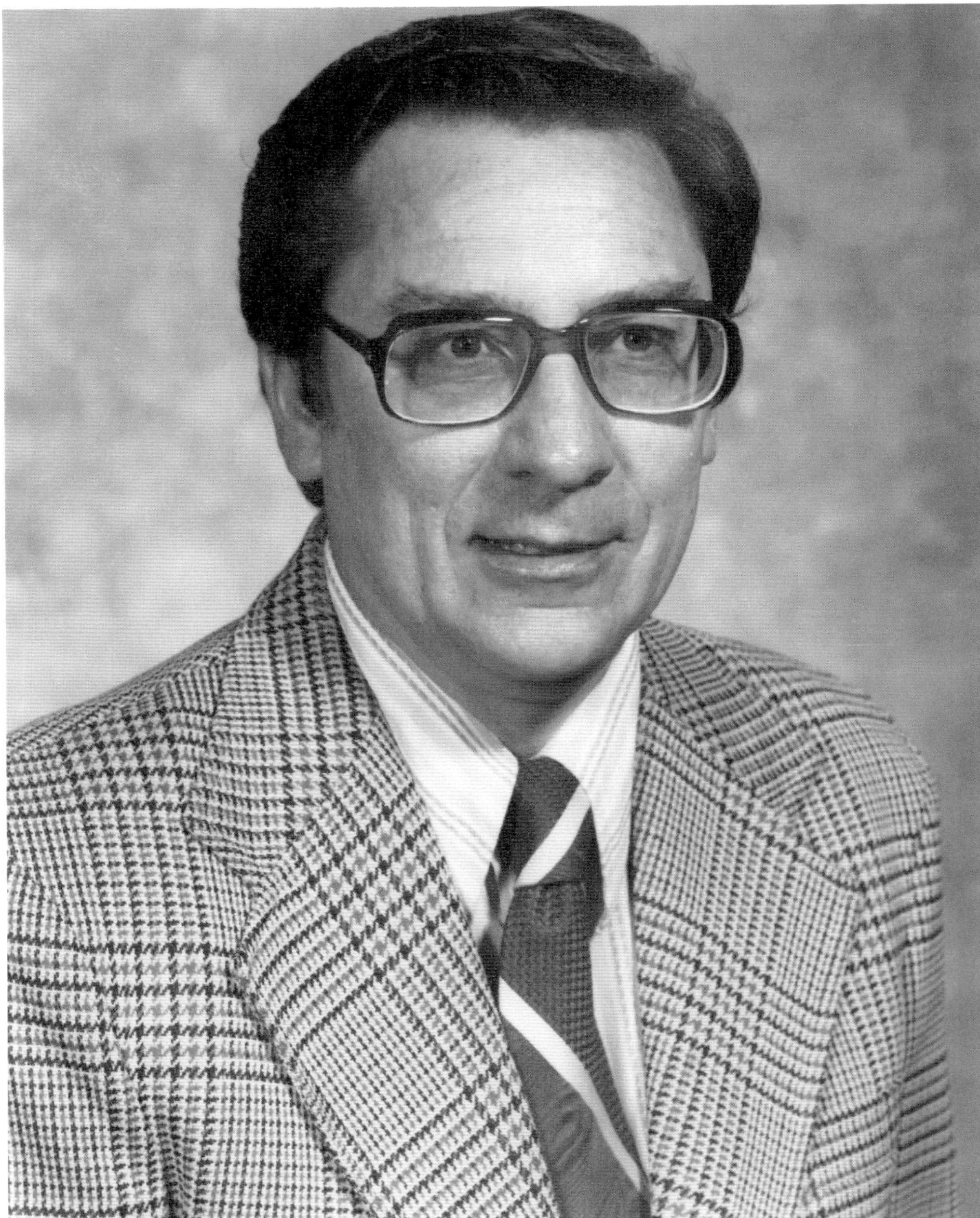

Durward Schuetz

Durward Schuetz was a longtime teacher and principal and later superintendent of school district No. 171 at the south end of Lansing. He retired in 1993. A fine arts program continues to this day that was named for Durward and his wife, Pat, who were big supporters of the arts. Schuetz was well liked by his staff. During his administration, the school district grew from one small building, Sunnybrook School, to two large state-of-the-art schools, Nathan Hale Elementary School and Heritage Middle School. (Courtesy of Durward Schuetz.)

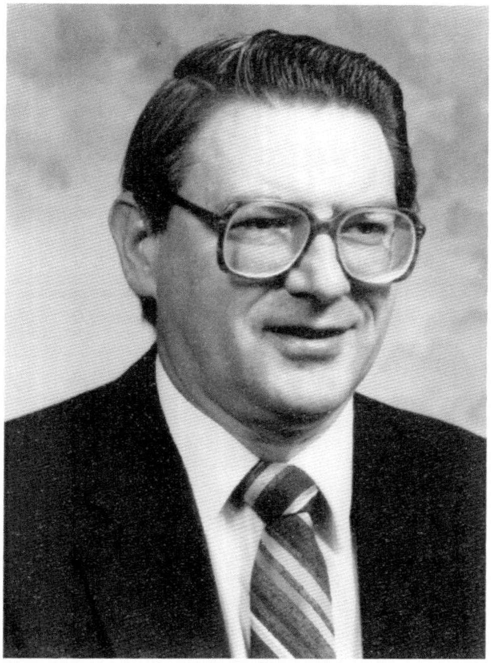

Harold Gronewold

Hal Gronewold's career began in the former location of St. John Lutheran School, where he served as a longtime teacher and principal. For more than two decades, he taught third, fourth, seventh, and eighth grades and was coach of the boys' sports teams. He also served as a principal at St. John. He is very involved at St. John Lutheran Church currently, where he preaches, visits shut-ins, plays on the dartball team, and sings in the choir. He is also an elder and an usher. (Both, courtesy of Eileen Gronewold.)

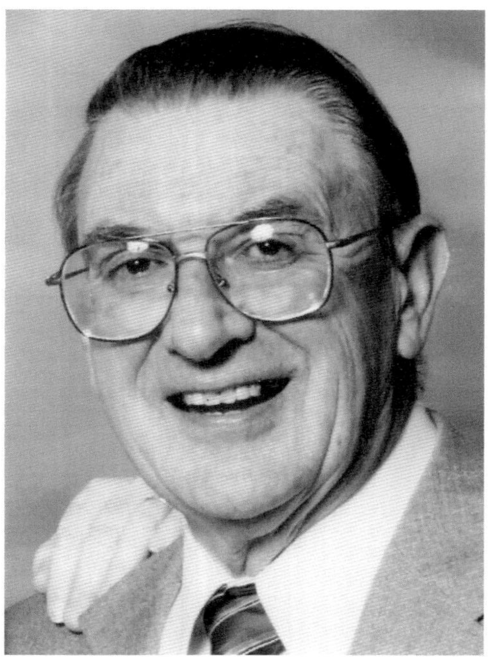

Cindy Neickula

Hundreds of students have passed through Cindy Neickula's classroom as their educational foundation was set by her loving and encouraging teaching style. A graduate of National Louis University and Olivet University, Neickula has been a kindergarten teacher for 25 years, with the last 12 at Oak Glen School in Lansing. She has presented workshops to groups of up to 300 on integrated learning at various teaching conferences. She has been nominated for the Golden Apple Award, the Disney Teaching Award, and the Kohl/McCormick Early childhood Teaching Award, and she is a recipient of the Lansing Sam's Club Teacher of the Year Award. Married to her husband, Joe, for 34 years, the couple has three kids. Their son is a doctor, one daughter is an X-ray technician, and one daughter is a kindergarten teacher. She has three grandchildren. (Courtesy of Cindy Neickula.)

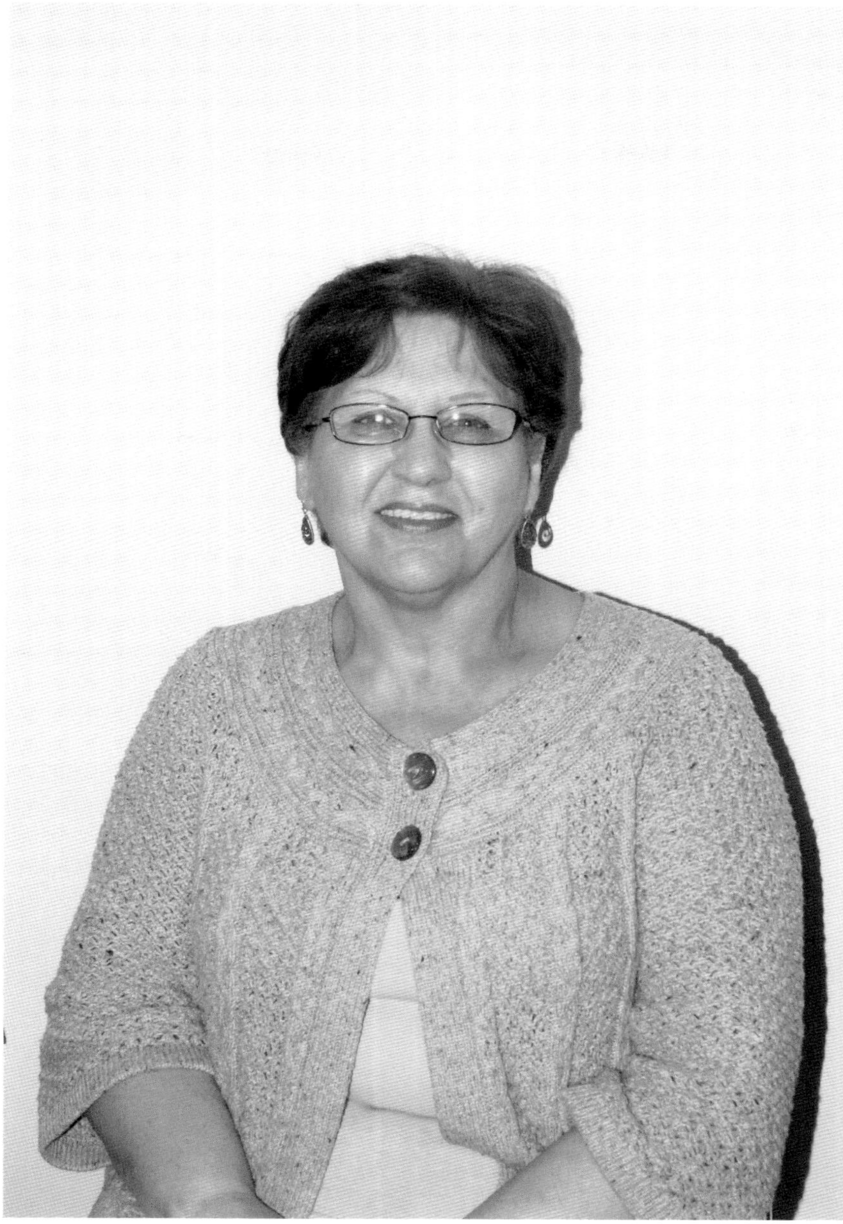

Toni DeLaurentis
A retired fourth-grade teacher from Oak Glen School in Lansing, Toni enjoyed teaching her kids about history and organized a yearly field trip to Springfield to learn more about Abraham Lincoln and the state capital. In her retirement, she gives lectures about Illinois agriculture at area schools. A member of the Lansing Historical Society, she worked with every Lansing school to involve them in a contest for a chance to paint a table-top replica of the trimotor planes that were placed throughout town during the Tri Motors in Plane View public art project. She was a 2010 recipient of the ATHENA Award. Her husband, Tony, has served for several years as a village trustee. The couple has three children and five grandchildren. (Author's collection.)

Richard Dust

A retired social studies teacher from Thornton Fractional South High School, Richard Dust spent 37 years teaching and has served on the school board for school district No. 215 for three years. He is currently the board president. He also coached cross-country, track, and softball and was a National Honor Society sponsor. He is an active member of the First United Methodist Church of Lansing and volunteers doing deliveries for Meals on Wheels. Dust is a lifelong Lansing resident who attended Coolidge School, Memorial Jr. High School, and Thornton Fractional South High School. His wife, Barb, also taught for many years in Lansing. They have three daughters and two grandchildren. (Author's collection.)

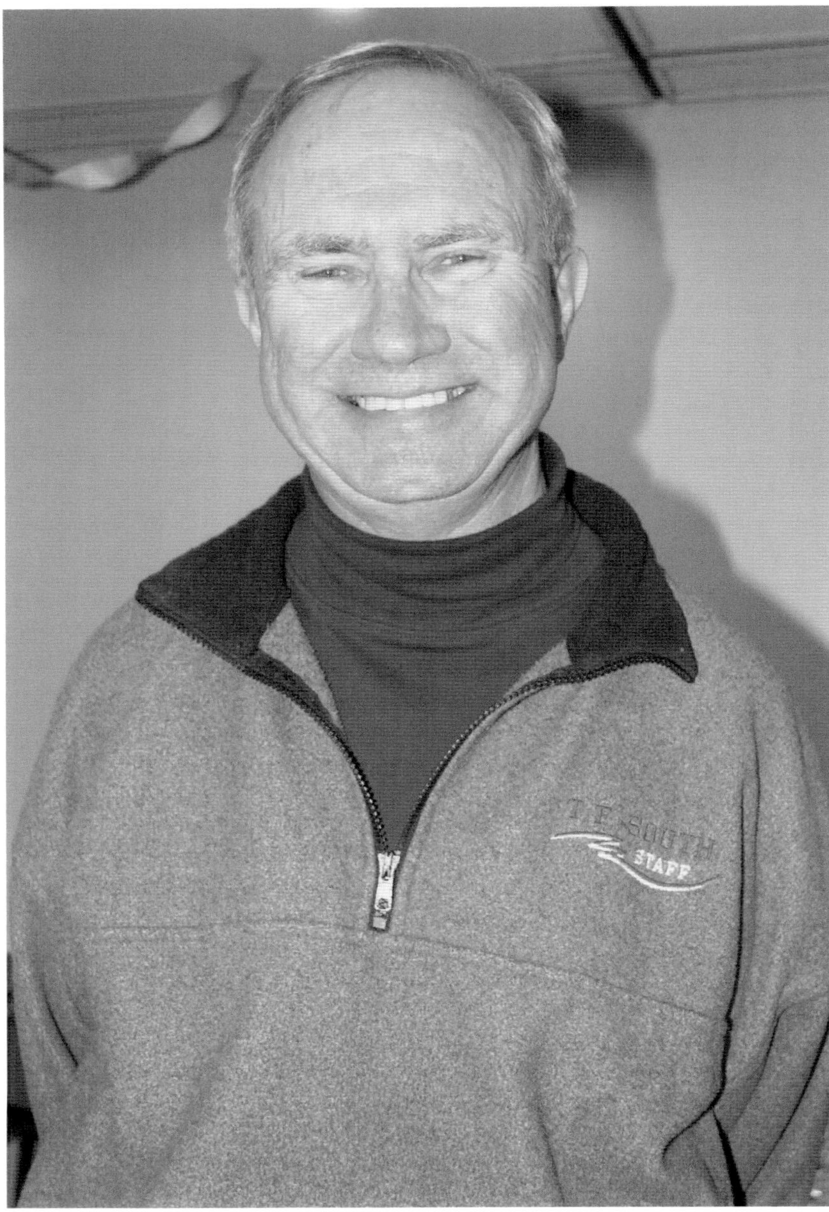

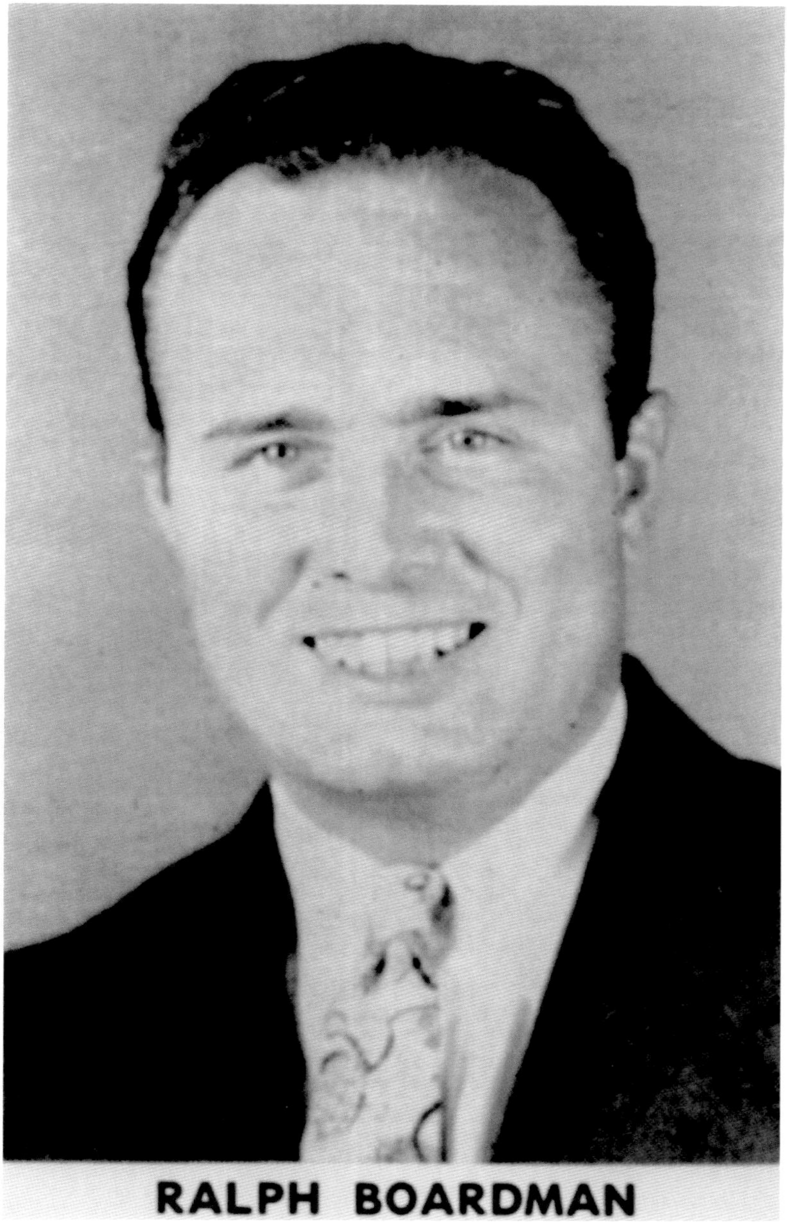

Ralph Boardman

A longtime teacher at Trinity Lutheran School, Ralph Boardman became school principal, succeeding William Kraegel. At the time he began teaching at Trinity Lutheran School it was a two-room school house, and he taught the upper grades while also coaching and keeping coal in the furnace. Later, he became principal while still teaching eighth grade. His career spanned more than 30 years there. He has been very interested in history and recording the history of the school and church. He and his wife, Nellie, had three daughters. Nellie was also very involved in the school and church and served as the church secretary. He is also a veteran of World War II. (Courtesy of the Lansing Historical Society.)

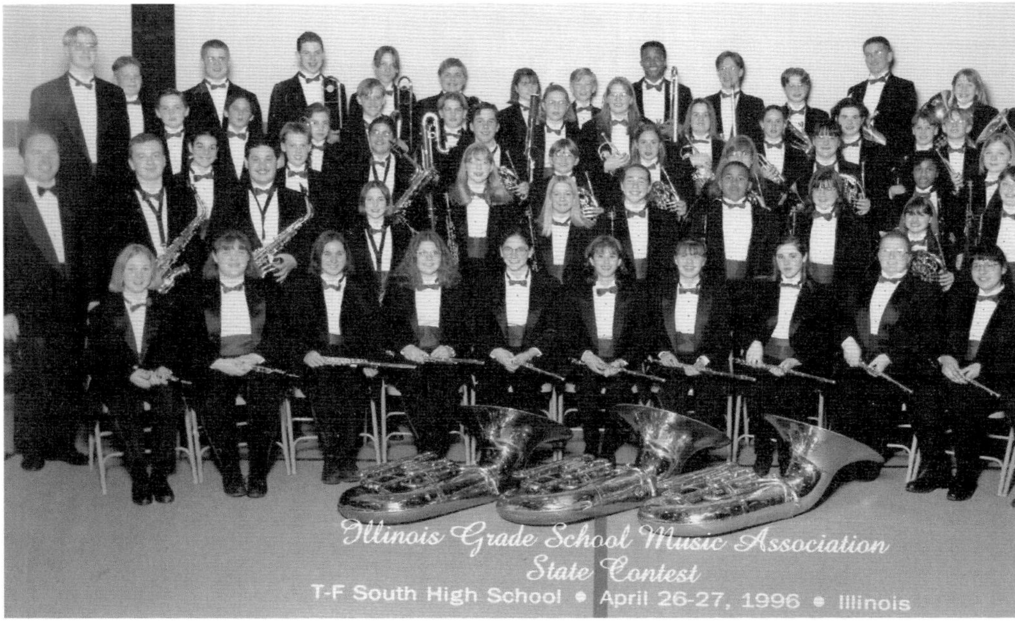

David Allie

As a band director in his 36th year of teaching at school district No. 158, David Allie has impacted countless students. He has served as band director at Memorial Junior High School and also instructs fifth-grade students in the district on instruments before entering Memorial Junior High School. (Both, courtesy of David Allie.)

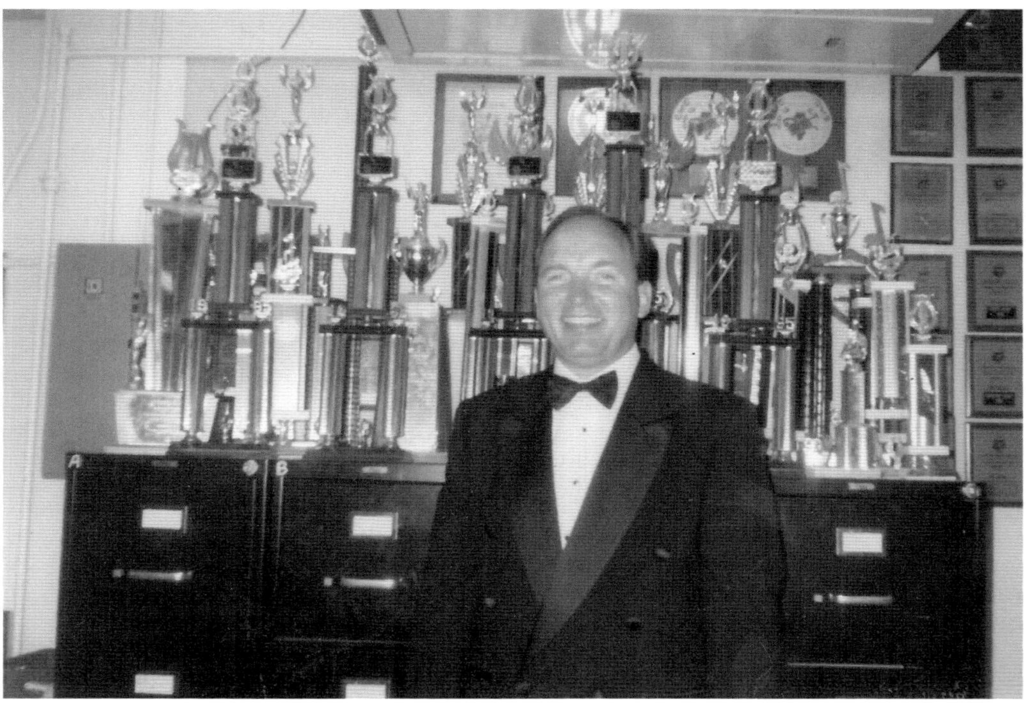

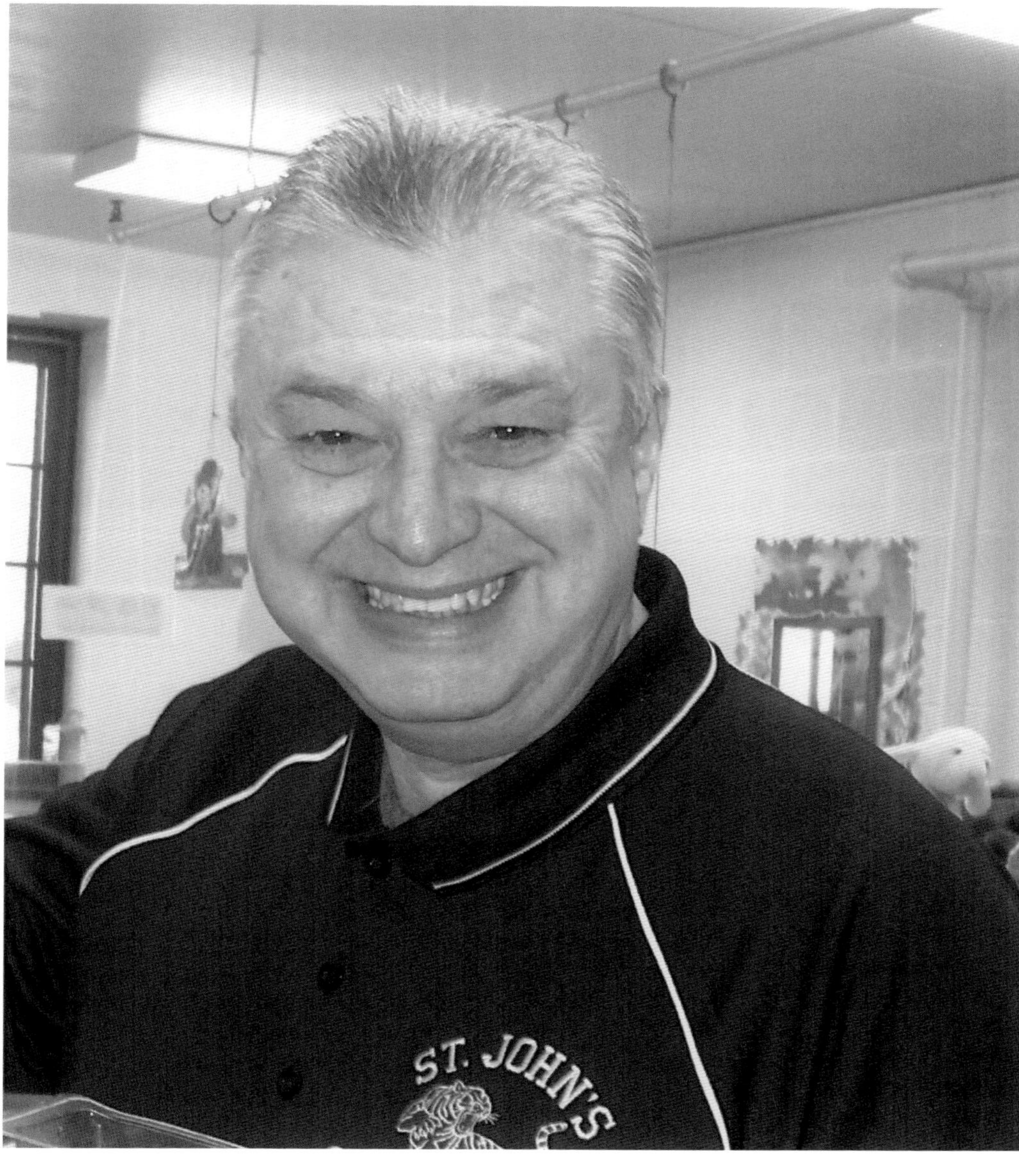

David Swanson

Dave Swanson became principal at St. John Lutheran School in 1984, the first principal to serve in the new school building, along with teaching seventh and eighth grade. A native of Cleveland, Ohio, he is a 1970 graduate of Concordia Teachers College in River Forest. His first call to teaching was in a Chicago school. He then taught at St. Peter Lutheran School in Joliet and then Salem Lutheran School in Homewood. He spent 27 years of his 42-year career at St. John School, where he also served as athletic director. He also coached girls' basketball at Thornton Fractional South High School, with eight years as the freshman coach and two years as the assistant varsity coach. (Author's collection.)

Carol Joza

A warm and friendly personality and attitude that "all children are a blessing" drew families to St. John School for their children's first formal classroom setting where Carol Joza has served as the three-year-old preschool teacher. She has taught many siblings over the years and has seen the program go from a half-day, part-time schedule to a full-time schedule. Integrating lots of field trips and hands-on lessons, Carol has taught dozens of preschoolers the education basics while also introducing them to religious education. (Author's collection.)

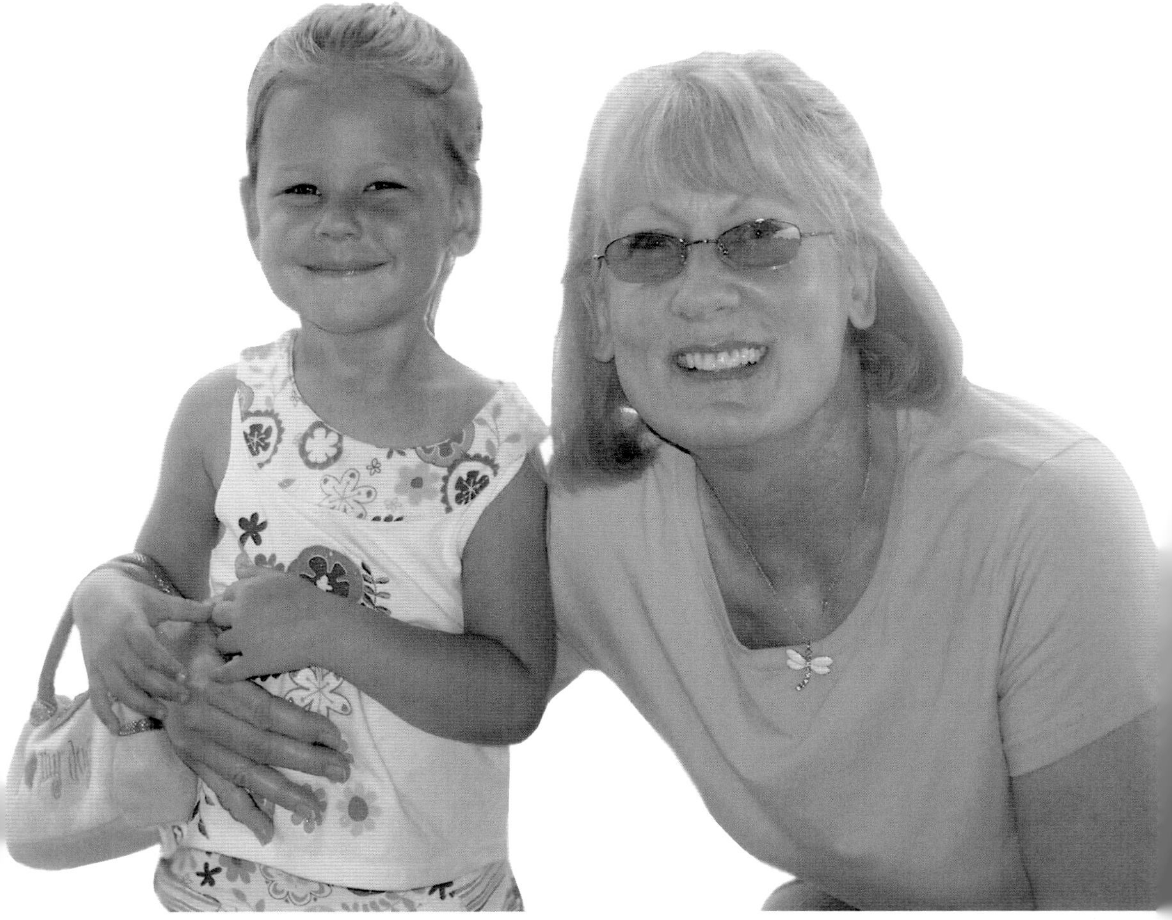

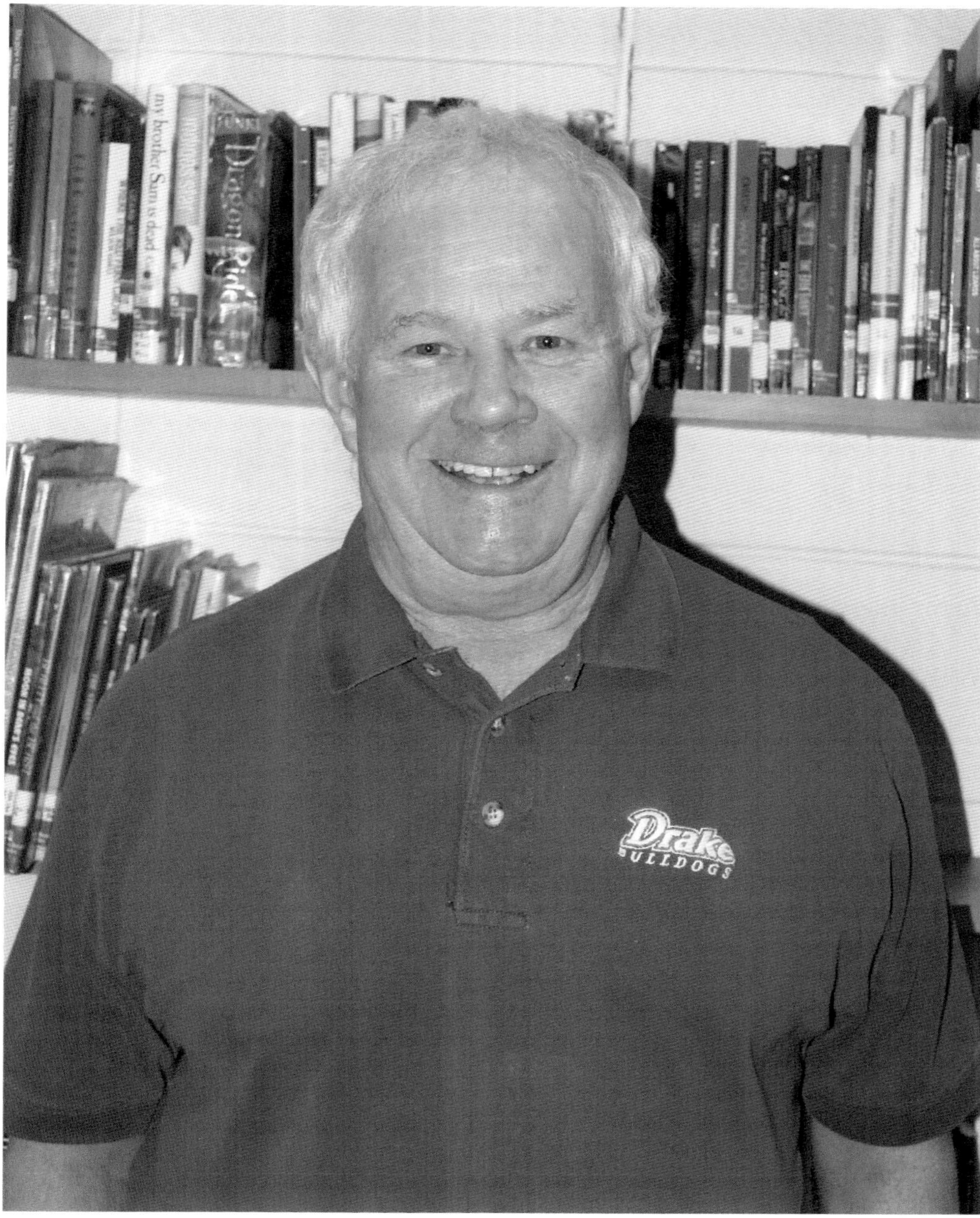

Jerome Kern

Jerry Kern has served on the school board for school district No. 158 for 40 years. He served on the Lansing Chamber of Commerce Board of Directors for four years and was a member of the Lansing Economic Development Board for five years. He currently serves on the planning and zoning board of appeals and has served on that board for eight years. He is retired from the engineering department of Acme Steel. He and his wife, Mary (May), have three children and six grandchildren. (Author's collection.)

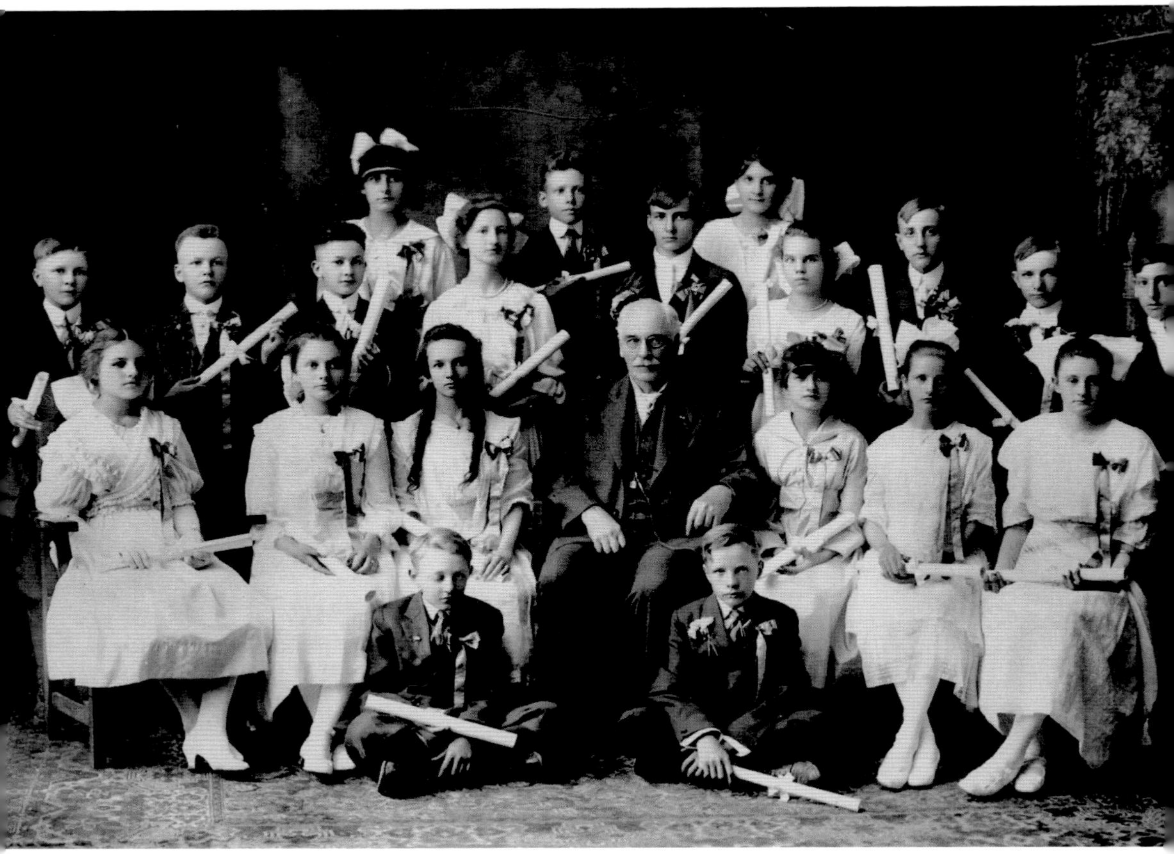

D.W. Gamble

For several years in the first part of the 20th century, D.W. Gamble served as a teacher and principal of the Lansing Public School. Gamble is pictured here with the 1917 graduating class. Pictured from left to right are (first row) William Maat and Nelson Norrgran; (second row) Elizabeth Dietrick, Alice DeVries, Emma Drunecke, D.W. Gamble, Frances Lucas, Ann Cook, and Nellie Van Heert; (third row) Evert Schultz, Walter Schultz, Alfred St. Aibin, Artha Fieldhouse, Cornelius Vroom, Pauline Lange, William Wietzer, William Fiene, and Delphus LaTulip; (fourth row) Elizabeth Erfert, Raymond Fieldhouse, and Esther Mueller. (Courtesy of the Lansing Historical Society.)

CHAPTER FOUR

Groups and Organizations

Since the early days of Lansing, citizens have sought to be part of civic and social organizations with intentions of benefiting the greater good of the community. The first half of the 20th century saw chapters of many organizations become a part of Lansing, from the Lions Club to the Scouting groups to the Lansing Old Timers. The police and fire departments were established, with eager residents volunteering to play a part in ensuring the safety of their neighbors. Social groups used the talents of their members for humanitarian efforts and community betterment. Community events were planned to bring residents together and foster a sense of pride, including annual happenings like the steak fry, Santa House, and Good Neighbor Parade. As the years have moved forward, some organizations have faded and others are still going strong, continuing the sense of togetherness and public service.

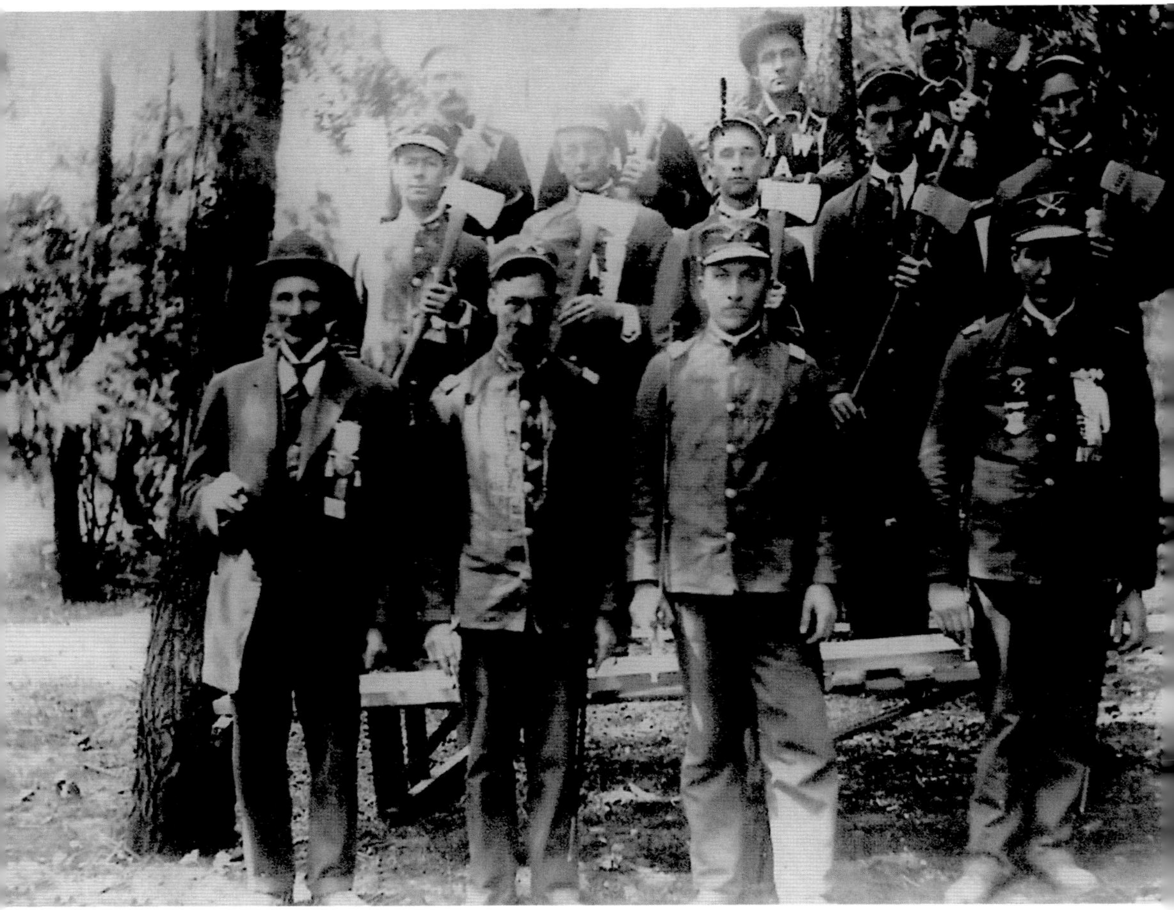

Modern Woodmen of America Camp No. 9344

One of Lansing's early organizations was the Modern Woodmen of America Camp No. 9344 of Oak Glen, Illinois, which held meetings at Busack's Tavern in Lansing. The man on the far left in the first row is Edward Krumm, who was the owner of Edward F. Krumm Building Materials. This photograph was taken in 1907. (Courtesy of the Lansing Historical Society.)

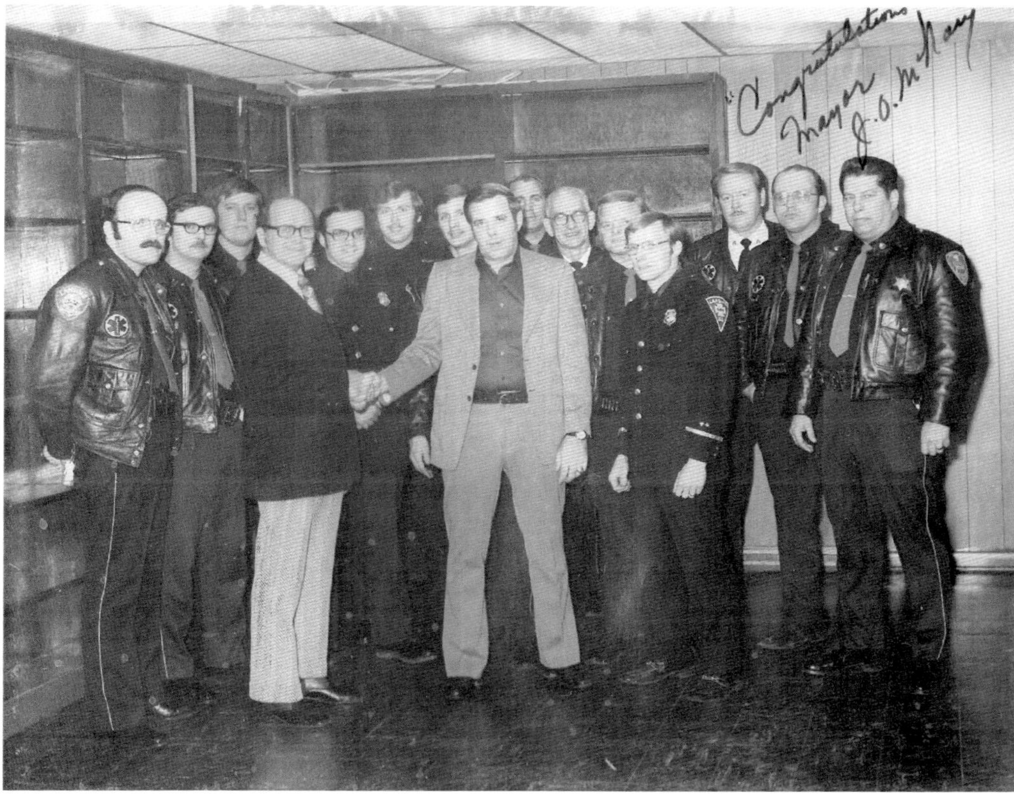

Lansing Police Department

This undated photograph shows Lansing police officers with Mayor Jack McNary. The top of the image reads "Congratulations! J.O. McNary." Ed Van Laningham served as Lansing's fire chief from 1931 to 1957 and was the only full-time police officer for many years. In 1936, he hired Jack Smith as the first part-time "special" officer. By 1957, when John Braschler became chief, there was a staff of five full-time officers and a supplemental part-time staff. In 1974, Dean Stanley became chief and the department saw many changes and the addition of new equipment. During his tenure, the department moved from its small quarters inside the former village hall building at Lake and Henry Streets to the current facility on 170th Street. In 2001, Daniel McDevitt became chief, leading his department during the September 11 tragedy. The current chief is Dennis Murrin, whose father and grandfather were both police officers in Lansing. (Courtesy of the Lansing Historical Society.)

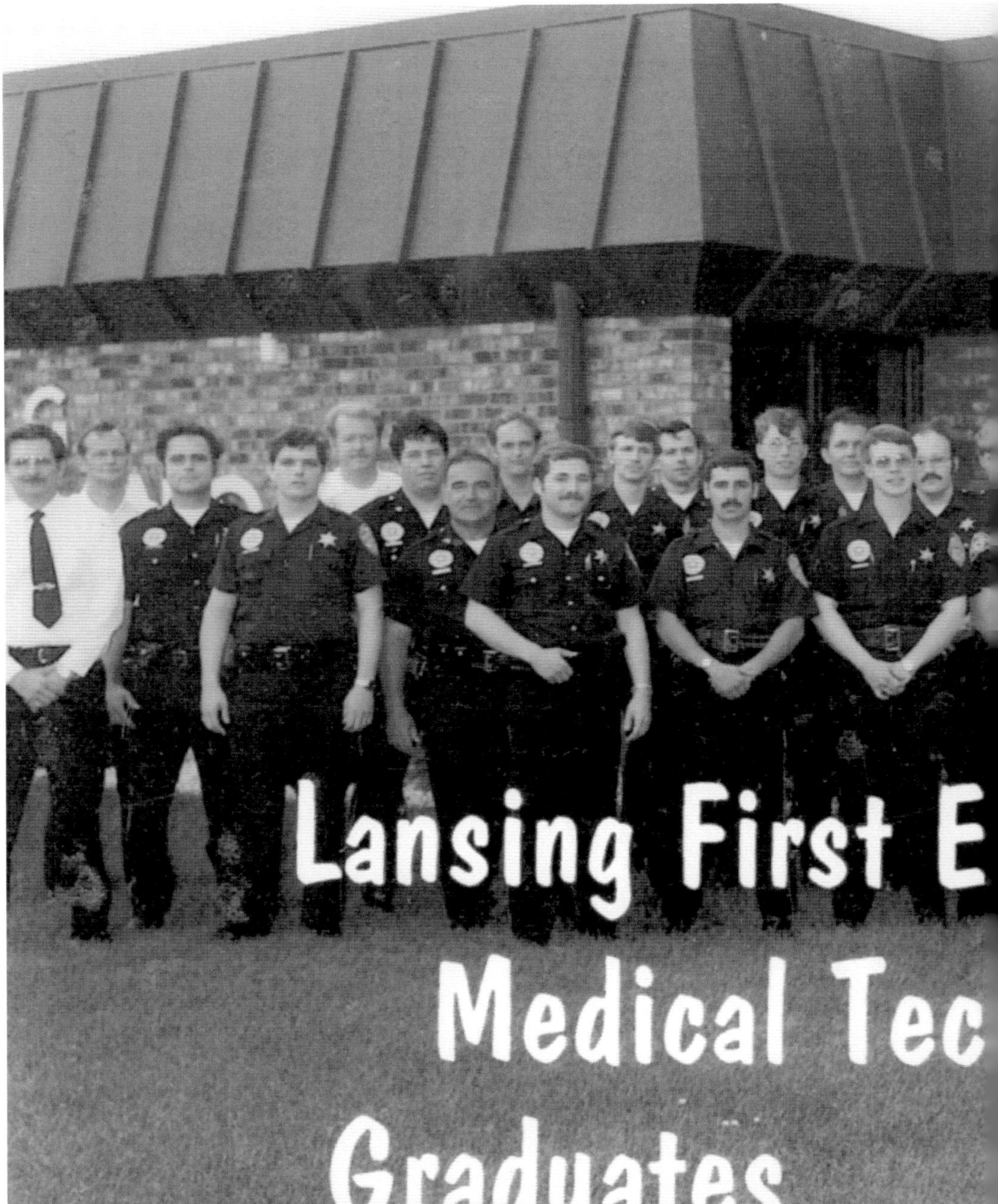
Lansing First E
Medical Tec
Graduates

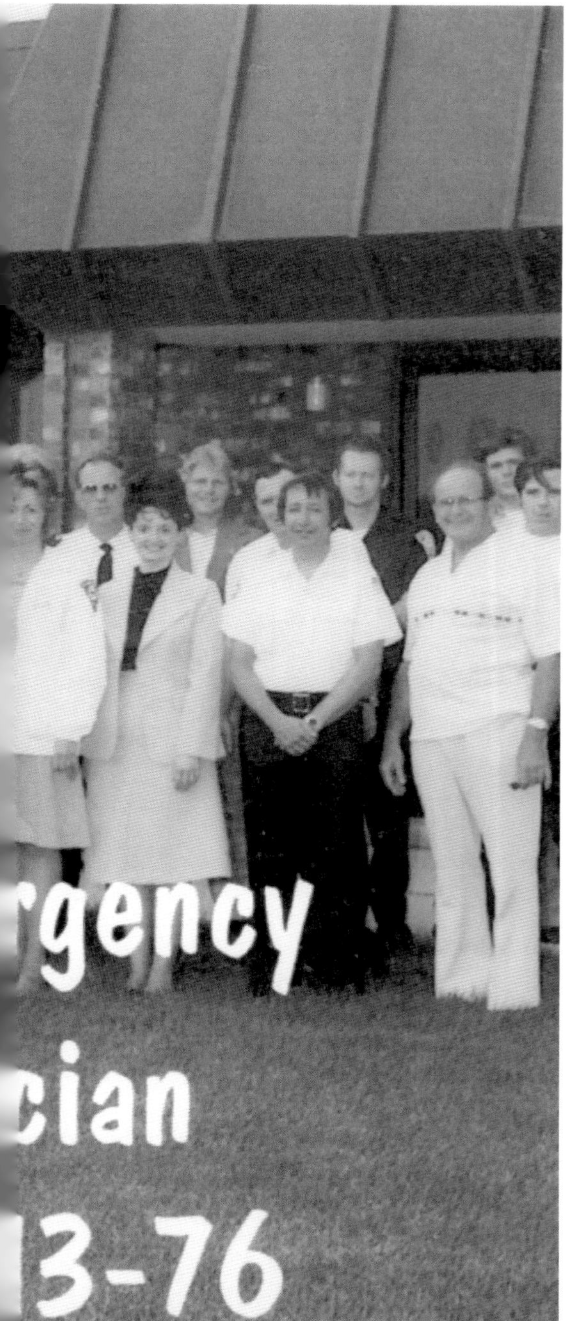

Lansing Emergency Medical Services
In 1976, Lansing's EMS program went into operation and became one of the first municipalities in Illinois to have a fully trained paramedic staff. The first phase consisted of 81 hours of training, including 15 emergency room hours, and the second phase involved 108 classroom hours and 52 clinical hours through Ingalls Hospital. A combination of 35 police officers and firefighters made up the first graduating class of Lansing paramedics. (Courtesy of Patty Eidam.)

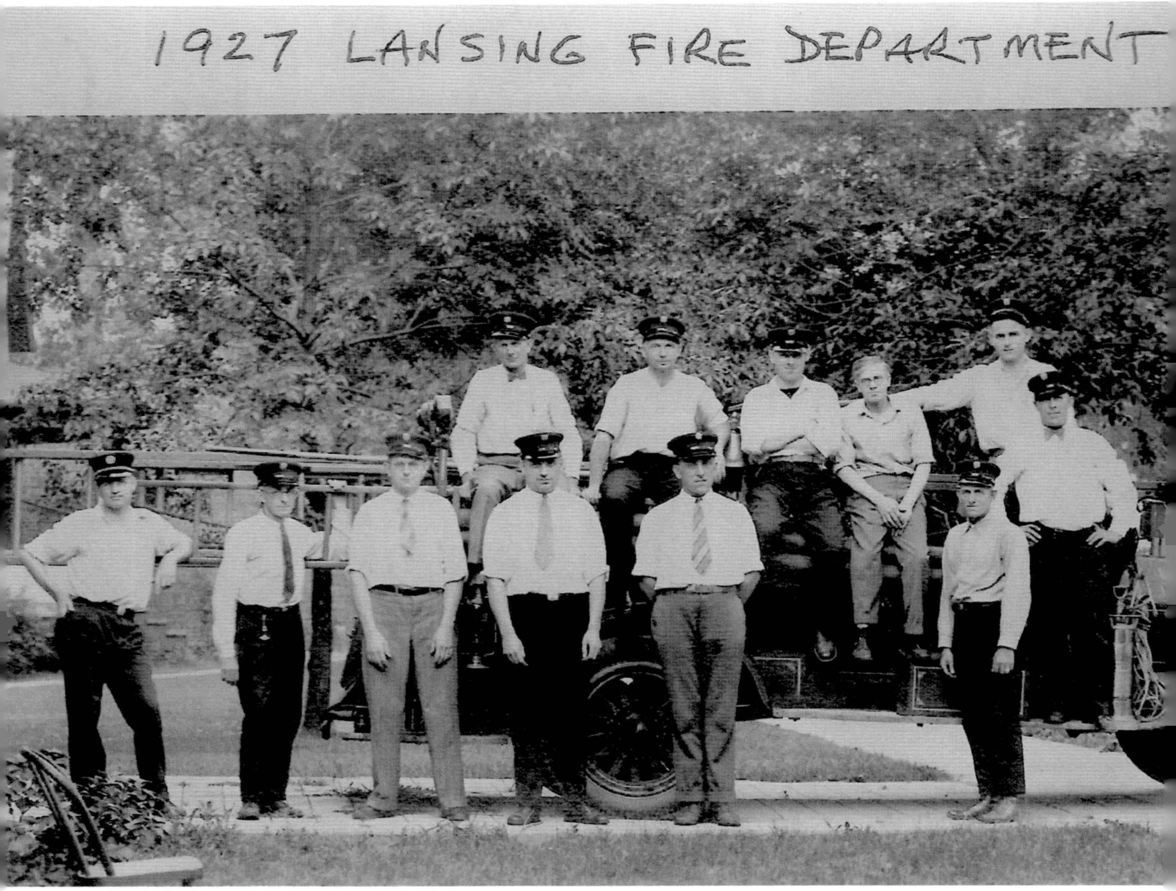

Lansing Fire Department
The Lansing Fire Department dates back to 1922 when William Winterhoff organized a group of 60 men to join the volunteer department. He donated a flatbed truck from his Ford dealership that became Lansing's first fire engine (pictured). In 1955, the Fire Prevention Bureau was formed. The original station was housed in the former village hall building at Lake and Henry Streets and a second station opened in 1958 on Chicago Avenue. A third station was dedicated in 1975 at the south end of town and a fourth station was later added as part of the police facility on 170th Street. In 1970, Ralph J. Schauer became the village's first full-time firefighter. Today, the department, under the direction of Chief Dan Gregorovic, operates as a full-time department with three shifts working 24 hours on and then 48 hours off, with a supplemental staff of paid, on-call firefighters. (Courtesy of the Lansing Historical Society.)

Lansing Lions Club

The Lansing Lions Club was chartered by Lions Clubs International on June 29, 1937. Over the years, club members have become involved in numerous community betterment and humanitarian projects, including providing squad cars to the Lansing Police Department, Jaws of Life to the Lansing Fire Department, light at the Lansing Old Timers Sports Complex, and scholarships to Lansing students. Pictured are members of the Lansing Lions Club at the annual Veterans Appreciation Dinner that is organized by the Lansing Junior Woman's Club and supported by a financial donation from the Lions Club. (Author's collection.)

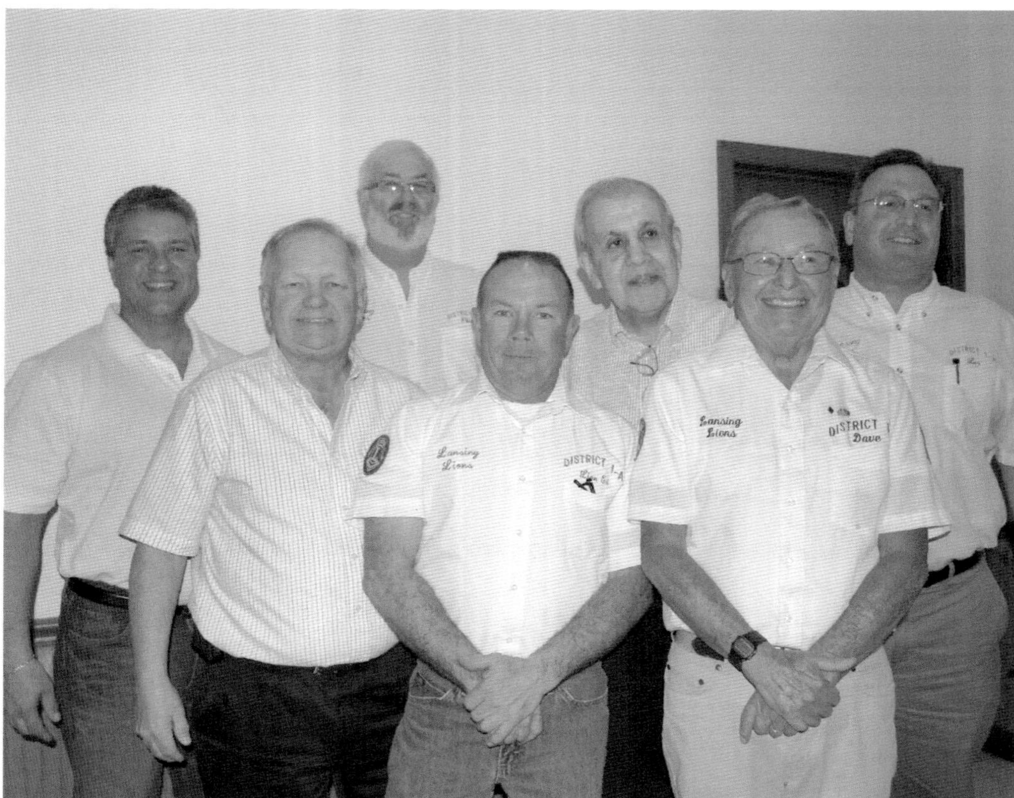

Lansing Veterans Memorial Ceremonial Honor Guard
The year 2012 marked 20 years that the Honor Guard has been in existence, having first met at the Lansing Airport to organize a group to appear at solemn events to honor those who have served their country. The group holds an annual Memorial Day service at the Lansing Veterans Memorial at the Lansing Airport and participates in other events and parades. (Author's collection.)

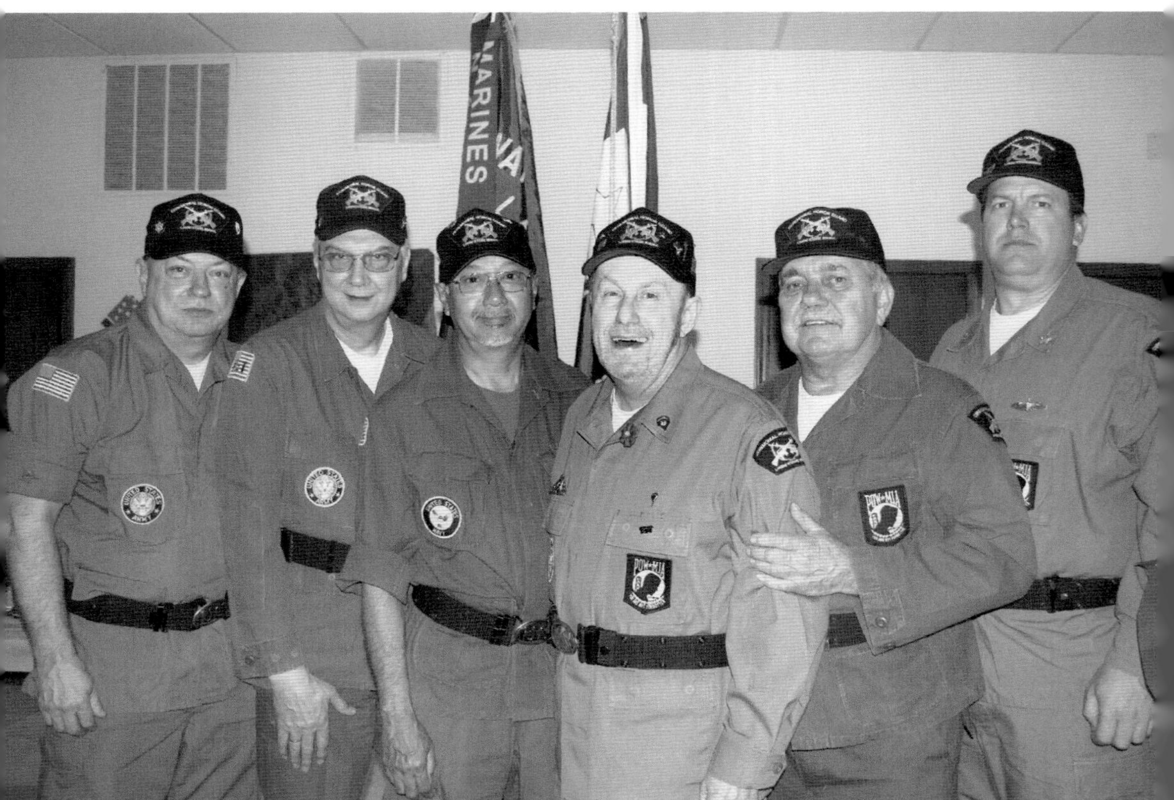

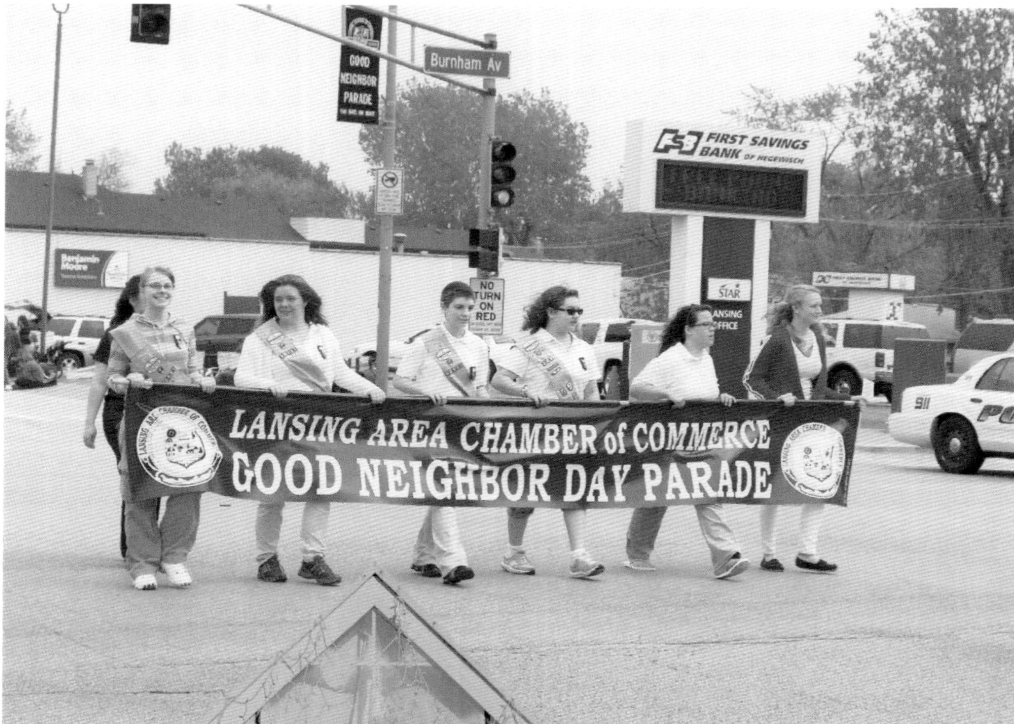

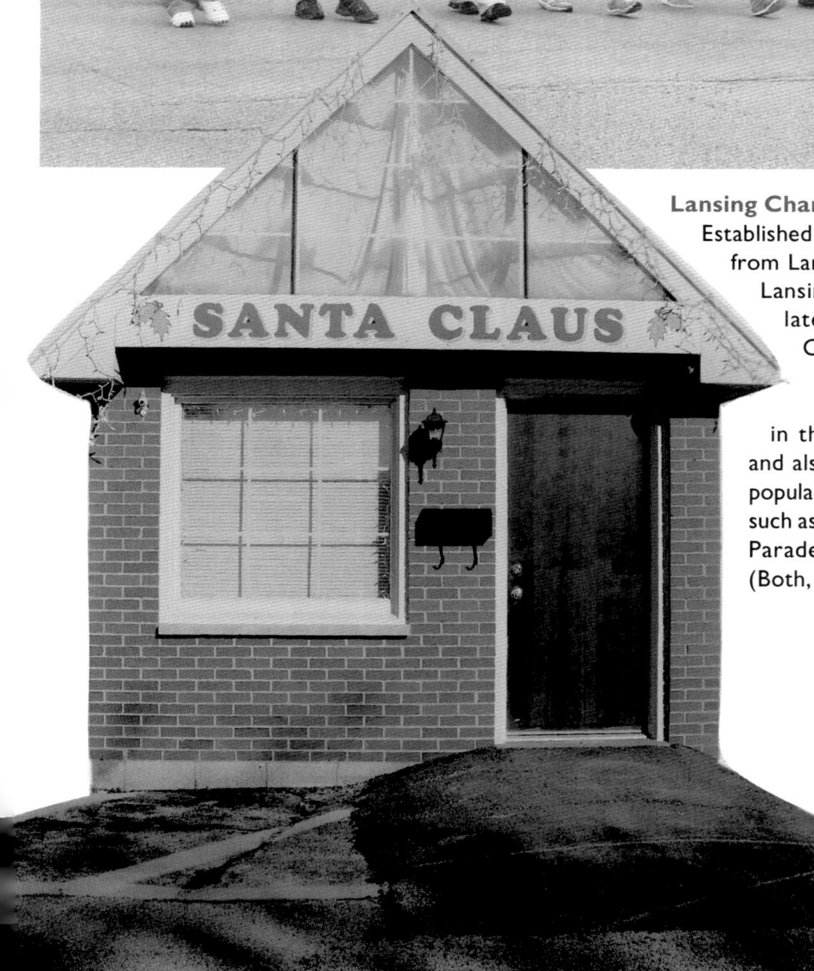

Lansing Chamber of Commerce Established in 1947 by 40 merchants from Lansing and Oak Glen, the Lansing Business Association later became the Lansing Chamber of Commerce. The group has provided support to its members in the business community and also arranged some of the popular annual events in Lansing, such as the Good Neighbor Day Parade and the Santa House. (Both, author's collection.)

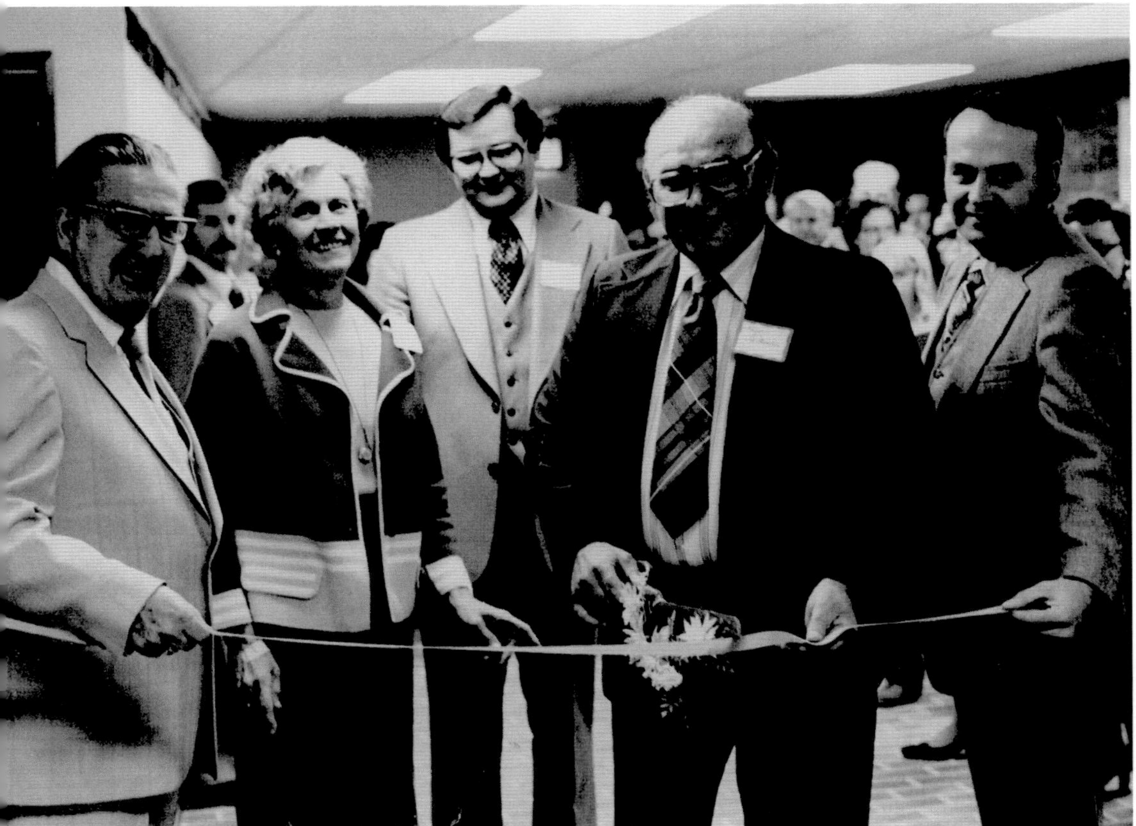

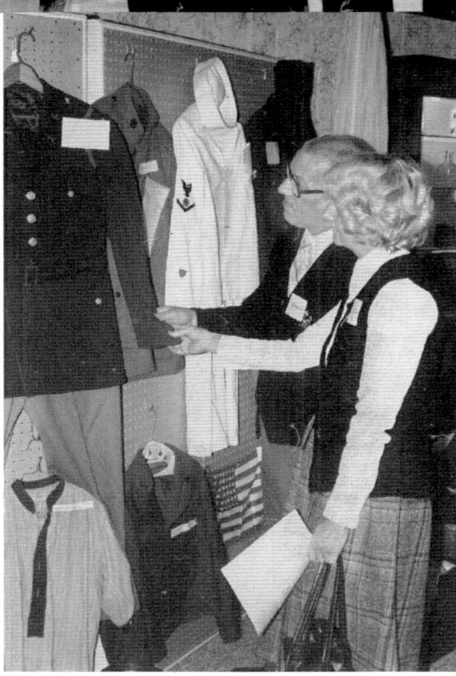

Museum Dedication
In 1980, the Lansing Historical Society, which had been established in 1976, finally moved into a permanent home in the lower level of the Lansing Public Library. Here Mayor Louis LaMourie does the ribbon cutting in the lobby of the museum, which continues to operate today in the same location. At the November 23, 1980, opening and dedication of the Lansing Historical Museum, an open house was held for the community to get a look at the first exhibits. Here, Art and Donna Galanis inspect some military uniforms on display. (Both, courtesy of the Lansing Historical Society.)

Lansing Historical Society
The Lansing Historical Society continues to engage residents in history through monthly meetings and programs and museum exhibits. Pictured is the 2012–2013 board (from left to right): Paul Schultz, Don Olsen, Marilyn Kooy, Barb Dust, Jackie Ore, Carrie Steinweg, and Richard Dust. (Courtesy of Patty Eidam.)

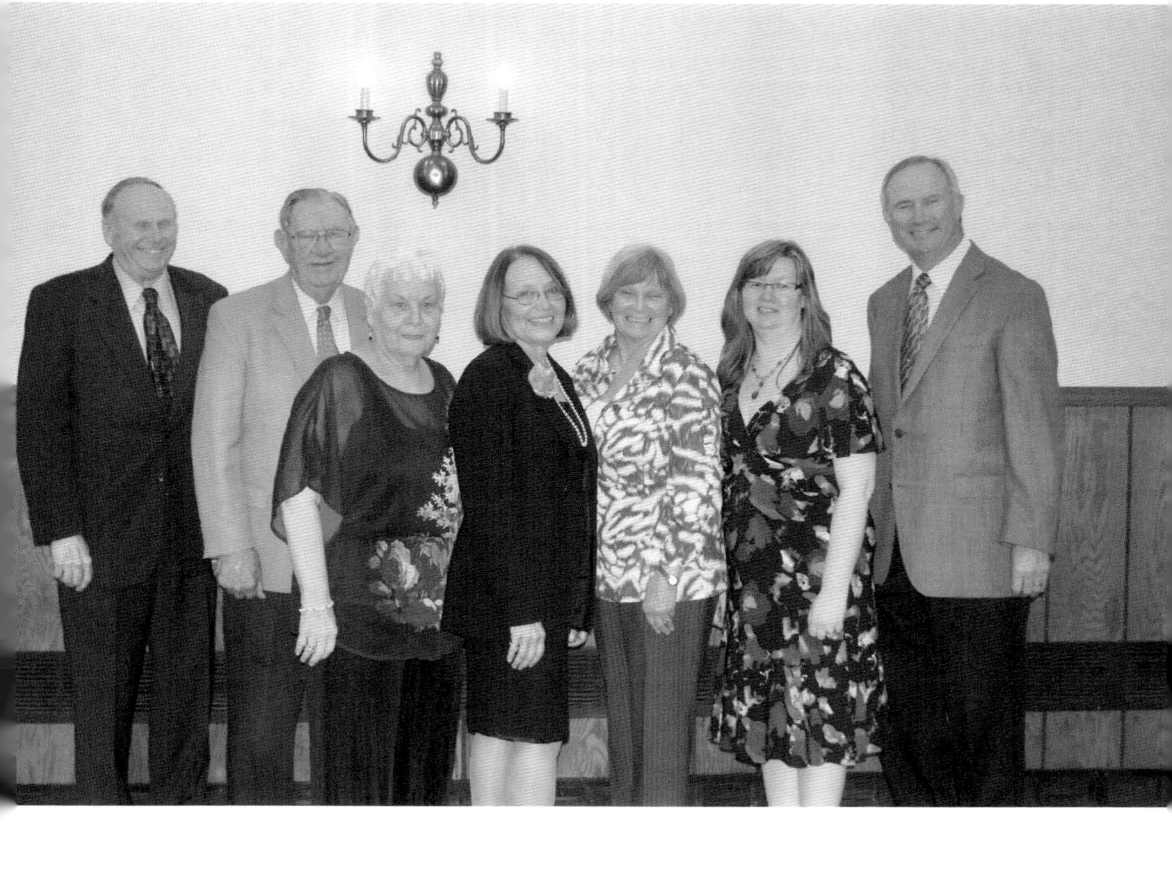

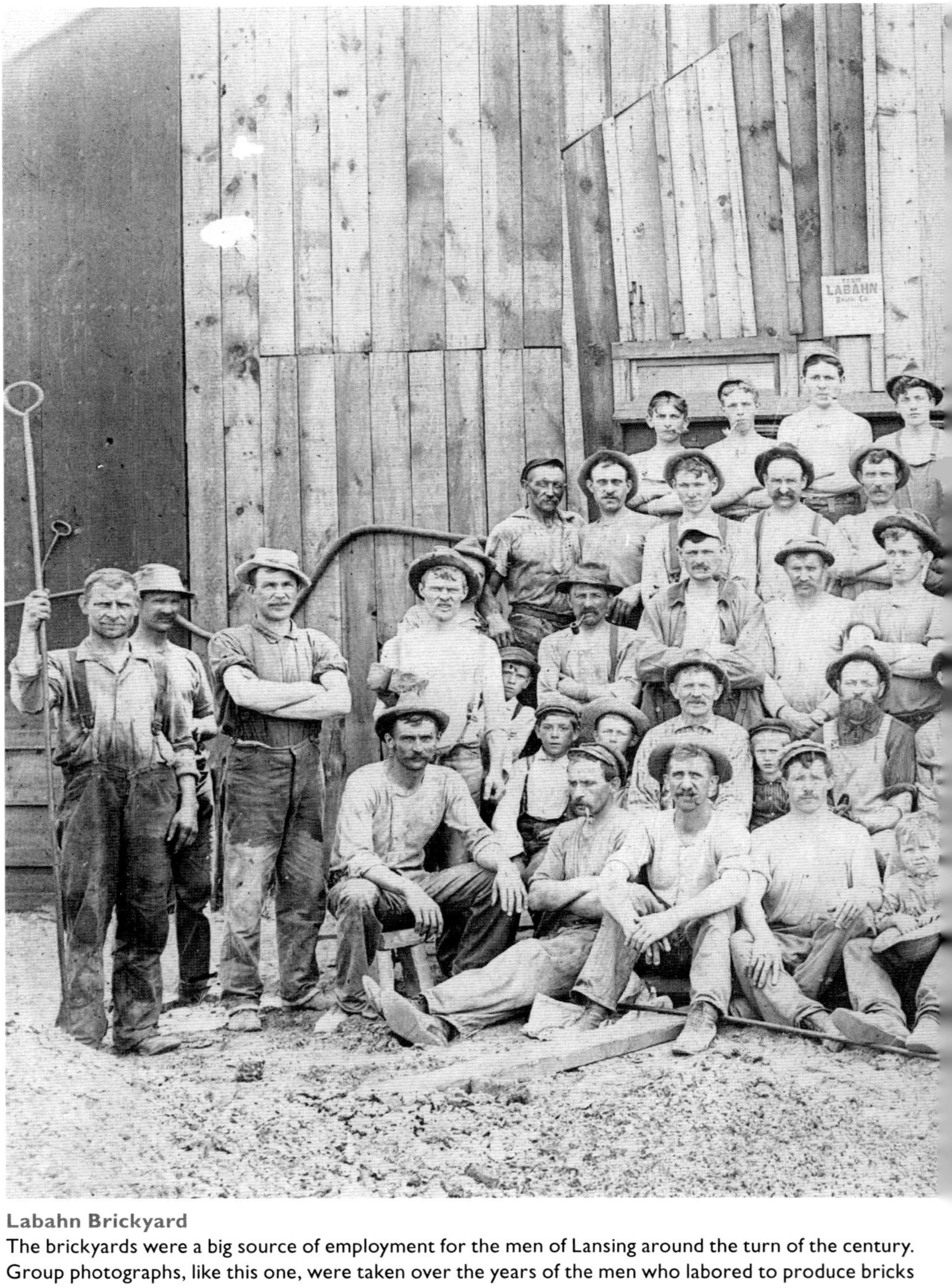

Labahn Brickyard

The brickyards were a big source of employment for the men of Lansing around the turn of the century. Group photographs, like this one, were taken over the years of the men who labored to produce bricks that were used in constructing many homes and structures in the area and beyond. Some of the employees in this Labahn Brickyard group photograph are: (top row) John Schuldt (fifth from left); (second row

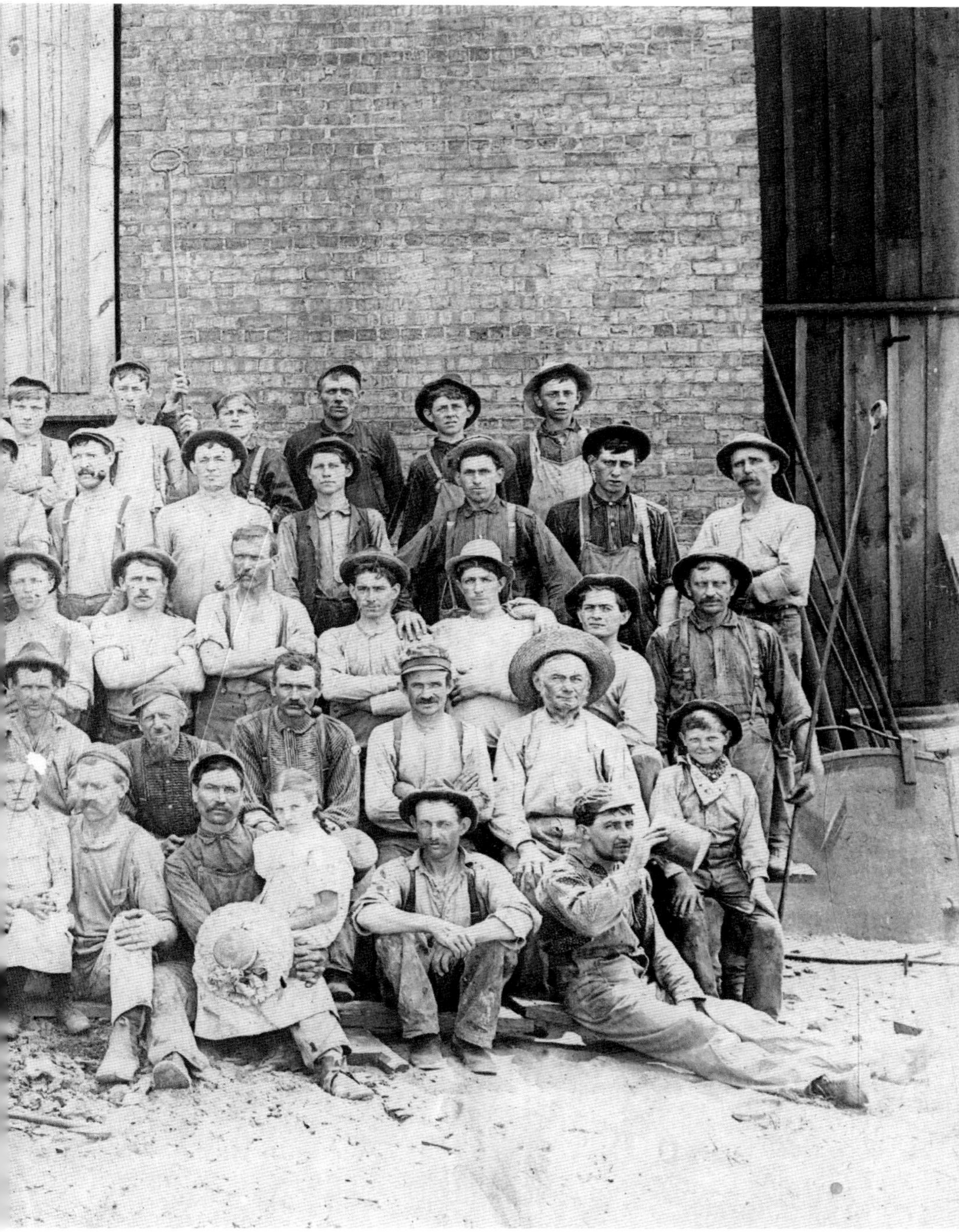

from the top) B. Beckman (ninth from left); (middle row) William Lange (seventh from left), Chas Wolf (ninth from left), Chas Miller (tenth from left), Fred Mueller (13th from left), and Chas Nittenhage (14th from left); (fifth row) Clarence Schultz (fourth from left); (bottom row) Clarence Schultz (fourth from left, on lap of Albert Schultz), Helmuth Vierk (third from left), Ernest Schultz (fourth from left), and Fred Vierk seated on the stool. (Courtesy of the Lansing Historical Society.)

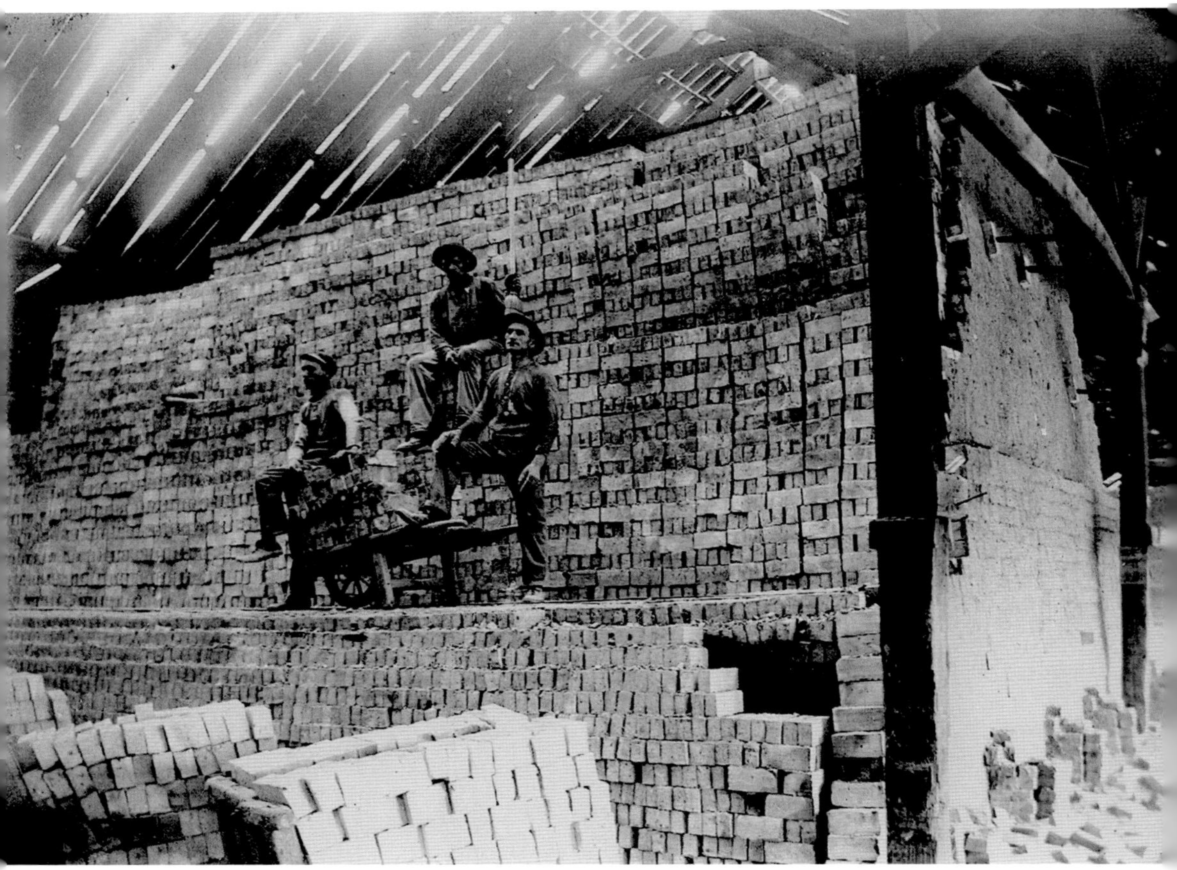

Brickyards
The men photographed here are unidentified, but the photograph shows what a large amount of bricks were produced here at one of several brickyards that operated in Lansing. (Courtesy of the Lansing Historical Society.)

Girl Scouts

The Girl Scouts have been an active group in Lansing since the first Brownie troop started in 1938 with 16 girls. In 1939, the Lansing Girl Scouts hosted the first cookie sale. The money from the sale was used for attendance at Camp Paxton. In 2011, the Calumet Council celebrated 100 years of Girl Scouting in the United States. Pictured here are a group of Girl Scouts who were on hand to assist with the opening and dedication of the new Lansing Historical Society Museum in 1980. (Courtesy of the Lansing Historical Society.)

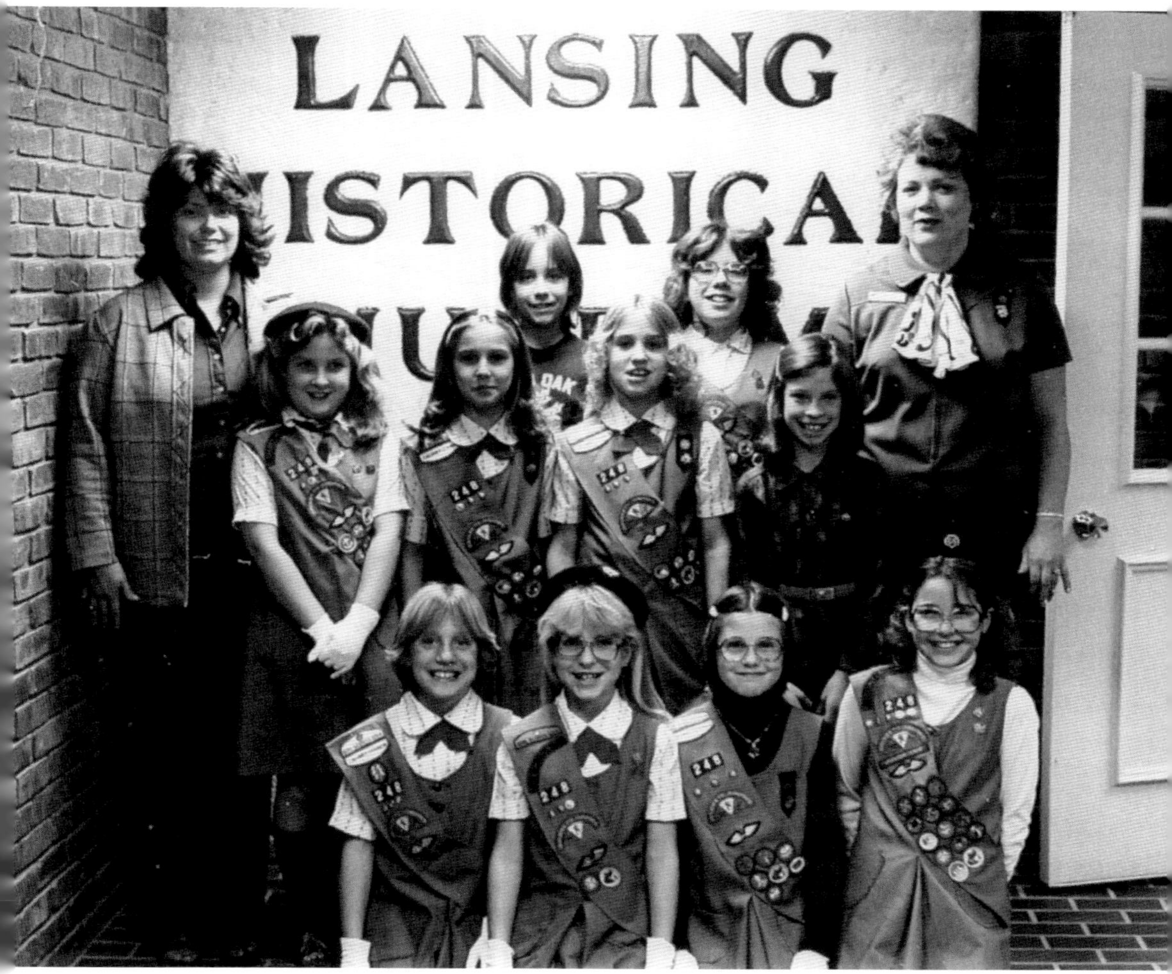

Lansing Junior Woman's Club

The Lansing Junior Woman's Club was organized in 1947 by nine local women. The club is part of the General Federation of Woman's Clubs. Janice Pew served as the first president of Lansing Juniors. The members have dedicated themselves to making Lansing a better place by emphasizing the safety and well being of children. The club has sponsored scholarships, essay contests, clean-up projects, and, for 25 years, produced and directed annual children's plays. In recent years, the club has become heavily involved in veterans' causes and hosts an annual appreciation dinner for veterans and their guests at the American Legion. (Author's collection.)

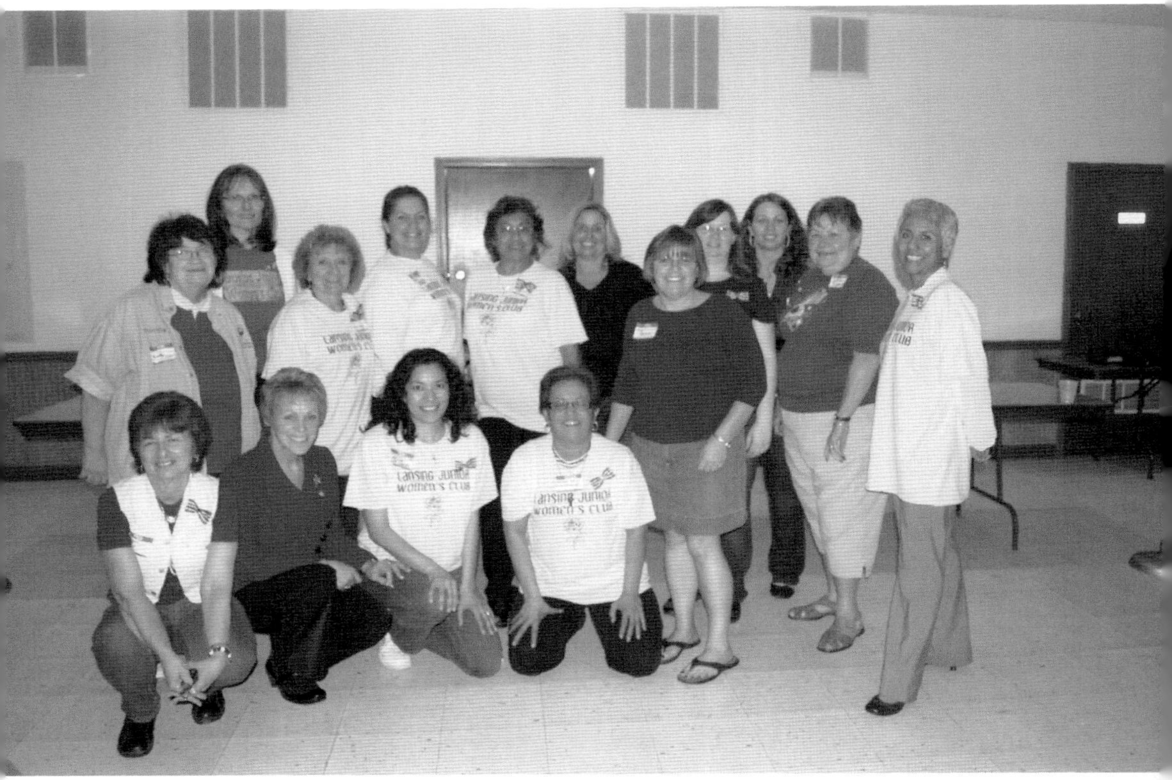

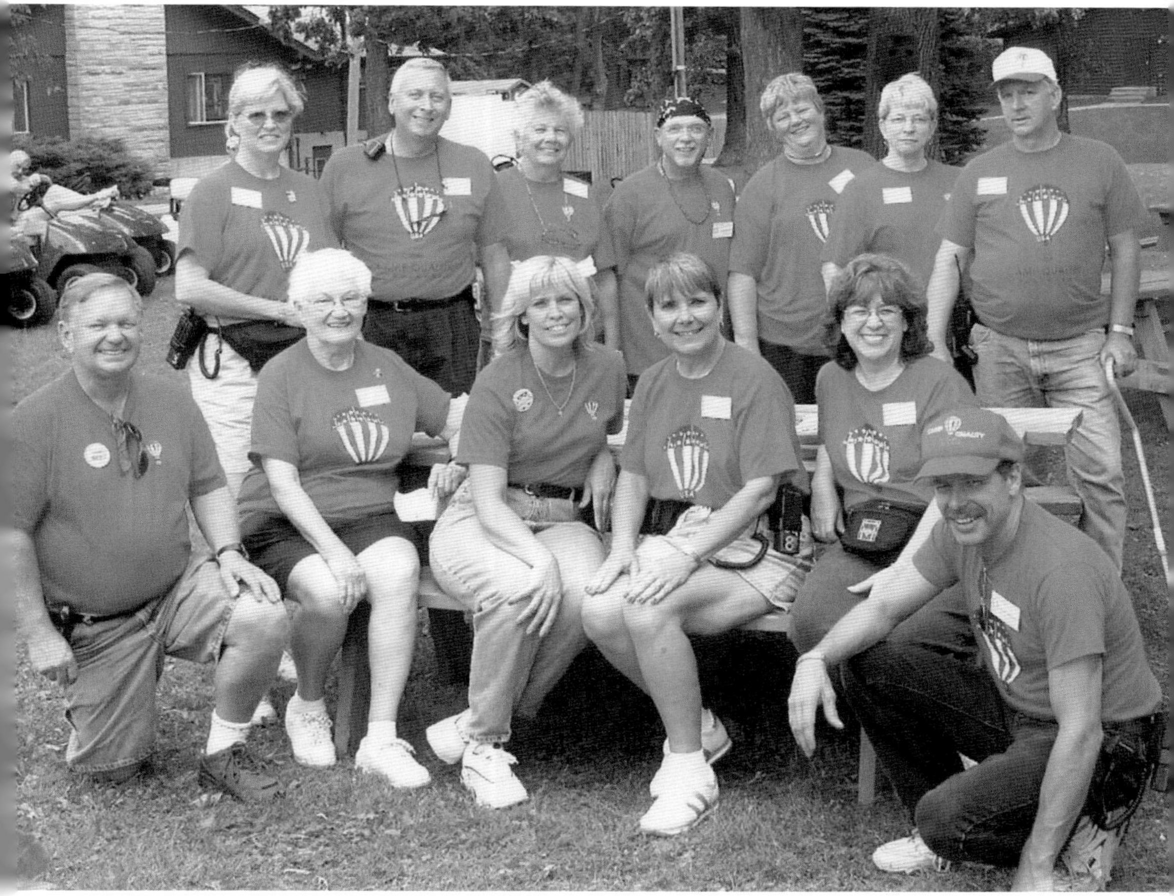

Camp Quality

Started in 1995, Camp Quality Illinois, which is based in Lansing, is a weeklong summer camp for kids with cancer. After Ed Leverenz attended a camp in another state and approached officials at Community Hospital about funding, later that year, the first Illinois camp took place. Thirty-one children attended the first camp, and today it has grown to accommodate about 80 campers and companions and a full volunteer and medical staff at its location in Frankort, Illinois. Pictured are, from left to right, (first row) Tom Lockton, Pat Beilfuss, Shannon Szelinski, Diane Nowaczyk, Linda Reece, and Scott Szelinski; (second row) Carol Oostman, Chris Nowaczyk, Liz Daley, Bud Ream, Sandy Wilkening, Karen VanKley, and Don Reece. (Courtesy of Camp Quality.)

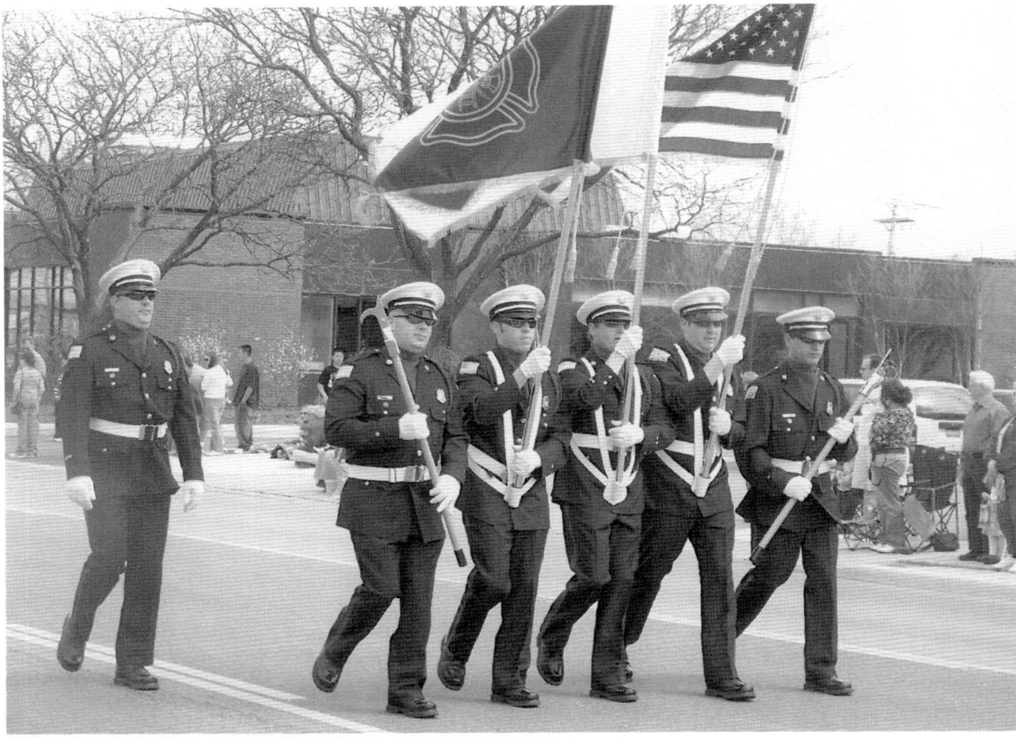

Lansing Fire Department Honor Guard

The Lansing Fire Department Honor Guard was organized in the 1990s and members have participated in parades and other events. Several department members have also become part of the Band of Brothers Pipes and Drums in recent years, which is a group of firefighters who play bagpipes and drums at various events. (Author's collection.)

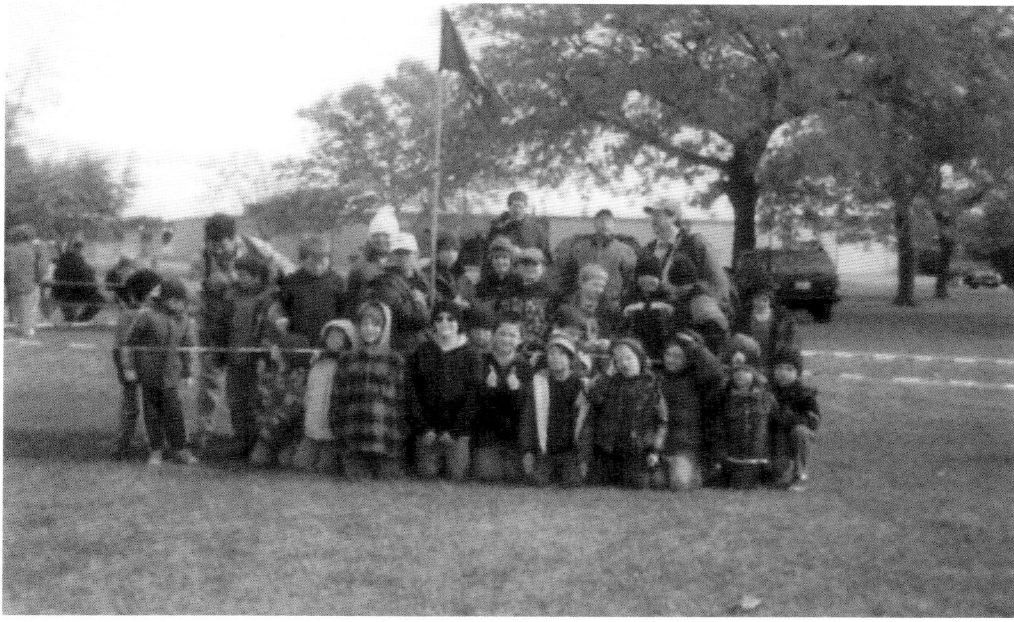

Cub Scouts

Boy Scouts began in Lansing when William Thaldorf established a troop of 15 boys and served as the first scoutmaster. Sponsored by the Lansing Public Schools, they formed in 1973 with sponsorship from the American Legion. Pictured are Cub Scouts from St. Ann Pack No. 247. (Courtesy of Paul Steinweg.)

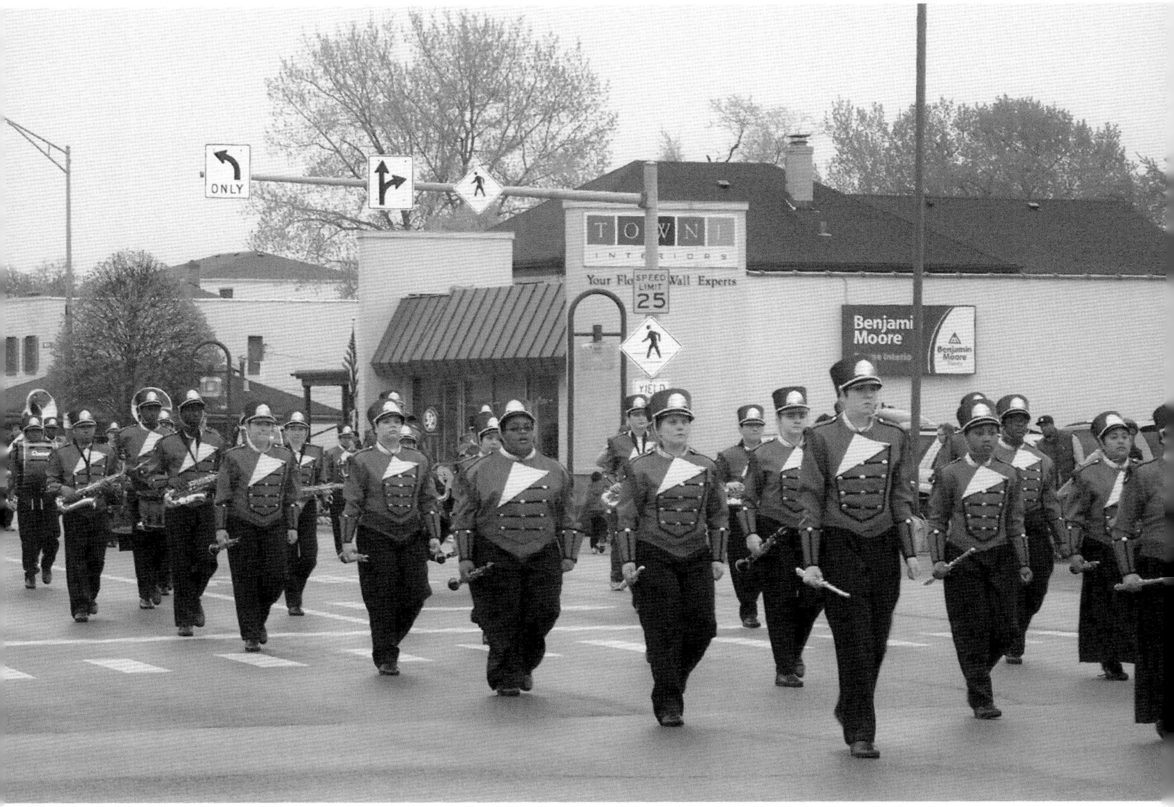

School Bands
Several local schools have intensive music programs with bands that perform not just at school functions but around the community and in events like the Good Neighbor Day Parade. Pictured is the Memorial Junior High School band. (Author's collection.)

Illiana High School Marching Band

Illiana High School's marching band is another musical group to participate each year in the Good Neighbor Day Parade. The current band director is Pat Menninga. (Author's collection.)

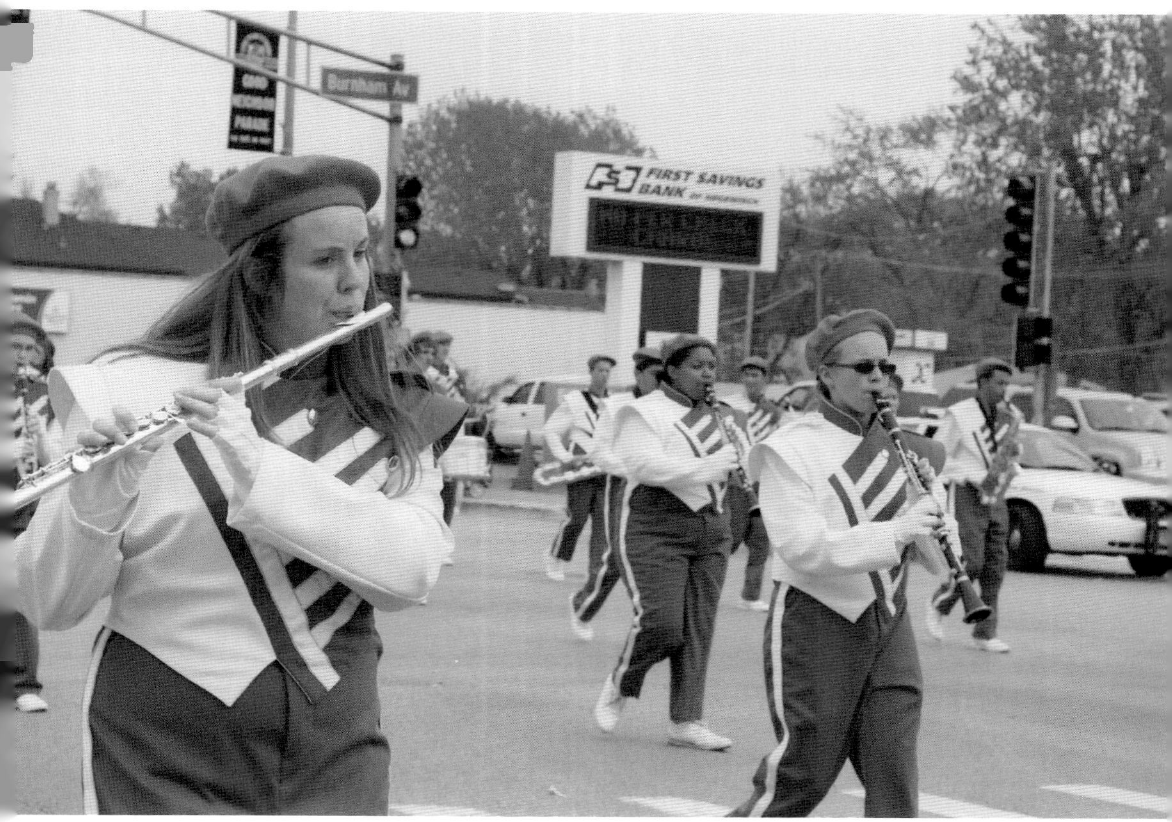

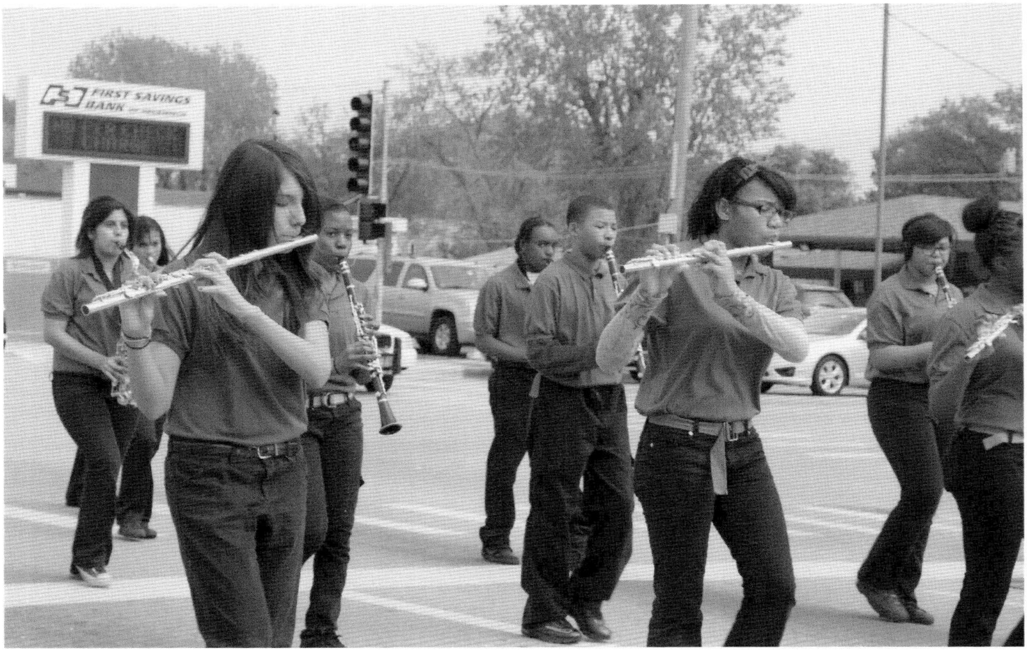

Heritage Middle School

Heritage Middle School, which serves students in the south portion of Lansing and Lynwood, can also be seen marching in the Good Neighbor Day Parade. The band is under the direction of Jenna Lake. (Author's collection.)

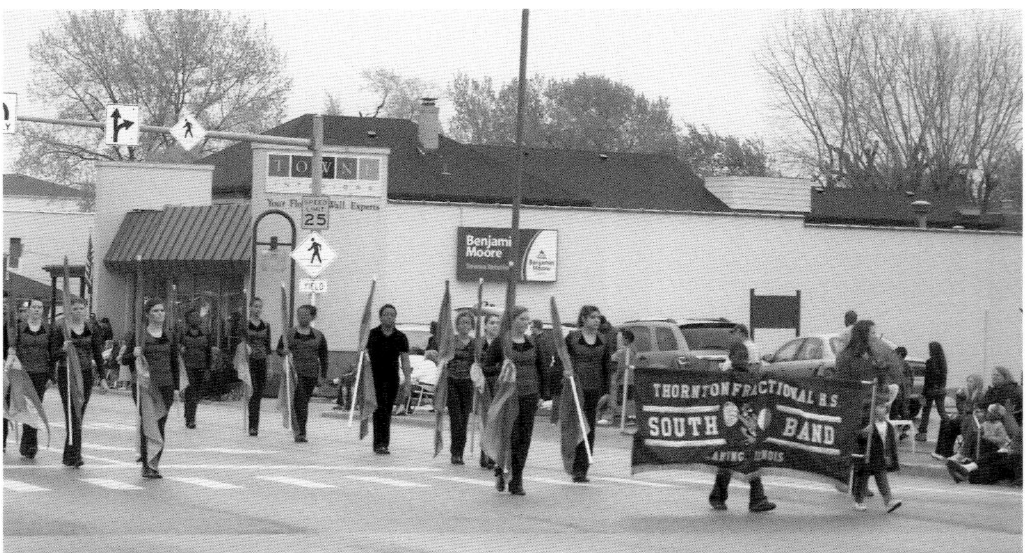

Thornton Fractional Color Guard and Band

Thornton Fractional South's Color Guard and Band appear annually on the first Saturday in May at the Good Neighbor Day Parade. Mike Madonia has been the band director at Thornton Fractional South High School since 1991. (Author's collection.)

Boy Scouts
Two Boy Scout troops exist in Lansing, Troop 271, which meets at the American Legion, and Troop 276, which meets at Heritage Middle School. Pictured are Scouts from both troops as they helped with the annual Veterans' Appreciation Dinner. (Author's collection.)

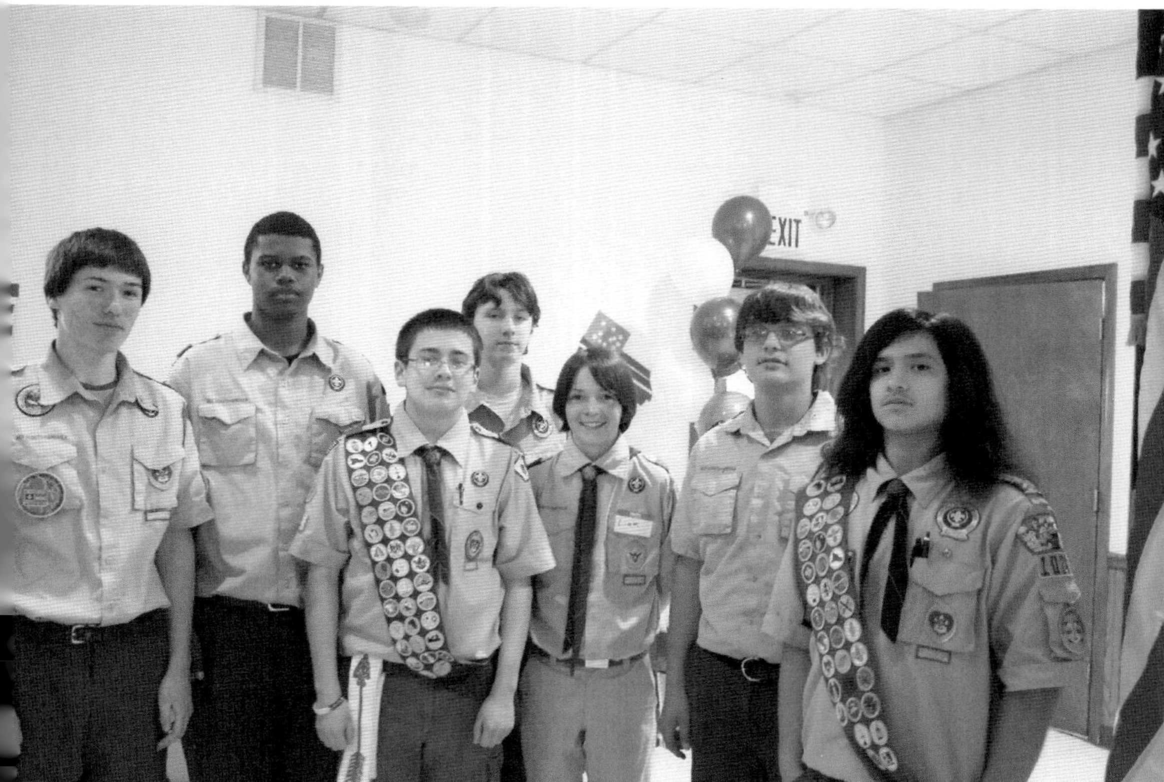

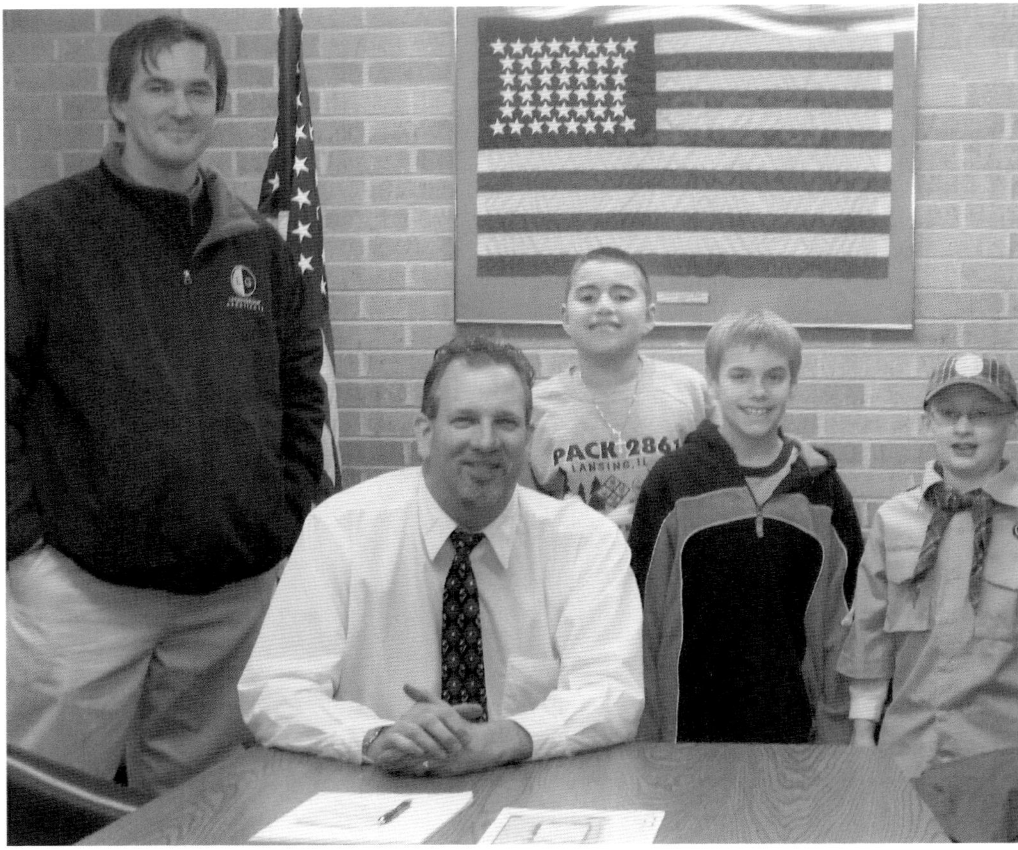

Cub Scouts

Scouts take part in many activities within the village. Here are some Cub Scouts from Pack 2671 learning about the design of the new Village Municipal Center with Mayor Dan Podgorski. (Courtesy of Paul Steinweg.)

CHAPTER FIVE

The Business Community

From blacksmith shops to big box stores, Lansing has been home to entrepreneurs of all kinds over the years. With Ridge Road and Torrence Avenue being the home of many small businesses, residents have been able to fill nearly all their needs simply by traveling one of Lansing's main roads. Some family businesses have stood the test of time, including Walter Schultz Insurance, the village's oldest family business, which began in 1923, and Ridgeway Chevrolet, which dates back to 1927. Gus Bock Hardware has had two owners since being established in 1926. The Lansing Sport Shop has been in operation for more than 50 years with a third generation now working at the store. The Fashionette, which dates back to 1955, still offers clothing and accessories for the ladies of Lansing. The chamber of commerce has served as a support and networking group for the businessmen and businesswomen of the village. From Henry Krumm's first business, the Union Hotel, to today's remaining mom-and-pop establishments, Lansing has a variety of products and services to offer.

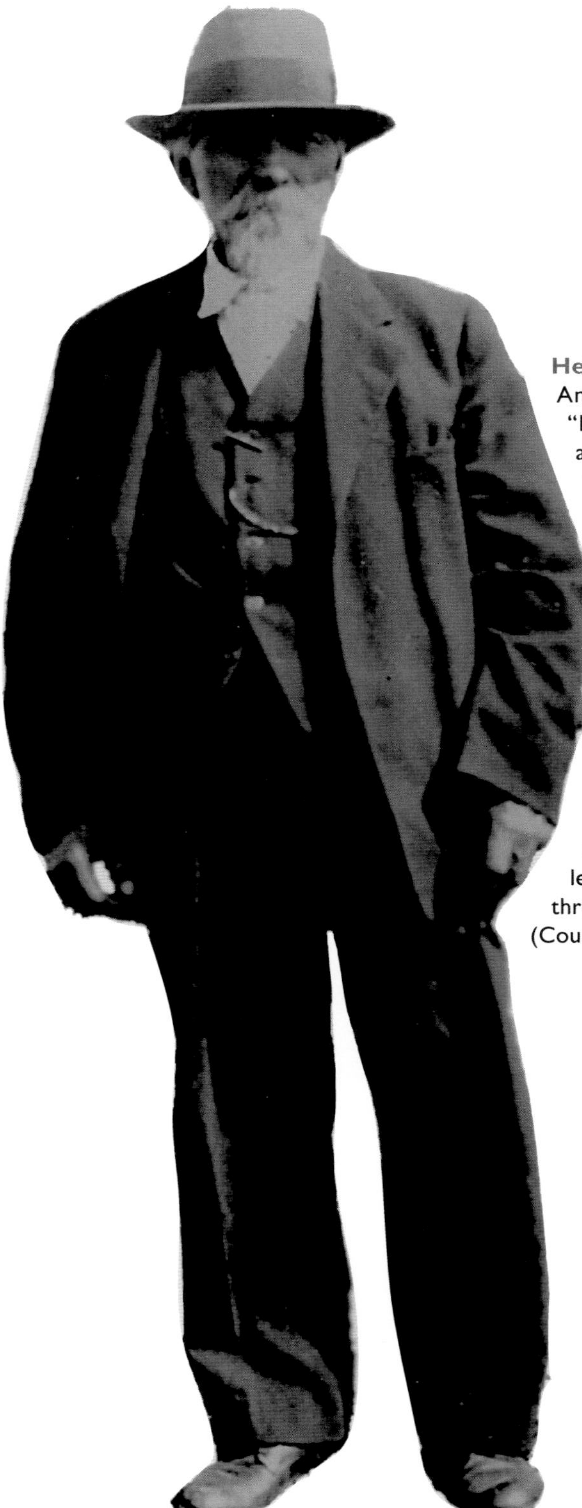

Heinrich Krumm

An immigrant from Germany, Heinrich "Henry" Krumm opened the Union Hotel around 1850 at the southwest corner of what is now called Wentworth Avenue and Ridge Road as Lansing's first documented business. The combination hotel, stagecoach stop, and tavern is believed to have been a stop on the Underground Railroad. The story, as told by Heinrich's daughter to her grandchildren, is that any leftovers prepared by Heinrich's wife, Sophie, were put out in the stable. In the morning, after the escaping slaves had been through, they would find that the food was gone and the dishes were washed and stacked. Heinrich had at least eight children, five being sons with three in the hotel business at the same time. (Courtesy of Herb Krumm.)

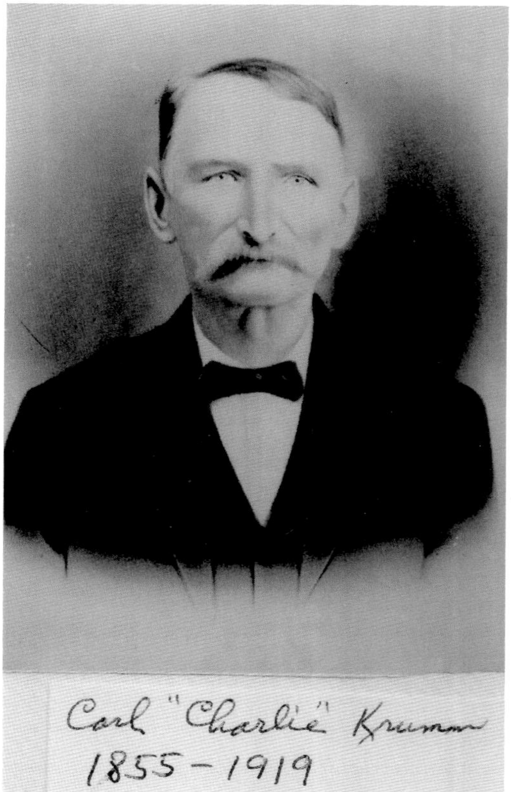

Charlie Krumm
One of the five sons of Heinrich Krumm, Charlie farmed in Sauk Village and Dolton before returning to the area in 1896 when he changed the name of the Union Hotel to the Lansing Hotel. His daughter Anna took over the hotel until it was sold outside the family in the 1920s. It continued as a hotel and tavern until it was destroyed by fire in 1943. Charlie had seven children. (Courtesy of Herb Krumm.)

Krumm Brothers
Edward (left) and Henry Krumm are being pulled by their horse Sam around 1900 on Edward's rubber-tired buggy. Sam pulled the two as they went door to door during the week selling coffee and tea. They later sold the company, which became Eureka Tea Company, and continued delivering teas door to door in the area until the 1950s. He later returned to visit those same customers when he started an egg and poultry business. (Courtesy of Herb Krumm.)

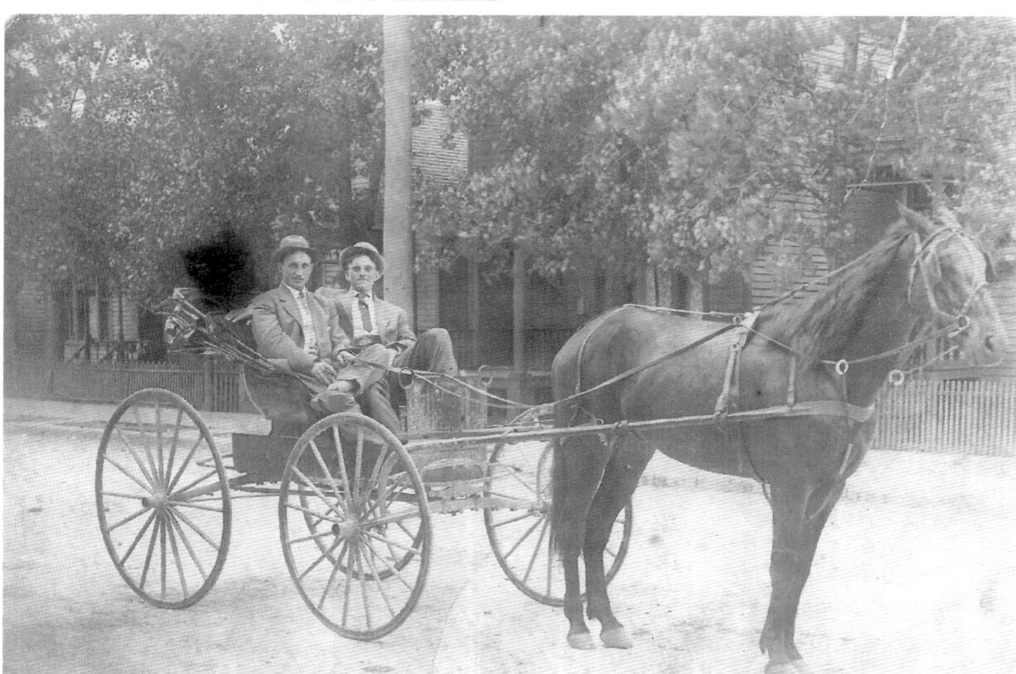

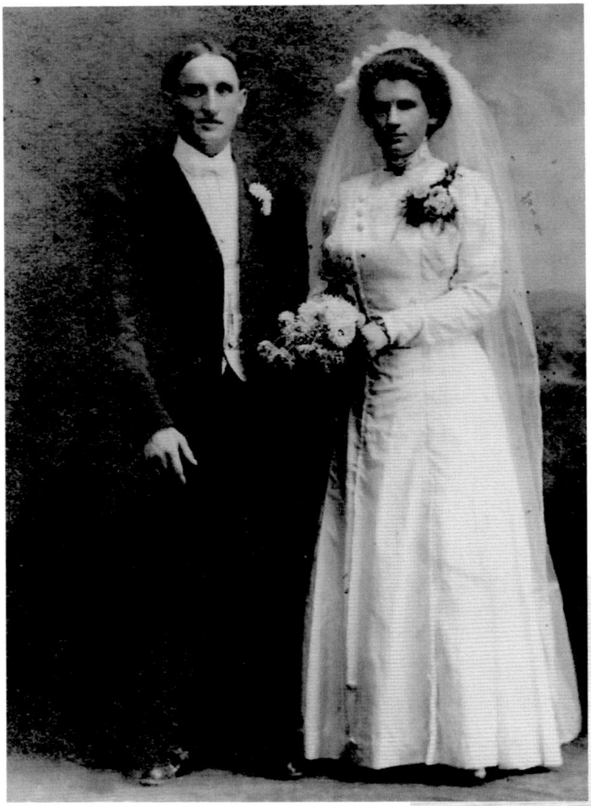

Edward Krumm

Edward Krumm remained in Lansing, working at one of the brickyards. At left, he is photographed at his wedding to Marie. In the late 1910s, Edward leased land from the brickyard after it closed and farmed. He also started delivering coal, which led to another business venture, Edward F. Krumm Building Materials. The company supplied cement for many of the local paved roads. The family, including son Art, also ran Ridgeview Coal on Henry Street, which later became Lan Oak Lumber. Below, Krumm is pictured in 1915 farming on land that was once owned by the brickyard at the current Knights of Columbus grounds. (Both, courtesy of Herb Krumm.)

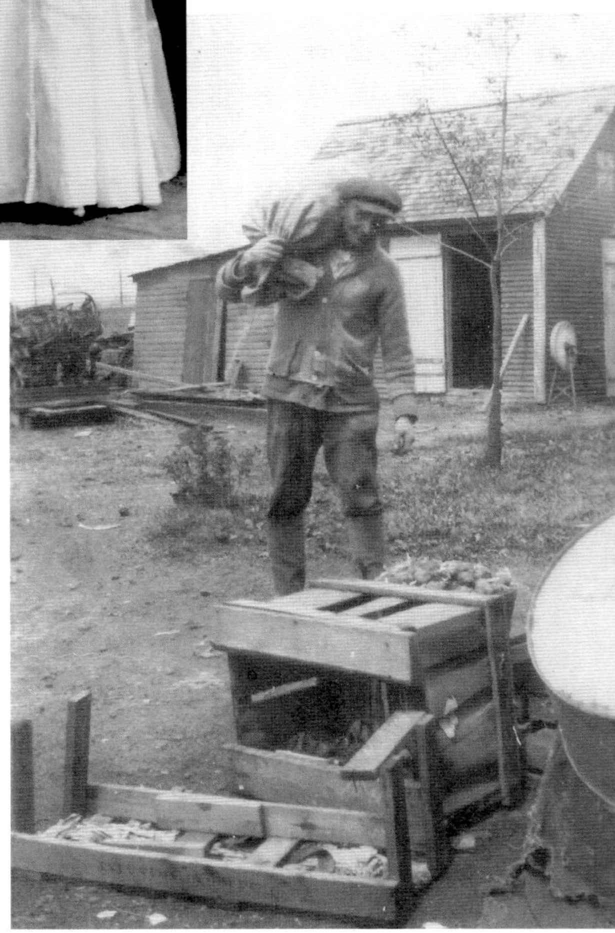

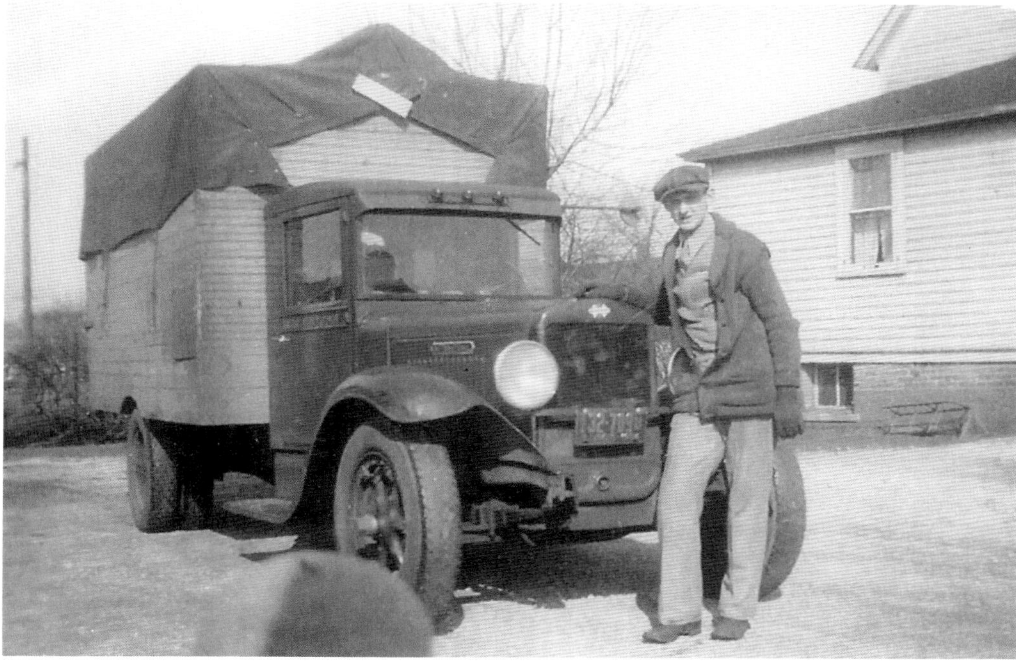

Art Krumm
Art Krumm, who continued in the family construction materials business, is pictured with an International truck that was used to haul materials. During World War II, he had two men who were POWs from the camp in Thornton that he was in charge of. They would help him load and unload the truck. (Courtesy of Herb Krumm.)

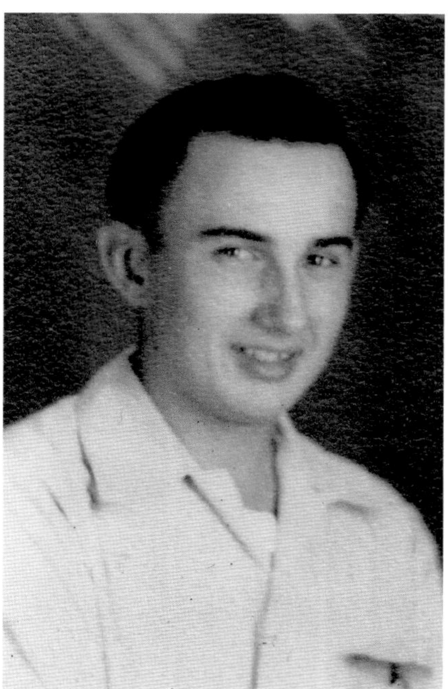

Herb Krumm
A brother to Art, Herb Krumm took over his father's egg and poultry business at the age of 16. He and his wife had a son and daughter. Herb has restored several of the vehicles once used in his family's business. (Courtesy of Herb Krumm.)

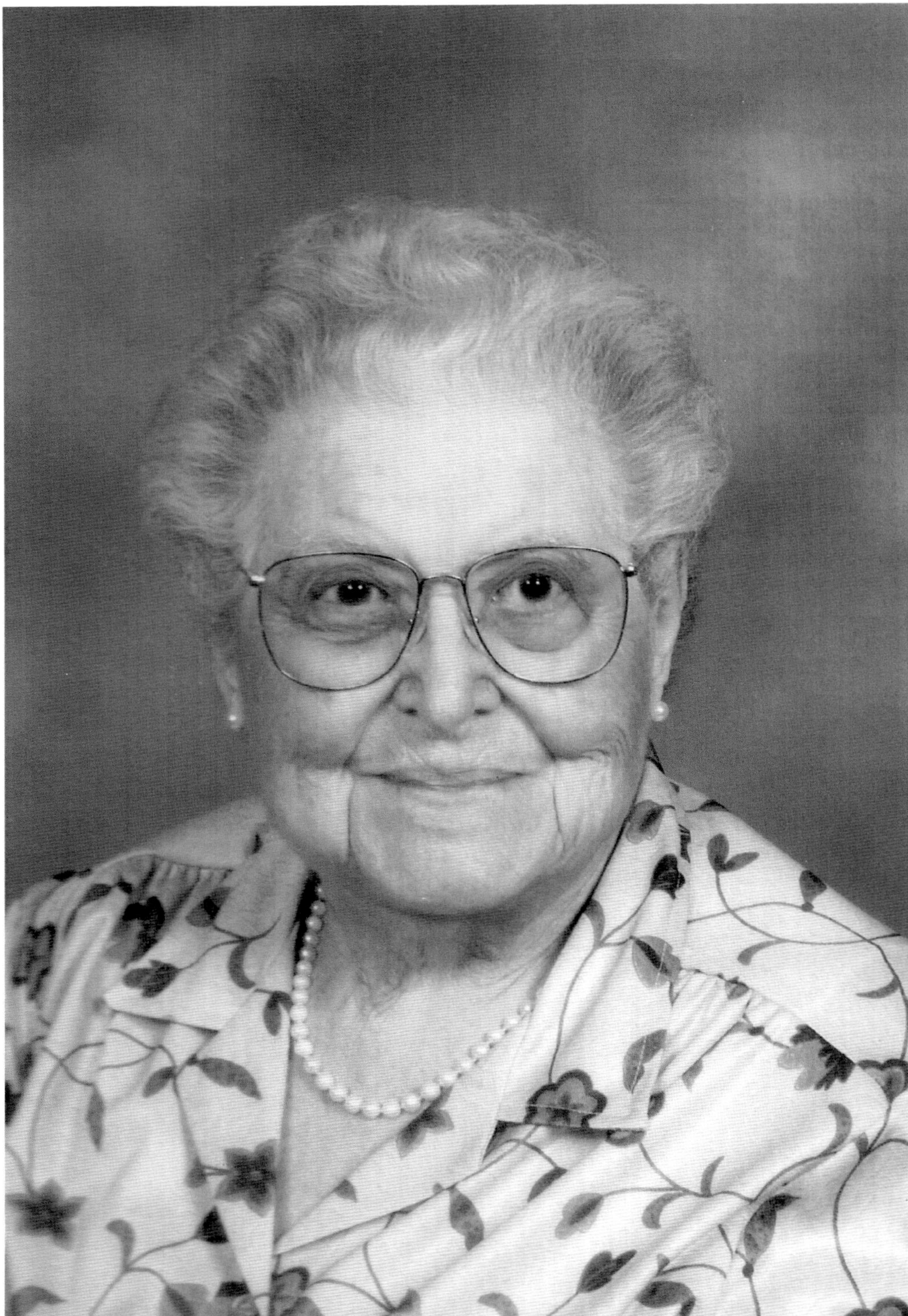

Josephine Schoettle (LEFT)
Born on New Year's Eve in 1909 in Esslingen, Germany, Josephine (Knupfer) Schoettle immigrated to the United States at age 20 on the steamship *Bremen* with her future husband, Julius. The two married in Chicago in 1931 and moved to a new home at the corner of 181st and Roy Streets in Lansing. The Schoettles became active parishioners at St. Ann Catholic Parish, hosting meetings at their home, and were part of the delegation that petitioned the cardinal to assign St. Ann Catholic Parish a full-time priest as well as construct a new church and school. A part-time job arranging flowers in her basement led her to open her own shop in 1958 and put an addition on the back of her home. She continued the shop until its closing in 2007 when she was 97 years old. Josephine was a charter member of the Daughters of Isabella, the women's auxiliary to the Lansing Knights of Columbus, of which her husband was a member. For her devotion and work at St. Ann Catholic Parish, she was awarded the Christifideles Award by the Catholic Church. She was a past president of the Lansing Business Women's Association and was involved in several other organizations. Josephine passed away just three weeks before her 102nd birthday and until that time was still active in several organizations and had a full calendar. (Courtesy of Jeff Schoettle.)

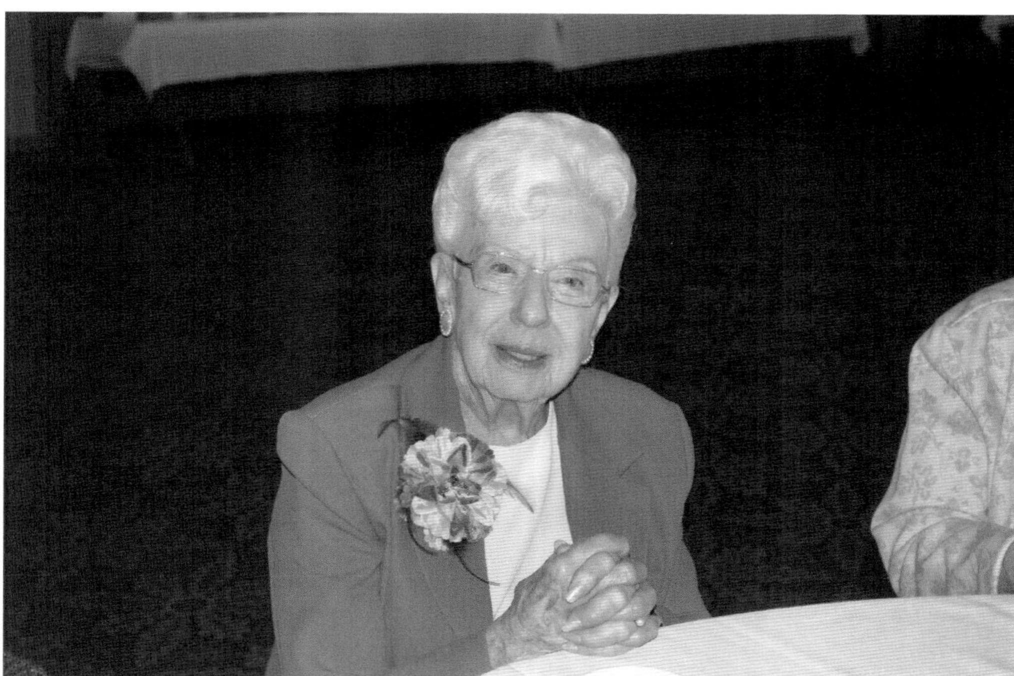

Jackie Protsman
In 1953, the Lansing Hosiery Shop opened on Ridge Road, owned by Florence Aumick. It continues today as The Fashionette, with daughter Jackie Protsman running the clothing store. Jackie has been active in the community, being a member and president of the Lansing Business Women's Association. (Author's collection.)

Walter W. Schultz

Brothers Walter and George Schultz shared a building on Torrence Avenue in Oak Glen that remains Walter Schultz Insurance. A third brother, Arnie, ran a deli and grocery store on Torrence Avenue and the street that the family resided on was named Violet Street after a sister named Viola. Walter served as the postmaster in Oak Glen for many years and in addition to a portion of the building serving as a post office, he also ran a real estate and insurance business. He was active in the Lions Club. Known for his generous nature, Walter was one of three men to donate land that would become Lansing's first park, Lan-Oak Park. He was also instrumental in securing funding for the construction of Lions Stadium. Walter Schultz Insurance began in 1923 and is the oldest family owned business in Lansing. He and his wife had one daughter, Diane. Diane's husband, Norm Abbott, later worked at the agency until his retirement. He is currently the mayor of Lansing. His daughter Cheryl now runs the business. (Courtesy of Norm Abbott.)

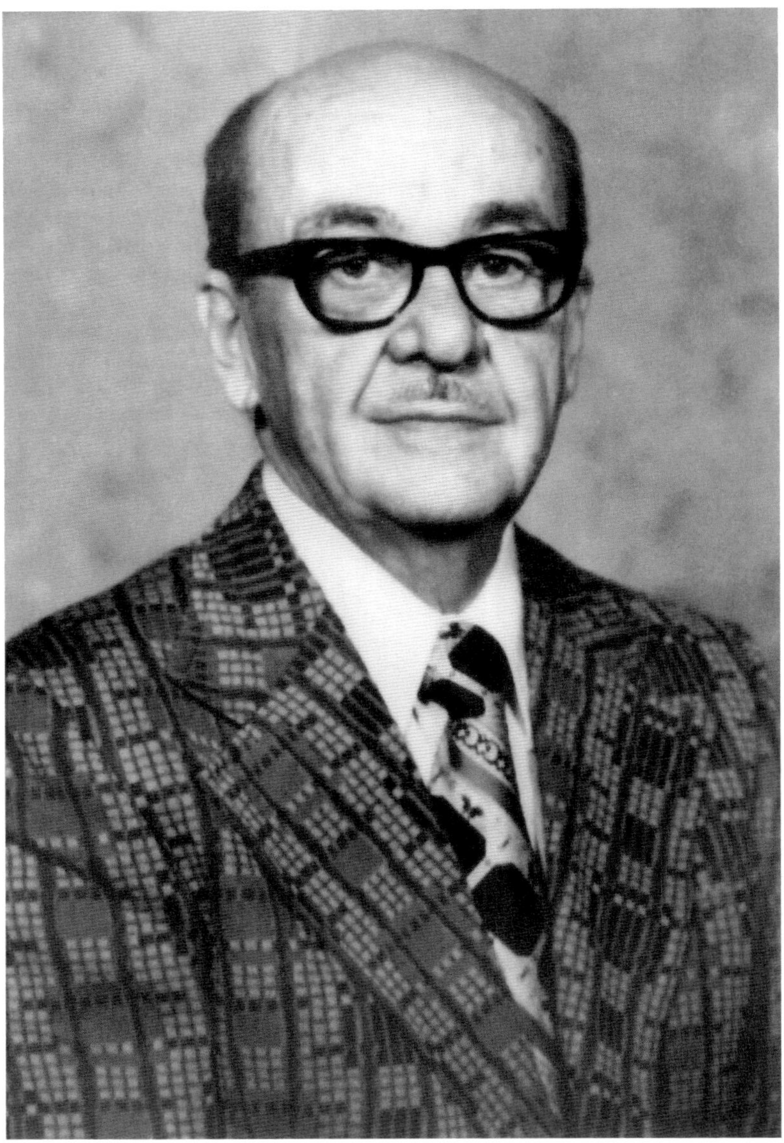

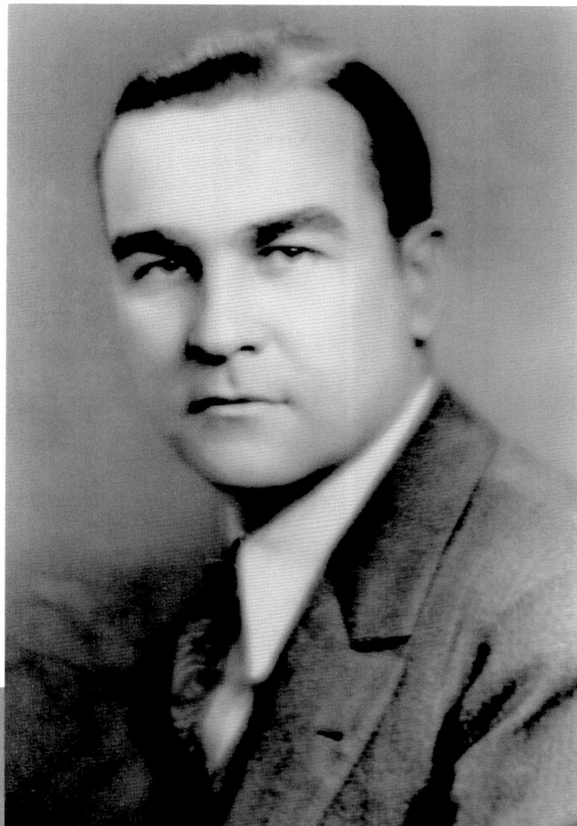

George Schultz
While Walter used half of the building as a post office, real estate office, and insurance agency, brother George had his own business in the other half of the building, Schultz Home Appliance, where appliances and gas for home use were sold. The business evolved into Schultz Gas and relocated to 175th Street. His only child, Don, joined him in the family business, which later was sold and became Amerigas. Below, George is pictured on the far left. To the right of him is his son, Don, followed by Clarence Vankangen and Nelson Swets, two employees at Schultz Gas Service. (Both, courtesy of Terri Marsee.)

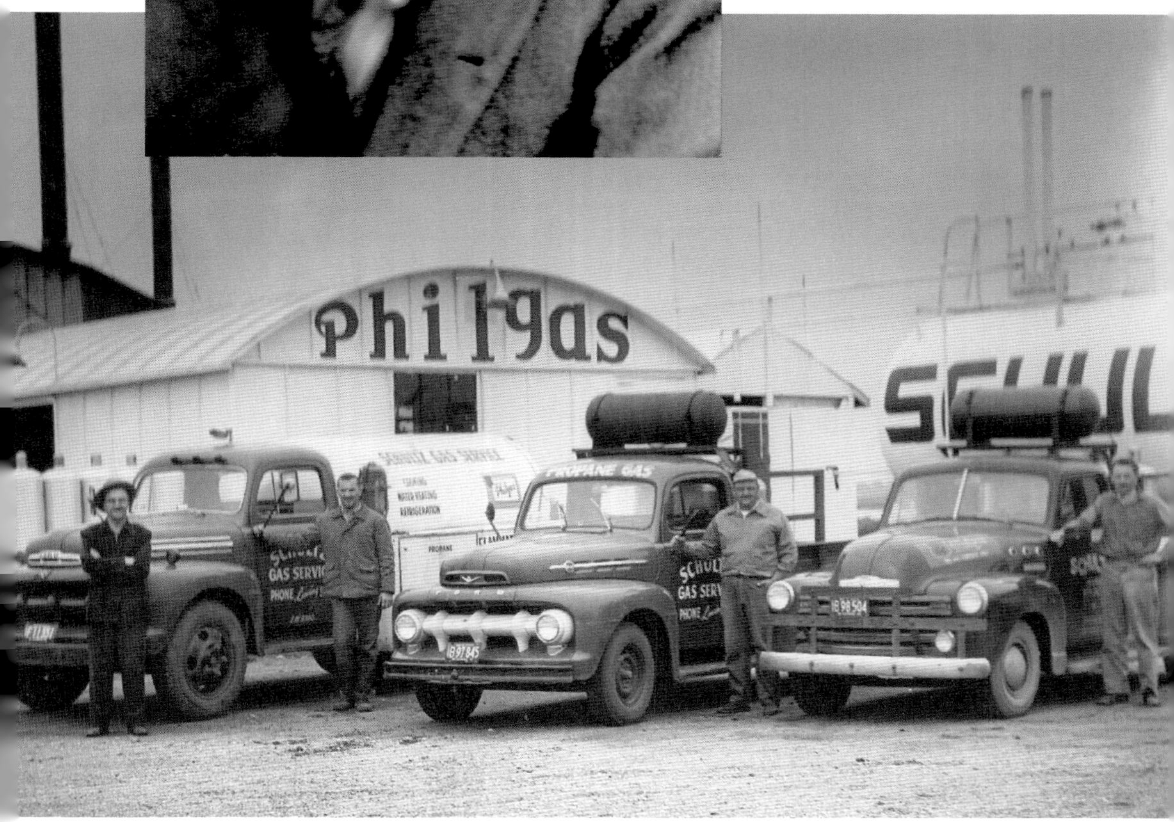

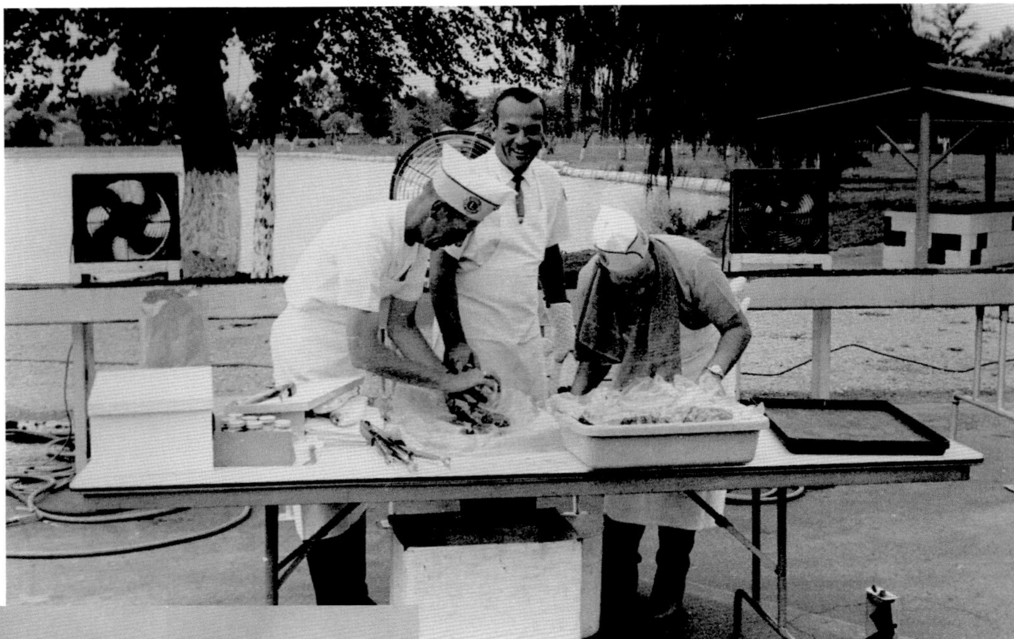

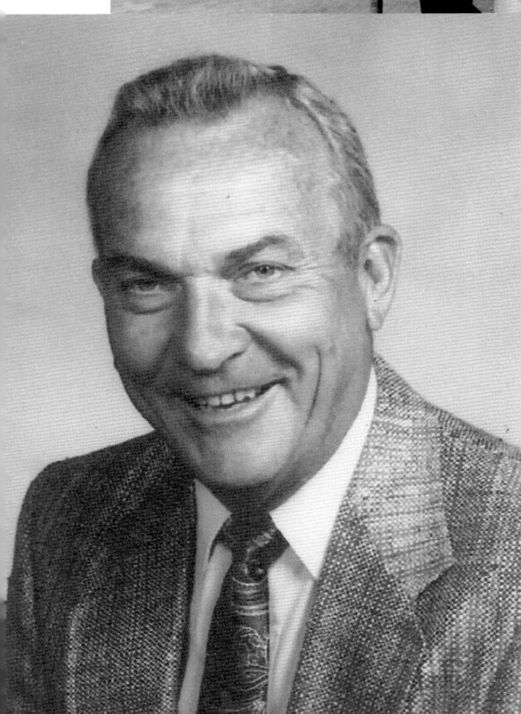

Don Schultz

Don Schultz attended Trinity Lutheran School and was a lifelong member of Trinity Lutheran Church. He graduated from Thornton Fractional High School in 1950 and served in the Korean War with the US Marine Corps. He joined the family business, Schultz Home Appliance, which later became Schultz Gas Service, Inc. He was a post commander of VFW Kenneth Brady Post 7660 from 1956 to 1957 and was instrumental in the construction of the former post building. He was also president of the Lansing Lions Club from 1963 to 1964. He was among the group that started the Lansing Lions Steak Fry and was chairman of the event for several years. He is pictured above at the Steak Fry, held on the Knights of Columbus Grounds, with Lansing police chief John Braschler on the left. The man on the right is unidentified. Don was also a coach and manager with the Lansing Little League, president of Trinity Lutheran Church Council, and was instrumental in the construction of the current church building in 1969. While in the propane business, he put on safety training classes for the Lansing Fire Department. His last business venture was E-Z Self Storage of Lynwood, which is run by his son Tom Schultz and daughter Terri Marsee. Don died in 2009 at the age of 77. (Courtesy of Terri Marsee.)

Joseph Lauer

Joe Lauer, who was originally from Hammond, attended the Indiana College of Mortuary Science. He came to Lansing in 1950 to work at the Schroeder Funeral Home on Ridge Road, which was founded in 1942 by Richard and Besse Schroeder. In 1968, he bought half-interest and became a partner in the funeral home, and it was renamed Schroeder Lauer Funeral Home. In 1973, he became sole owner of the business. In 1996, he retired and sold the business to Martin Kristo, who had been an employee of the business. The present owner is Robert Cole, a longtime resident of Lansing. Joe and his wife, Pam, have four children, 12 grandchildren, and two great-grandchildren. He was a longtime member of the chamber of commerce, a member of the Knights of Columbus and the Kiwanis Club, and an usher at St. Ann Parish for about 50 years. The bottom photograph shows a horse-drawn hearse in a Lansing parade from the Schroeder Funeral Home before Lauer became an owner of the business. (Right, courtesy of Joe Lauer; below, courtesy of the Lansing Historical Society.)

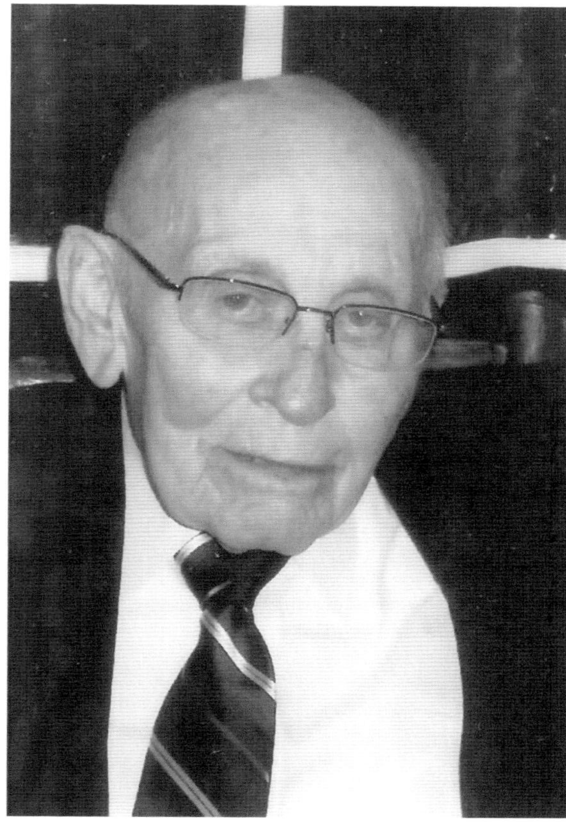

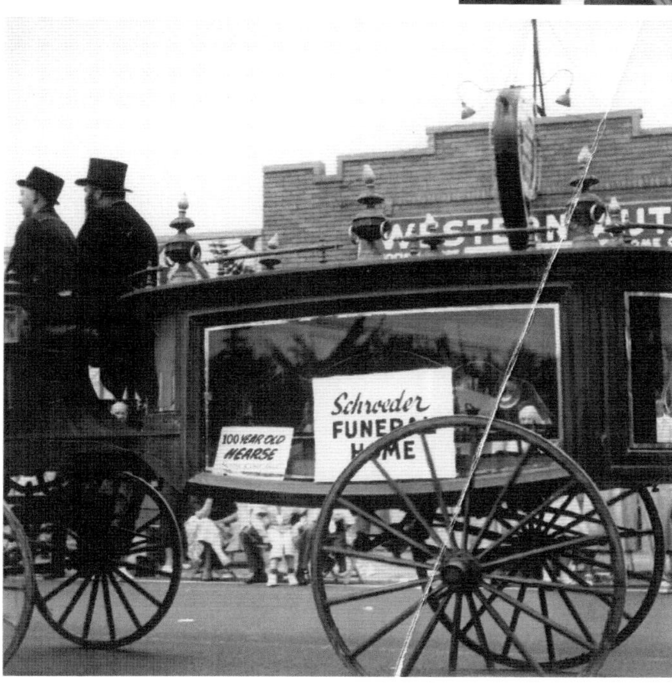

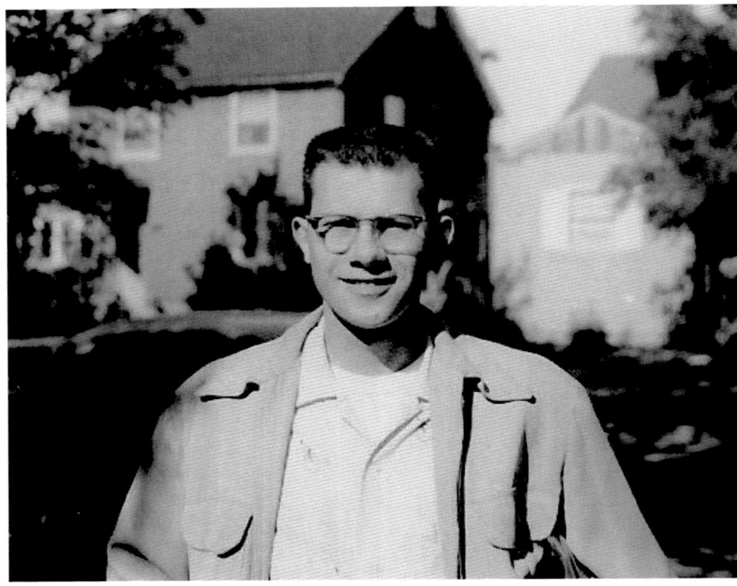

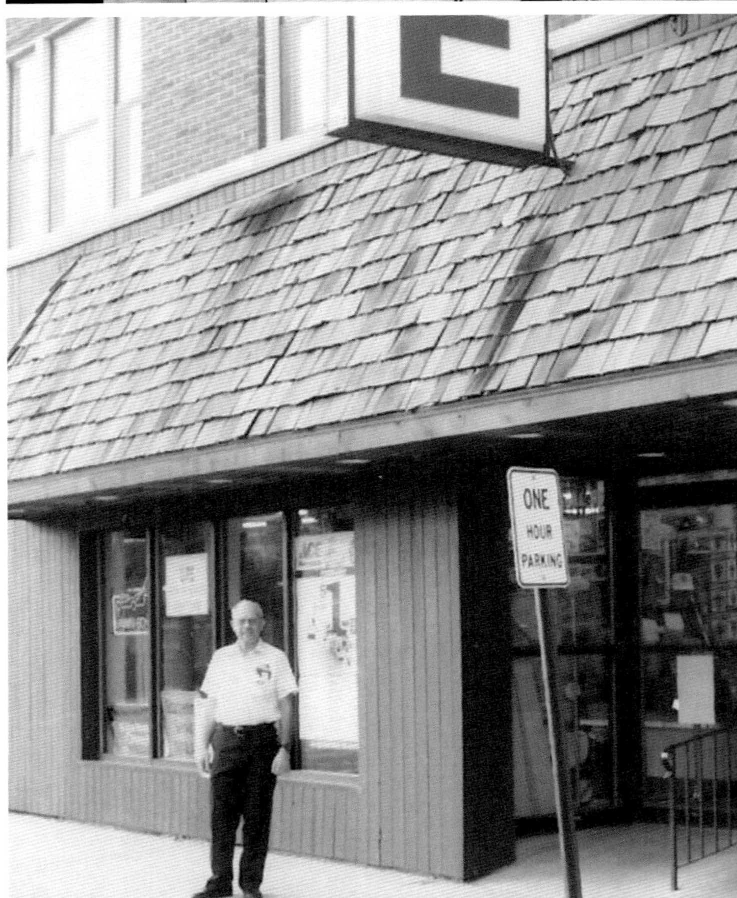

Burton Gardiner
Following service in the Korean War, Burton Gardiner and his brother Richard opened Gardiner's Ace Hardware in 1957 at the corner of Torrence and Indiana Avenues. He married Dorothy Koehn in 1958 and raised four children. His daughter recalled him coming home every day for lunch and opening up the business after hours if someone needed to make an emergency purchase. He sold the business in 1992 when he retired. Burt was a member of the chamber of commerce and has been a member of Trinity Lutheran Church since 1958. He served on the school board, board of elders, and the board of trustees for at least 25 years. He served on the board of directors of both First Savings and Loan and the Bank of Lansing for several years. He's been a member of the Lansing Rotary Club since 1958 with perfect attendance for 50 years. He currently has three homes, and one is still in Lansing. He is described as a "gentle" man who was a kind employer and excellent role model. (Both, courtesy of Patty Cherney.)

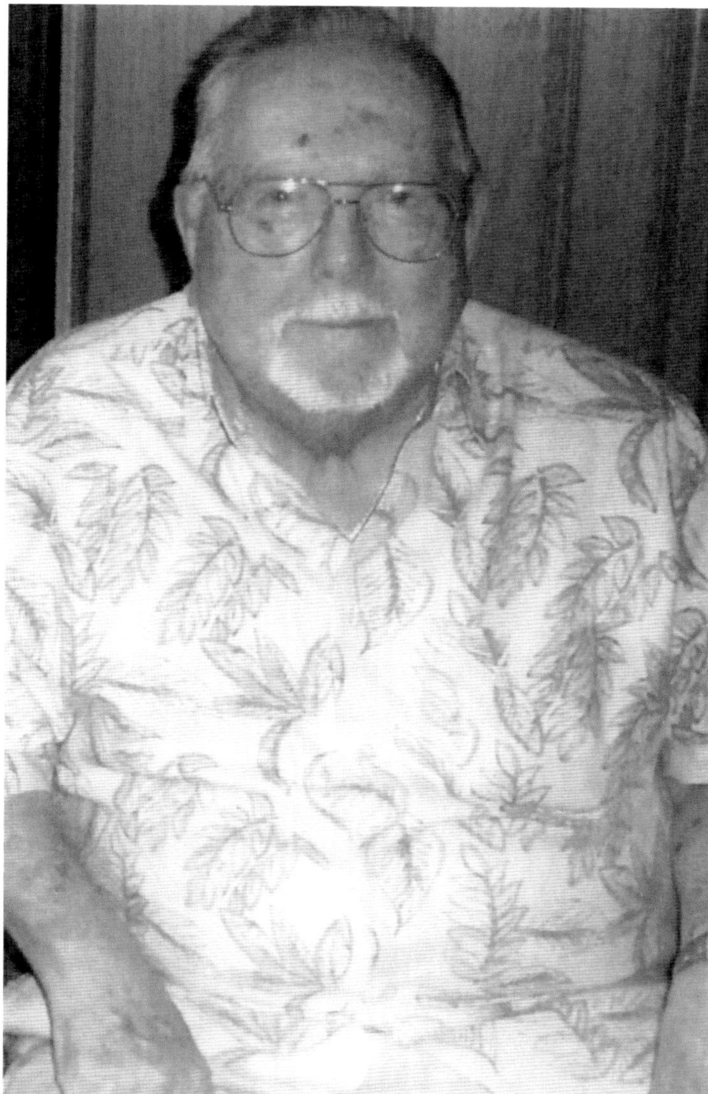

Anthony Rosati Jr.

Born in Philadelphia, Anthony met his wife, Phyllis, while stationed at Great Lakes Naval Station. He served in the Navy during World War II. After getting married, the couple settled in Lansing, and in 1954, he started Lansing Sport Shop, selling sporting goods, .45 records, and Rosati's Italian Water Ice from his Ridge Road storefront. The business has grown to add a three-story warehouse, trophy shop, and embroidery business. He retired in the late 1990s, and two of his 11 children, Anthony and Phil, bought the business. He was a member of the Knights of Columbus, was a charter member of the Lansing Sportsman Club, and a parishioner of St. Ann Catholic Parish.

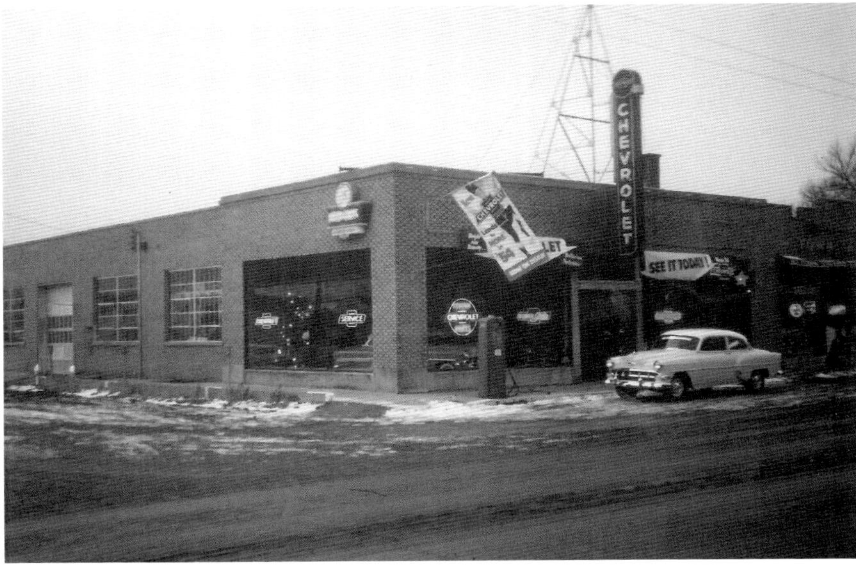

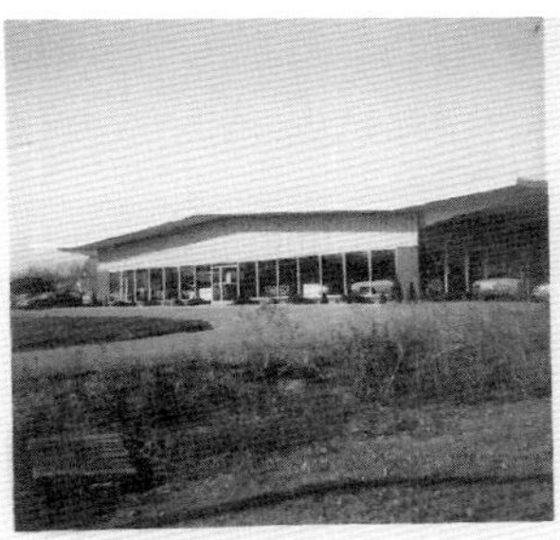

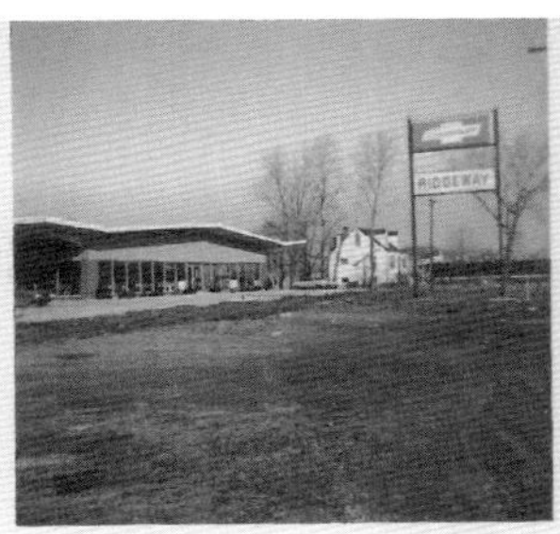

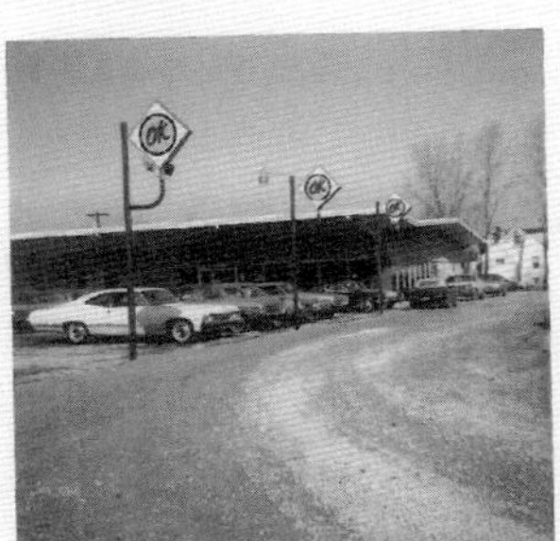

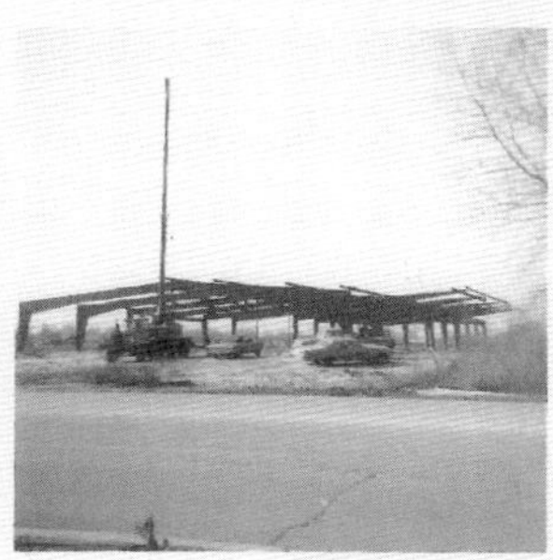

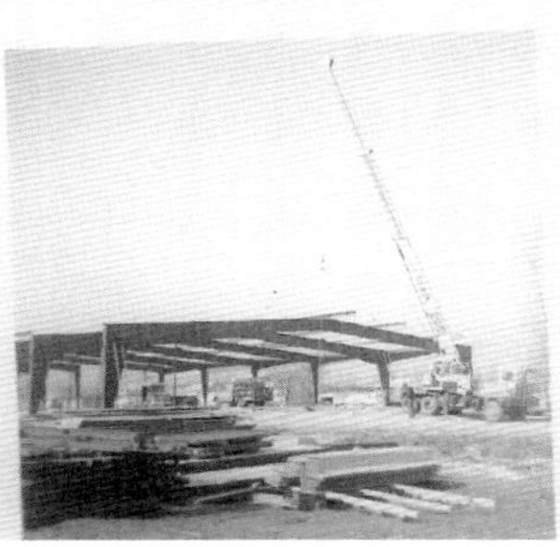

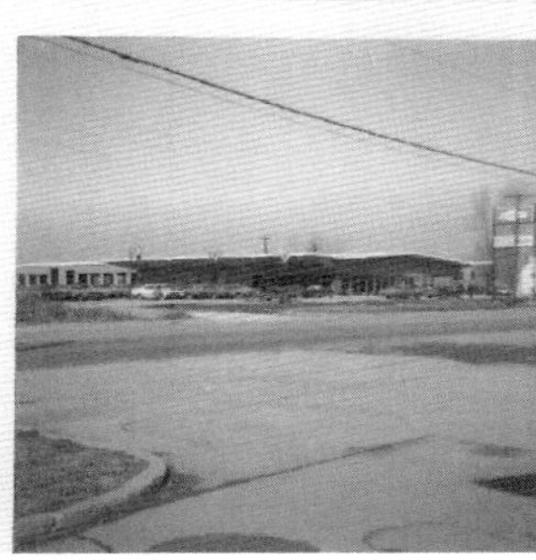

Ridgeway Chevrolet
Ridgeway Chevrolet, founded in 1927, is one of Lansing's oldest businesses. Its first home was at the corner of Torrence and Indiana Avenues in the building that now houses Besse Shirt Lettering. The photograph above shows the business at its original location. Still in the VanRamshorst family, the business was started by John VanRamshorst and was later run by his son Jack, who served as general manager until his retirement. Sons Bill and Bob currently operate the business with fourth-generation family members Amy and Doug also now working at the dealership, which has undergone a complete face-lift. Pictured at left is the current building while under construction in the late 1960s. (Both, courtesy of Bob Van Ramshorst.)

CHAPTER SIX

Serving the Community

Without individuals who are so giving of their time and talents, Lansing would not be the community it is today. In so many ways they have served the public: preparing hot meals for the elderly, mentoring groups of young people, serving in their churches, and creating programs in the parks and throughout the community that bring people together. These volunteers give tirelessly of themselves, without any expectations in return. Five years ago, the Lansing Volunteer Recognition Committee began hosting an annual dinner to recognize those whose efforts as volunteers impact the community. The event grows larger each year as does the number of people who continue to give to their community.

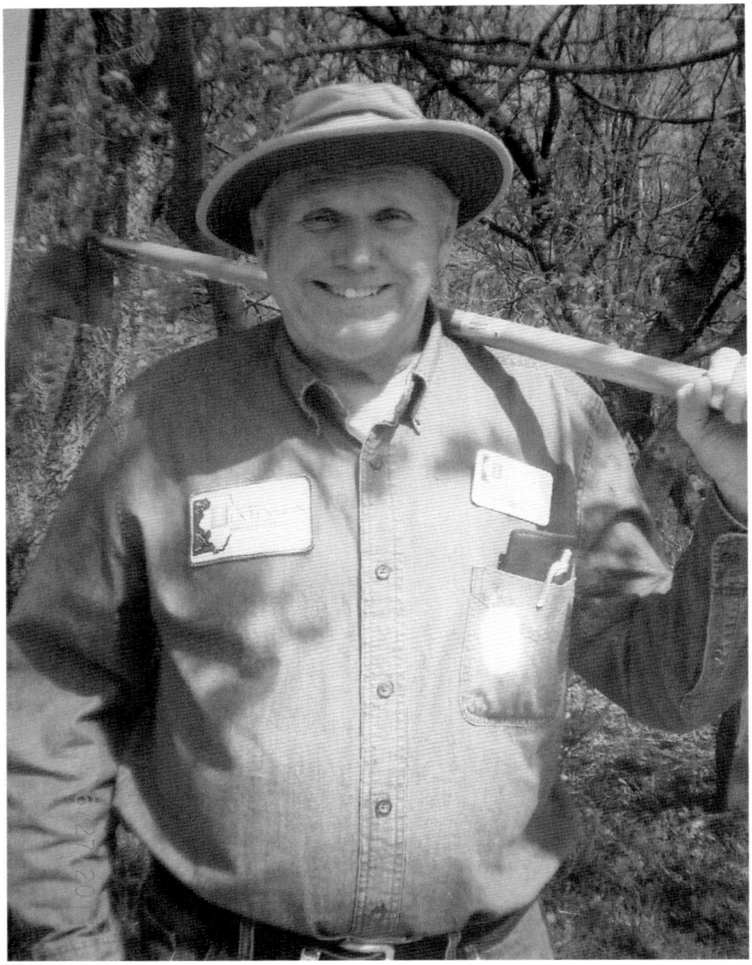

Paul Schultz

Arriving on Christmas Day in 1938, Paul Schultz was one of three children born to Harry and Rose Schultz. He attended Coolidge School and graduated from St. Ann School. He is a 1957 graduate of Thornton Fractional High School. He served in the Air Force as an air policeman. In 1962, Paul married Carol Fleck; the couple had three children and now have four grandchildren. A former postal carrier who worked the Ridge Road route, he got to know many people in Lansing. He retired in 1995 after 34 years of service. In 1971, the couple was on the founding committee of the Lansing Preschool Cooperative. Paul became involved in Operation Snowball at Thornton Fractional South High School from 1979 to 1982 and was active in the Boy Scouts of America for 12 years, serving as a cub master for packs at St. Ann and Coolidge Schools. He served as scoutmaster for Troops 247 and 271. Paul was chairman of the history committee for the 1993 Lansing Centennial and served on the Old Village Hall Cornerstone Committee. He is a life member of the Lansing Historical Society and has served as president and vice president and is currently on the board of directors. For 30 years, he has conducted an annual historical walk of the Lansing business district on Ridge Road each June. He is an active member at St. Ann Catholic Parish, where his grandfather Edward Koselke was one of the founders. In 2009, he became a Master Gardener, receiving certification from the Illinois Extension Service. He volunteers at Sand Ridge Nature, caring for three interpretive gardens. In 2010, he was named a Paul Harris Fellow by the Rotary Clubs International for his volunteer work. (Courtesy of Carol Schultz.)

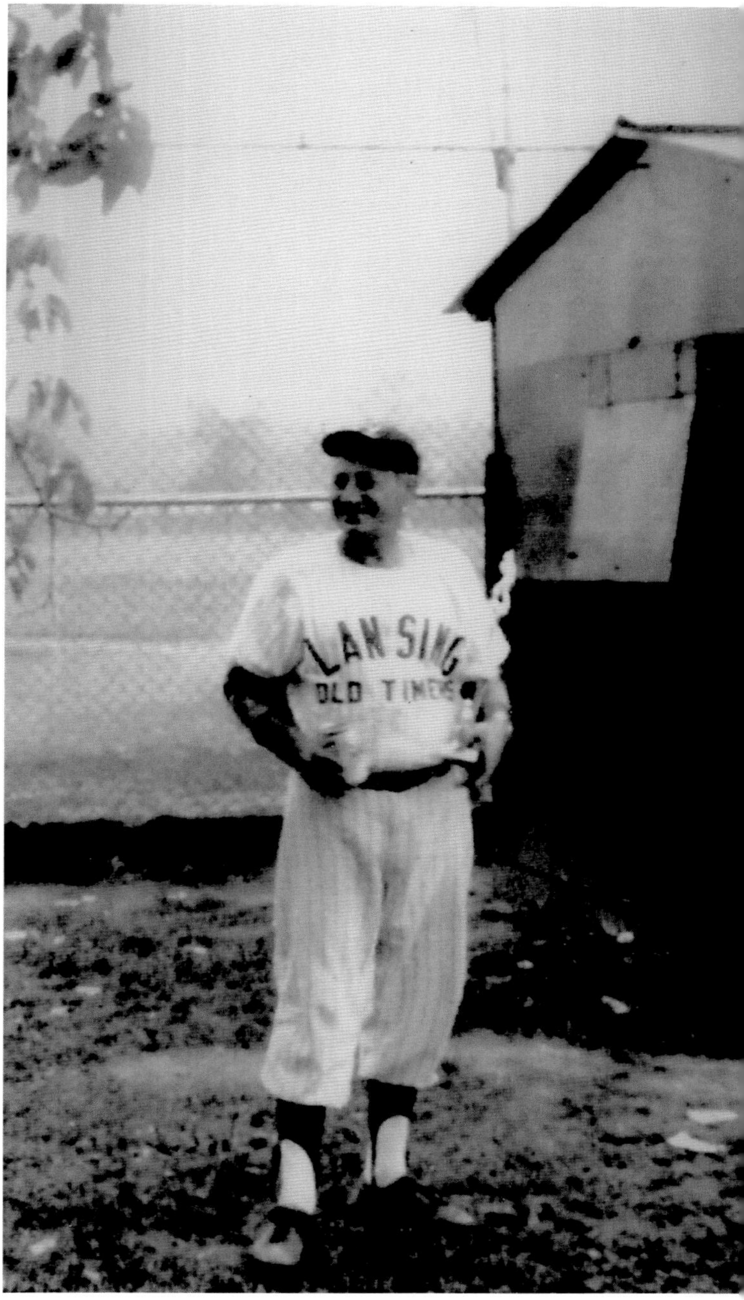

Edward Carlson
Born in 1911, Edward Carlson married Helen Banas in 1932 and moved to a home in Lansing. A former steel worker, Carlson was always interested in baseball and played for a minor league club. In 1944, he was one of a group of men who formed the Lansing Old Timers Athletes and Fans Association, and he later served as president of the club. Original uniforms were purchased by Evert Schultz, and years later, when new ones were needed, Carlson approached merchants and each one purchased a uniform that the business name would be on, a sponsorship arrangement that continues with the Old Timers youth sports teams today. The Lansing Old Timers (LOT) also had a senior team from 1945 to 1966, which won Illinois state championships in 1962, 1965, and 1966 and advanced to the National Semi-Pro Tournament held in Wichita, Kansas. The LOT, which started with a senior team and four midget teams, has grown to a league that includes peewee league, Little League, Babe Ruth, challenger league, girls softball, and volleyball. In 1966, Ed was appointed the building commissioner and continued in that role until 1974. He also served as president of the Lansing Lions Club, and during his term, the popular steak fry fundraiser was born. He was a past worshipful master of the Arcadia Lodge. He and fellow Masons were instrumental in the building of the Lansing Masonic Temple, completed in 1967. He died in 1989. (Courtesy of June Cole.)

Don Jenkins

Born in 1920 in Streator, Illinois, Don Jenkins spent most of his early life in Joliet. He married Frances Kirinich and they had three children: Larry, Bonnie, and Bud "Harold." In 1933, Don went to work for his Uncle Harry Burger at his Munster supermarket, and he moved to Lansing in 1965. Don and Frances were members of the First United Methodist Church in Lansing, where Don served on several church boards. One day in 1977, a volunteer from a Meals on Wheels organization approached Don, then manager of the store, about a donation. He sought more information and brought a proposal to his church that a Meals on Wheels program begin in Lansing. The church agreed to loan its kitchen facilities, and other churches in town and several service organizations joined to help the program succeed. Don became the first administrator of the program and remained in that role until his death in 1990. Meals on Wheels continues today with volunteers preparing and delivering hot meals twice a week to elderly residents of the village. (Courtesy of Bud Jenkins.)

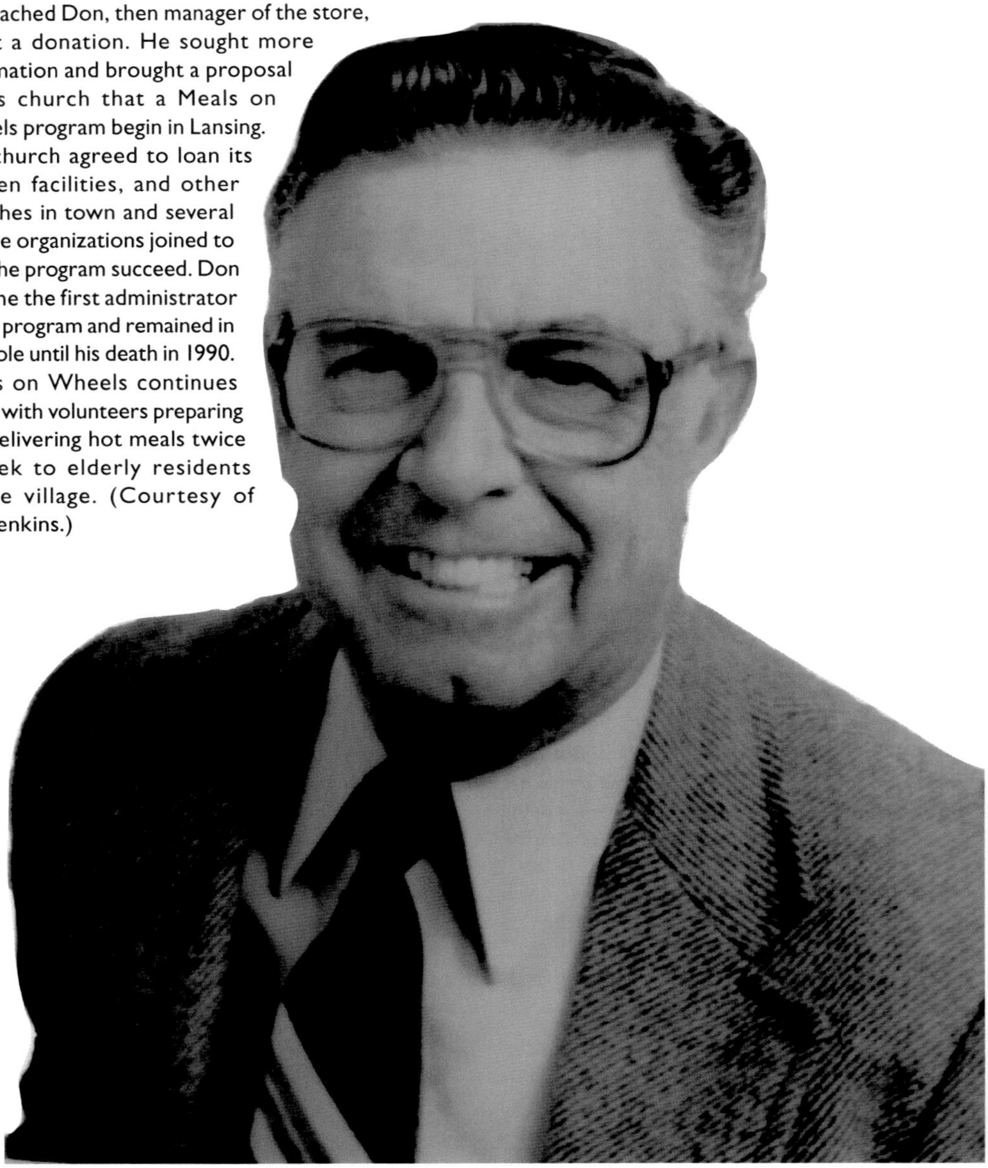

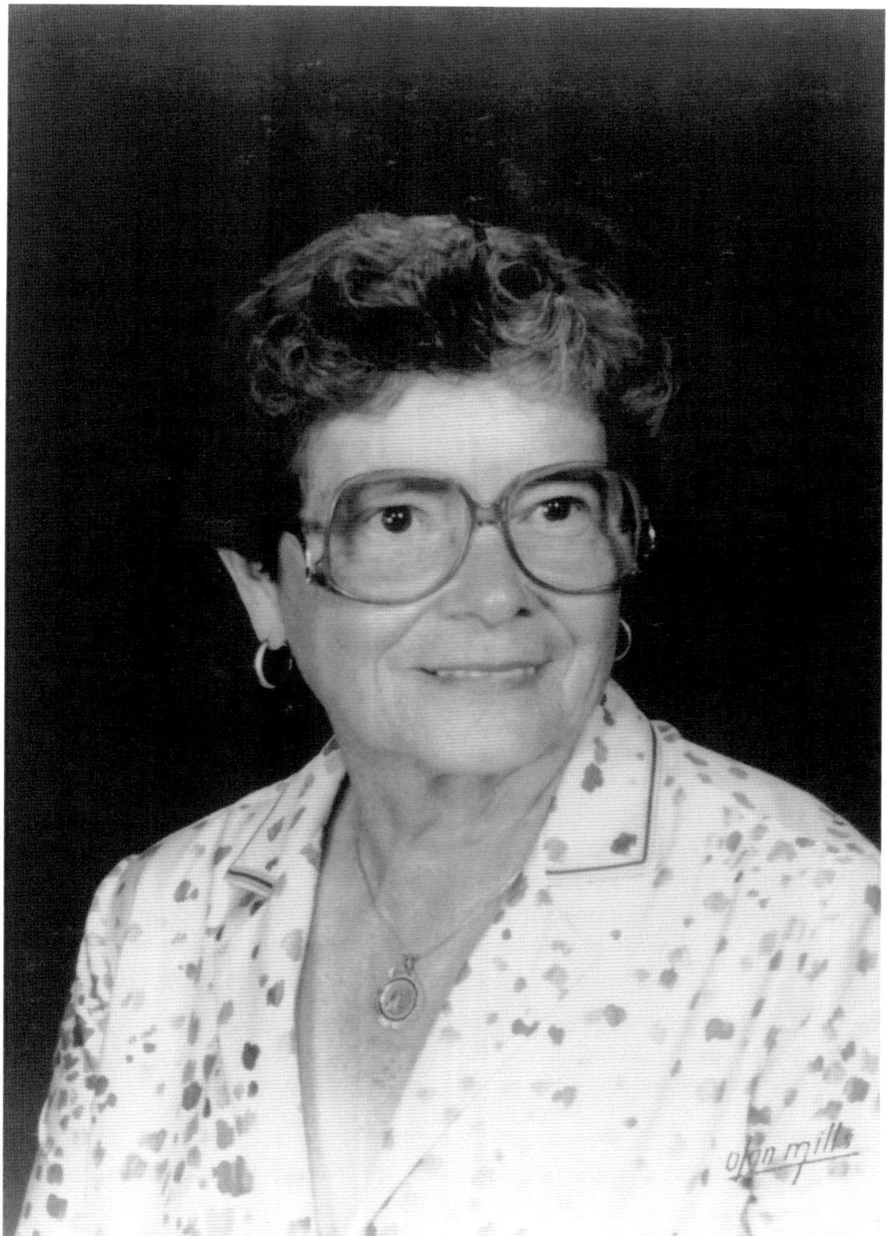

Julie Gault

A retired Thornton Fractional South High School biology teacher, Julie Gault organized the Lansing Historical Society as the country's bicentennial was commemorated in 1976. She served as president of the society and was presented with the Award of Superior Achievement by the Illinois State Historical Society in 1984. Gault fought against age discrimination after being forced into retirement at the age of 65 by school board policy, winning a case after seven years as she continued to substitute teach until the age of 75. In 1978, the US Court of Appeals ruled that public employees cannot be forced to retire on the basis of age alone, a ruling that resulted, in part, from Julia's case. (Courtesy of the Lansing Historical Society.)

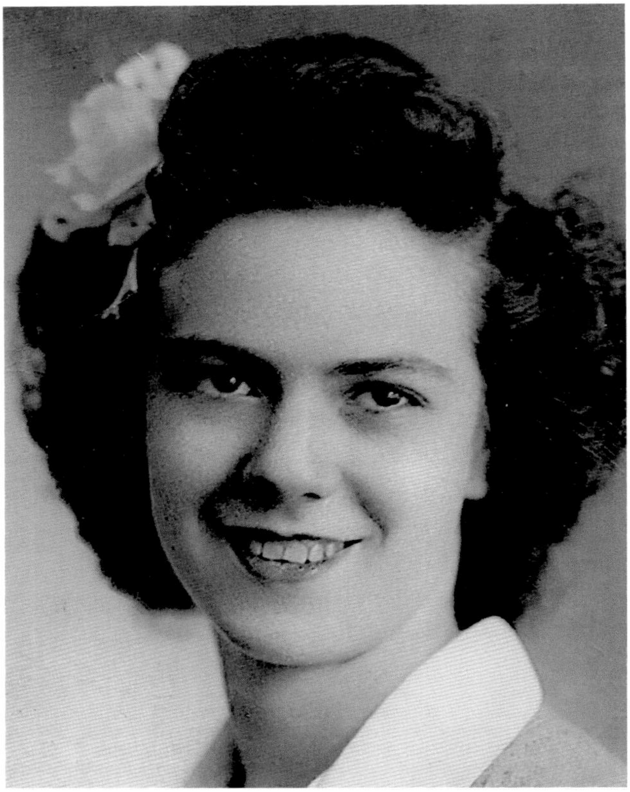

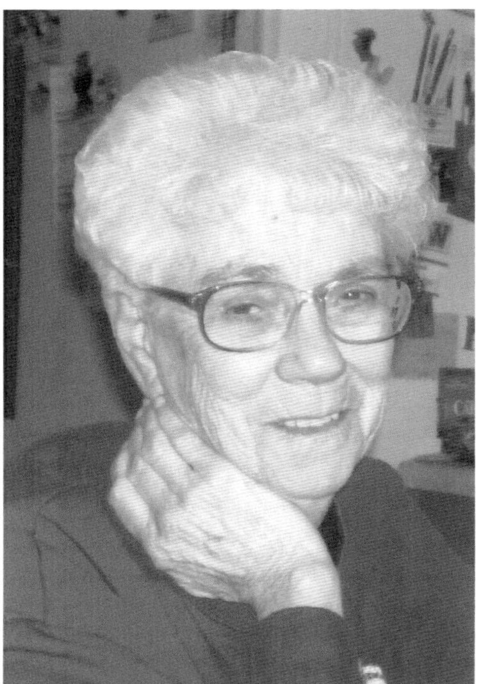

Joyce Dykhuis

Joyce Dykhuis (née Siegfried) has been a Lansing resident since the early 1950s. During the 1960s, she was one of two crossing guards at 178th Street and Burnham Avenue. Joyce spent many years at Lan-Oak pool teaching others to swim. When her children were in school, she participated in the PTA, where she held a variety of offices. For her dedication and service, Joyce received the Lansing Education Association Award in 1973. She also spent many years as a Girl Scout leader. As her children attended Coolidge, Memorial, and Thornton Fractional South schools and beyond, Joyce opened her home to foster children in need and exchange students from all over the world. For many years, she has served the public by being a judge in the various local, state, and national elections. She has also been a volunteer babysitter at the Markham courthouse. In 1975, she received the Jr. Woman's Club Woman of the Year award, and in 1996, Joyce was honored with the park district's Vince Award. She remains very active at Lansing Presbyterian Church, where she is one of the surviving original members as well as a past president of the Lansing Presbyterian Church Presbyterian Women's Organization. She helps the church serve free community dinners monthly, and for the past 15 years, has traveled to Kentucky for mission trips. Joyce is currently volunteering at Thornton Community Township Center and also at the Jones Community Center soup kitchen located in Chicago Heights. (Both, courtesy of Lori Siegfried.)

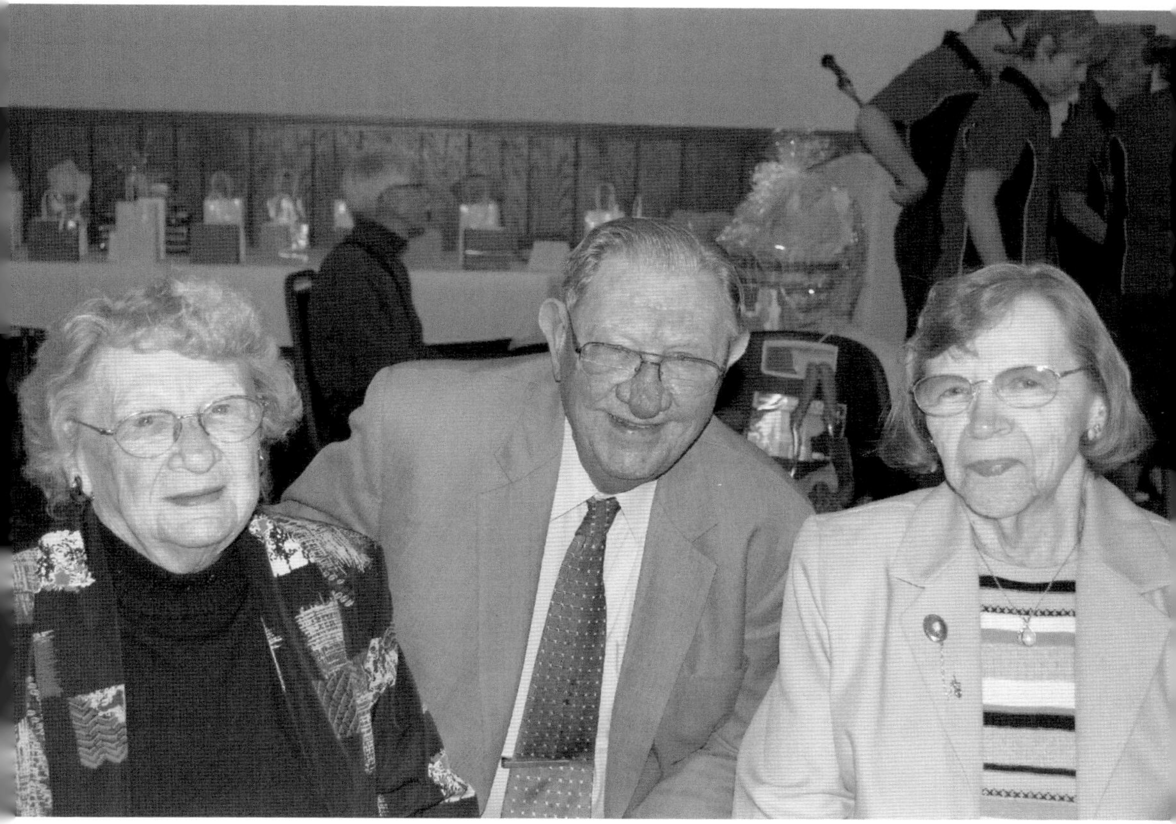

Olsen Family

There were seven siblings in the Olsen family: four boys and three girls. Another boy, Jack Broomhead, was raised with the Olsen family after his mother died during childbirth. The Olsen siblings were August Jr. (see pages 10–11), Laverne "Peggy," Floyed, Mildred, Don, Elaine, and Ralph. August died while serving in World War II. Ralph was a valedictorian at Thornton Fractional High School and taught math at Thornton Fractional High School and then Thornton Fractional South High School. Pictured are the three surviving siblings, from left to right, Millie Ogborn, Don, and Elaine Humbert. Millie worked at the Oak Glen Post Office station and then with Walter Schultz Insurance for 27 years. She has lived and worked her entire life within a four-block area. Don was valedictorian of Thornton Fractional High School. He is an active member of the First Reformed Church of Lansing and the Lansing Golden Ks. He has also been an active member of the Lansing Historical Society, serving as president, advisor, and director. Elaine moved from Lansing to Merrillville after she married and she still resides there.

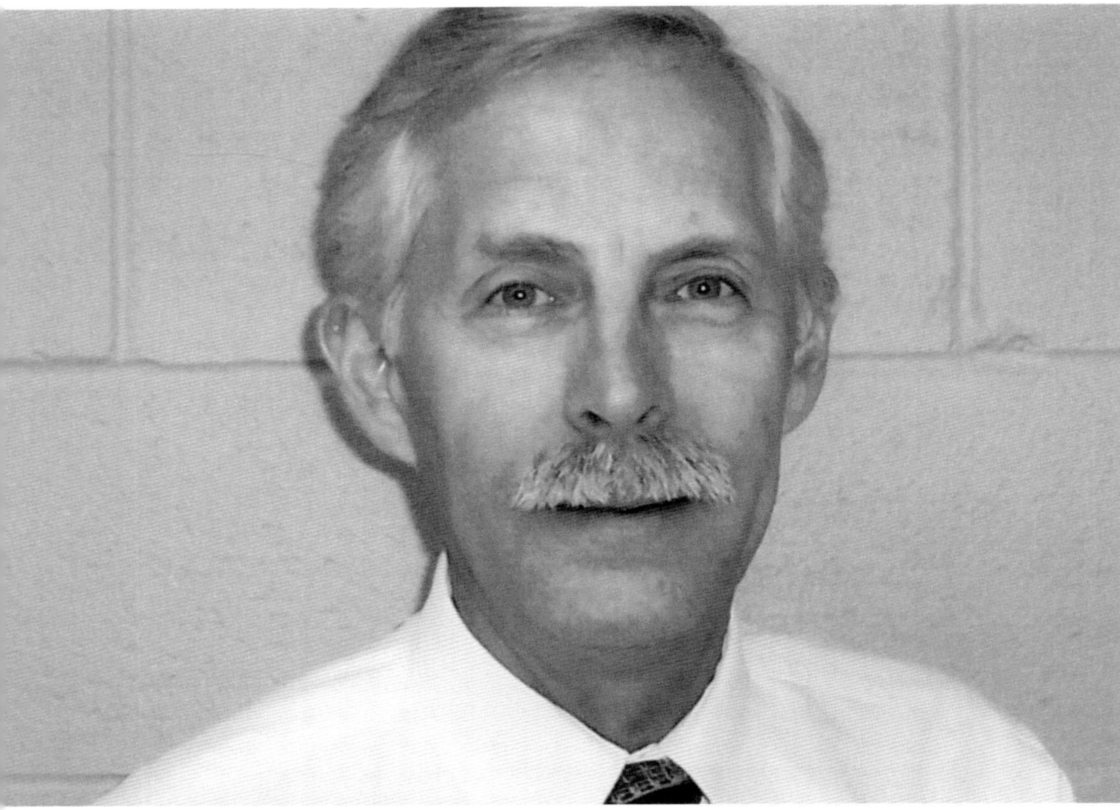

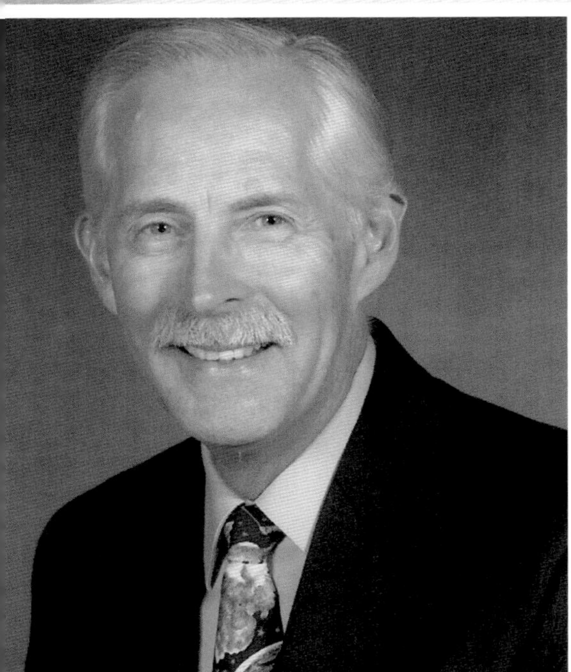

Dennis Flanagan

Dennis Flanagan served on the Lan-Oak Park District board and was instrumental in the creation of the Lan-Oak Park District Foundation and the cruise nights held on Ridge Road in the summer months. A classic car owner himself, the cruise nights were renamed Dennis Flanagan's Cruise on Ridge following his death. He was also active in other organizations in Lansing and served as the president of the Lansing Historical Society. (Above, courtesy of John Wilson; left, courtesy of Barb Flanagan.)

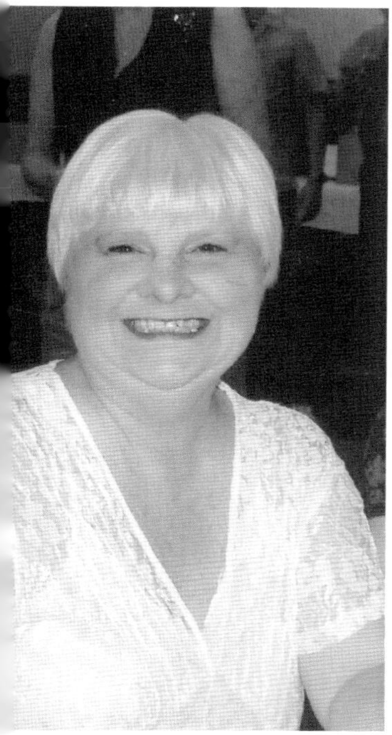

Jen Saia

A longtime member of the Lansing Historical Society, Jen Saia became curator of the Lansing Historical Museum, adding special touches to the traditional annual exhibits that draw in visitors, such as the June Brides and the Festival of Lights. Saia began the Lansing Historical Society tradition of hosting a luncheon for clients of LARC, an organization that provides support for adults with development disabilities. (Author's collection.)

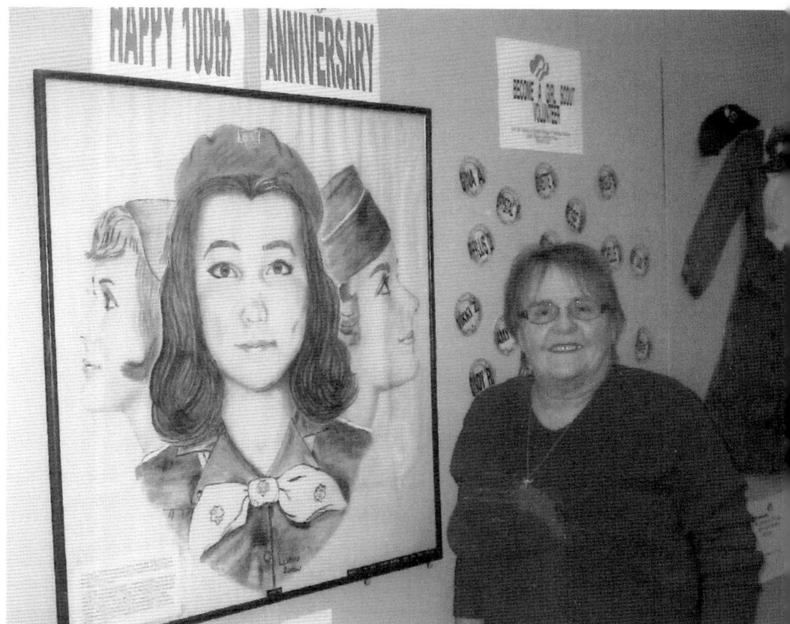

Janet Bockel

In the 1950s, Janet Bockel got involved in Scouts as a young girl, and right after high school, she became an adult volunteer with the troop she was in. She became involved as a helper with Boy Scouts when her son was young, and when her two daughters were old enough for Girl Scouts, she got involved as troop leader and has been involved in Girl Scouting ever since. Her family dates back to over 140 years in Lansing; she is a descendant of the Busack family. She's been involved in arranging Scout elves at the Santa House and organizing the Ten Penny Carnival and has been involved in PTA and band booster programs when her kids were in school. She served as Reavis PTA president for three years, Memorial Junior High School PTA president for two years, and Thornton Fractional South High School PTA president for one year. In 2012, she chaired the Girl Scout float celebrating 100 years of Girls Scouts, and an eight-foot-by-12-foot house was constructed of empty Girl Scout cookie boxes. She has been awarded the Curved Bar (the highest Girl Scout award) in 1960, the Outstanding Volunteer Award, and the Thanks Badge I and Thanks Badge II. She continues running a ceramics business at her home. (Courtesy of Janet Bockel.)

Winifred Edwards

In the late 1940s, Winifred Edwards began her long tenure as librarian. She worked in the old pump house that served as a library until a new building was erected at the corner of Ridge Road and Chicago Avenue, opening in 1957. It was cold and dark or hot and dark depending on the season because there were no storm windows, no insulation, and brick walls. She often had to find books by flashlight since only two dim light fixtures were used to light the building. In 1950, the building was refurbished with automatic oil heat and new windows that opened top to bottom to give the space some ventilation. Winifred retired in 1966. (Courtesy of Lansing Public Library.)

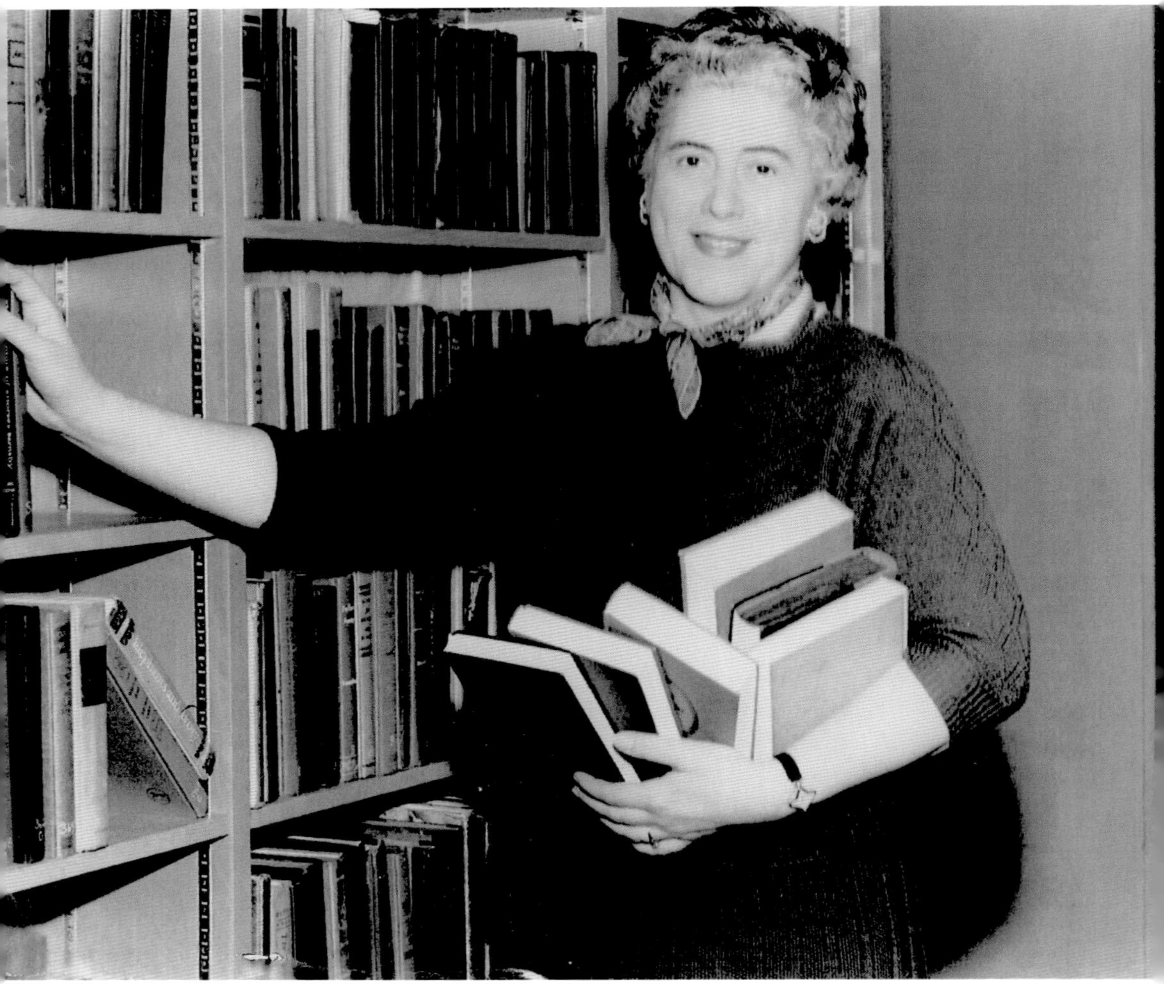

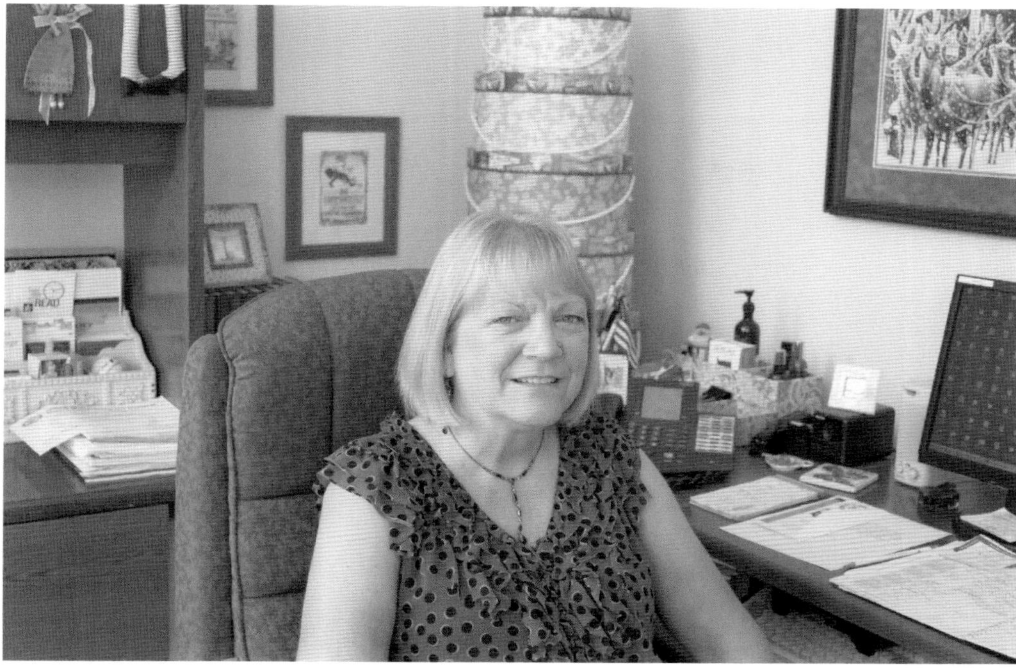

Debbie Albrecht

Debbie grew up in upstate New York and met her husband, Bill, a Lansing native, while attending college in Pella, Iowa. She married and relocated to Lansing, where they raised two sons who attended school district No. 171 and graduated from Thornton Fractional South High School. Debbie taught part-time at Lansing Nursery School for 10 years and later decided to go back to school to earn her master's degree in library and information science. In 1999 she began working as a part-time circulation clerk at the Lansing Public Library and the following year moved to a full-time position as youth services assistant. In 2004, she received her degree from Dominican University, graduating with honors. In May 2006, she was promoted to director and continues in that position. She oversaw remodeling of the library building and created several events to draw in residents, including the annual block party held on the front lawn of the library. She is a past president of the Children's Librarian Association of the South Suburbs, a board member of the Area Training for Librarians and Staff (ATLAS), and served on the selection committees for both the Rebecca Caudill and Monarch Awards. (Author's collection.)

Daniel Toren (RIGHT)

A resident of neighboring Lynwood, Daniel attended Lansing Christian School and Illiana Christian High School. He graduated from Hope College in 2010 with a degree in political science and worked with AmeriCorps managing a Chicago Public Schools after-school tutoring program for one year. He is currently a student at the University of Chicago Law School. He was a Cub Scout with Pack 271 in Lansing and then joined Boy Scout Troop No. 276 from the Lansing American Legion. He has always been interested in history and through his great-uncle Don Olsen, who is a lifelong Lansing resident and involved with the Lansing Historical Society, he discovered that the Lansing Historical Society wanted to place a historical marker at the site of the original Lansing General Store. Daniel raised the funds, identified the company that makes the metal markers, did the historical research, and wrote the text for the plaque. Local historian Ken Schoon was a great resource and attended the dedication ceremony in July 2005. Daniel organized the installation and had the other members of Boy Scout Troop No. 276 install the plaque. The picture on the bottom shows Daniel with (from left to right) Rev. Mel DeVries, Mayor Dan Podgorski, local historian Ken Schoon, and Daniel's great-uncle Don Olsen. In the top photograph, Daniel is to the right of the marker, and his brother Craig is on the far left. (Both, courtesy of Carl Toren.)

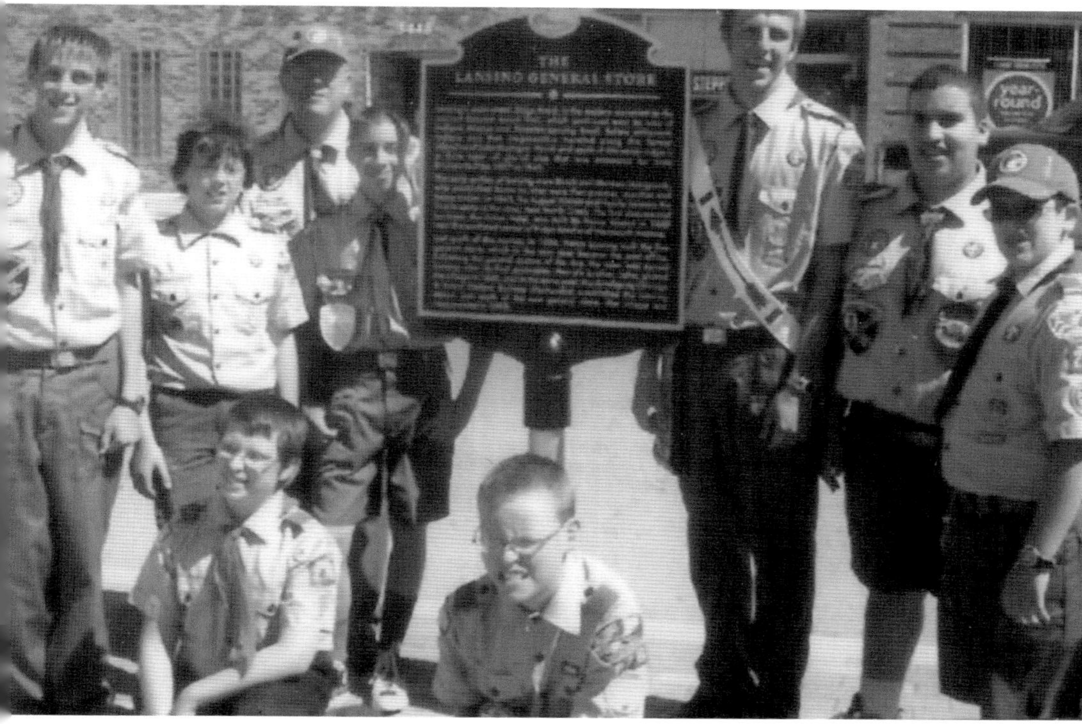
THE
LANSING GENERAL STORE

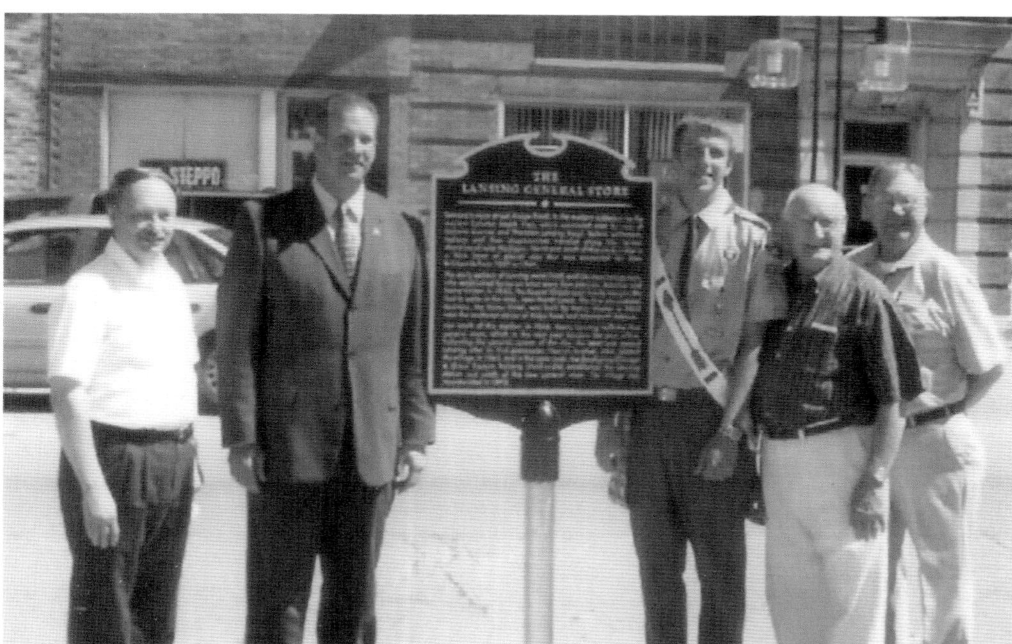
STEPPO
THE
LANSING GENERAL STORE

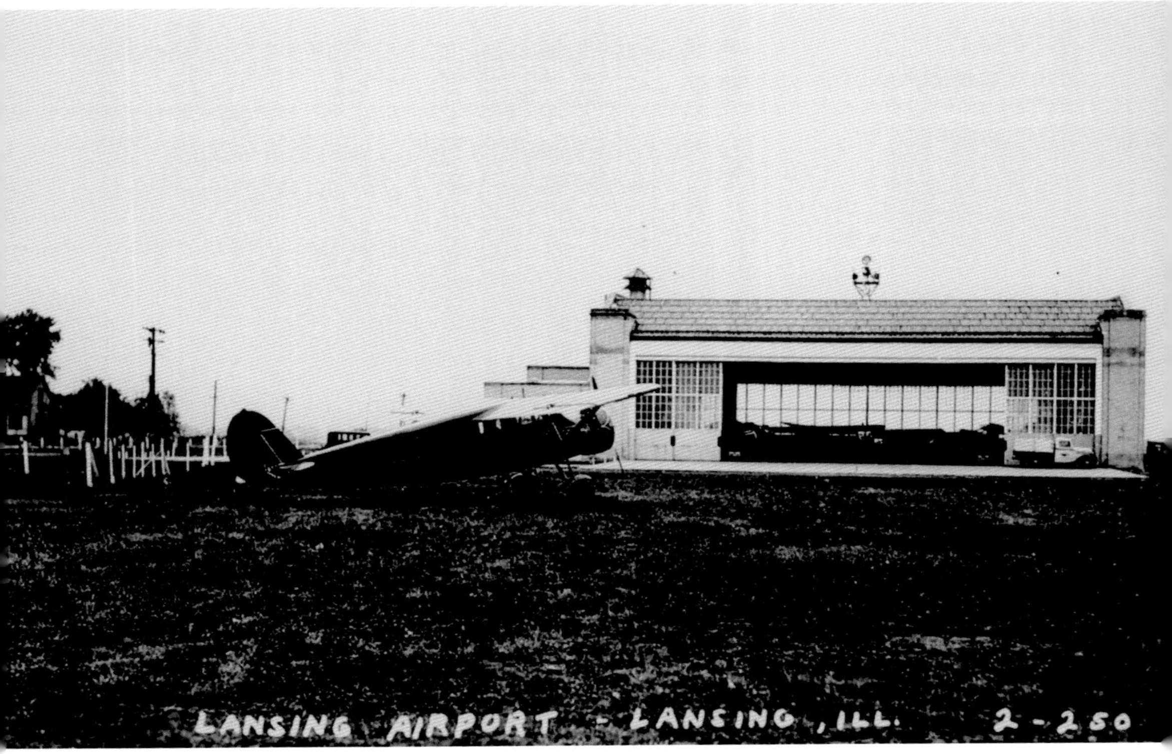

Henry Ford

Although he did not reside in Lansing, automobile maker Henry Ford's innovative and industrial spirit reached the village through the construction of the Ford Hangar, built in 1926. It was designed by Ford's famed architect, Albert Kahn, and was part of the Henry Ford Airport intended to connect Ford's industrial empire in Michigan and Ohio to his automobile plant in Chicago's Hegewisch neighborhood. The airport was sold in 1937 and later became the Chicago Hammond Airport. In 1976, the airport was purchased by the Village of Lansing. Due to the efforts of Lansing resident Harold Christian, the hangar was listed in the National Register of Historic Places on May 9, 1985. (Courtesy of the Lansing Historical Society.)

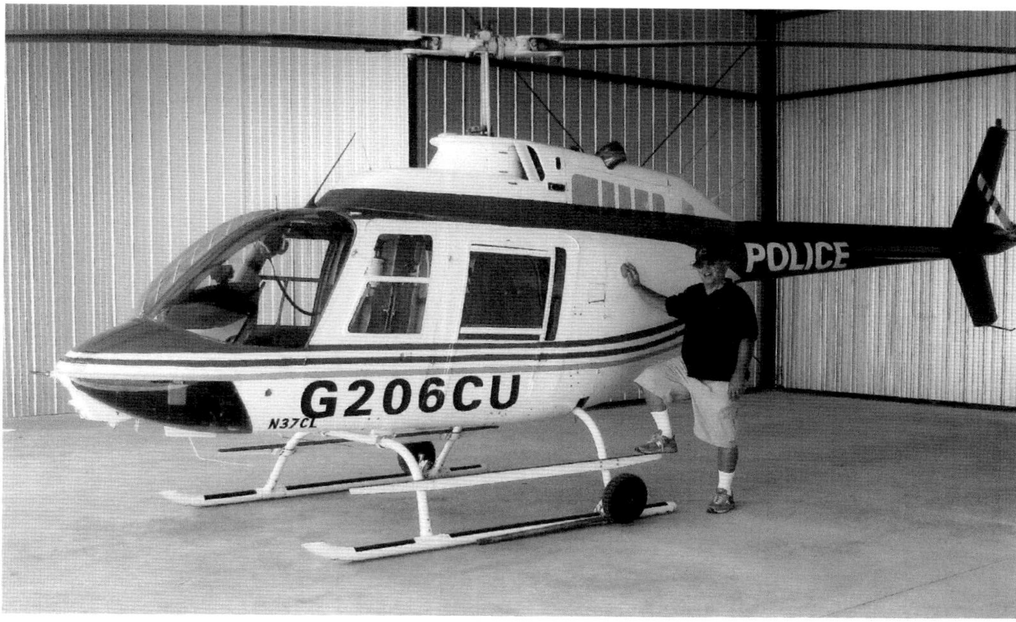

Bob Malkas

Bob Malkas stands in front of a helicopter used in the filming of the movie *The Dark Knight* in Chicago. Malkas served as airport commissioner for eight years before becoming airport manager. He served 23 years as manager, helping it grow from about 150 acres to the 650 acres it is today. Under his administration, it was twice named Reliever Airport of the Year by the Illinois Division of Aeronautics. (Both, courtesy of Bob Malkas.)

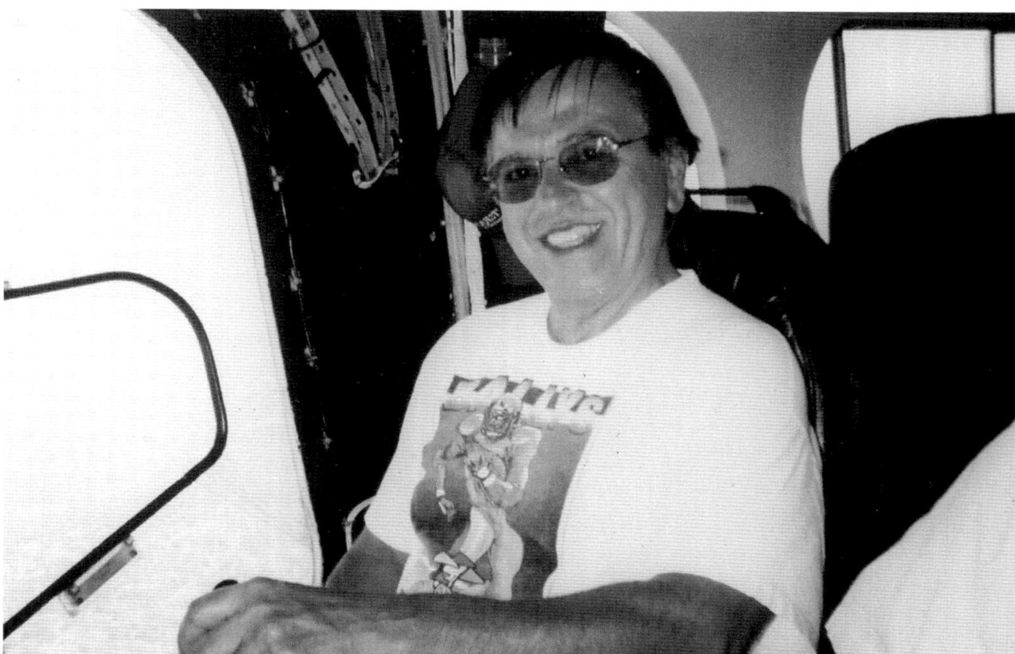

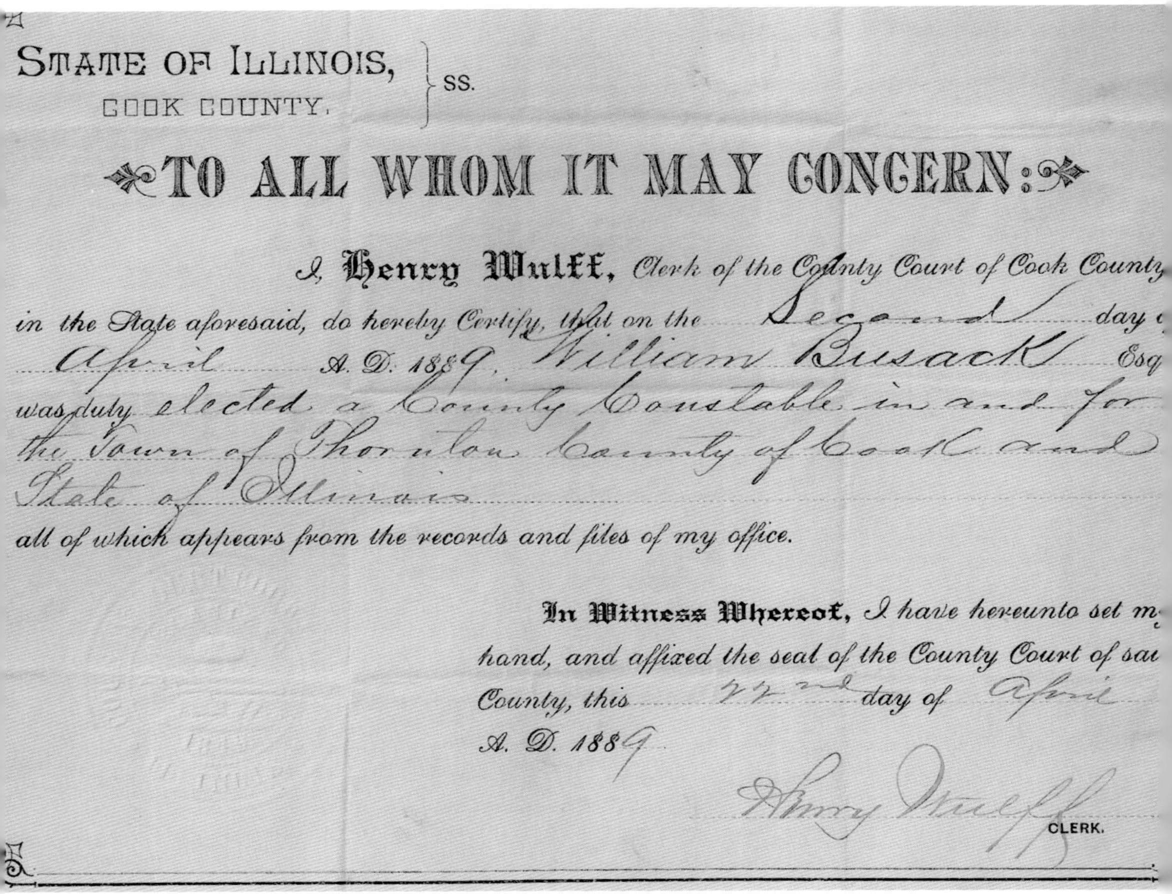

STATE OF ILLINOIS, }
COOK COUNTY. } SS.

TO ALL WHOM IT MAY CONCERN:

I, Henry Wulff, Clerk of the County Court of Cook County in the State aforesaid, do hereby Certify, that on the Second day of April A. D. 1889, William Busack Esq was duly elected a County Constable in and for the Town of Thornton County of Cook and State of Illinois
all of which appears from the records and files of my office.

In Witness Whereof, I have hereunto set my hand, and affixed the seal of the County Court of said County, this 22nd day of April A. D. 1889.

Henry Wulff
CLERK.

Busack Family

The Busack home at 3353 Ridge Road remains the oldest structure in Lansing. According to a 1959 news article from the *Chicago Daily News*, the home was built in 1860. It has served many purposes over the years, including town hall, railroad hotel, saloon, first jail, dance hall, and post office, and it has housed many businesses, including a barbershop and grocery store. Several family members played a role in the community as business owners. Christian Busack bought the home in 1875 and son William bought the building in 1893. This certificate shows William Busack's election as county constable for Thornton Township in 1889. The home has been acquired by the village, and as of the time of publication, plans were being made to demolish the building. (Courtesy of the Lansing Historical Society.)

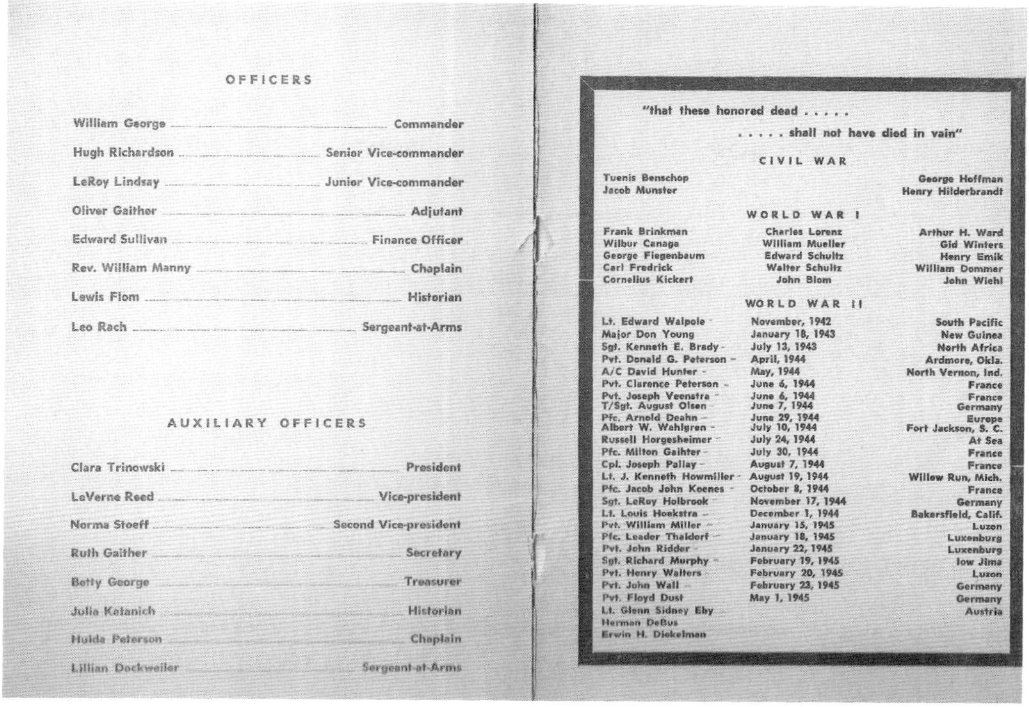

OFFICERS

William George	Commander
Hugh Richardson	Senior Vice-commander
LeRoy Lindsay	Junior Vice-commander
Oliver Gaither	Adjutant
Edward Sullivan	Finance Officer
Rev. William Manny	Chaplain
Lewis Flom	Historian
Leo Rach	Sergeant-at-Arms

AUXILIARY OFFICERS

Clara Trinowski	President
LeVerne Reed	Vice-president
Norma Stoeff	Second Vice-president
Ruth Gaither	Secretary
Betty George	Treasurer
Julia Katanich	Historian
Hulda Peterson	Chaplain
Lillian Dockweiler	Sergeant-at-Arms

"that these honored dead . . . . .

. . . . . shall not have died in vain"

CIVIL WAR

Tuenis Benschop	George Hoffman
Jacob Munster	Henry Hilderbrandt

WORLD WAR I

Frank Brinkman	Charles Lorenz	Arthur H. Ward
Wilbur Canaga	William Mueller	Gid Winters
George Fiegenbaum	Edward Schultz	Henry Emik
Carl Fredrick	Walter Schultz	William Dommer
Cornelius Kickert	John Blom	John Wiehl

WORLD WAR II

Lt. Edward Walpole -	November, 1942	South Pacific
Major Don Young	January 18, 1943	New Guinea
Sgt. Kenneth E. Brady -	July 13, 1943	North Africa
Pvt. Donald G. Peterson -	April, 1944	Ardmore, Okla.
A/C David Hunter -	May, 1944	North Vernon, Ind.
Pvt. Clarence Peterson -	June 6, 1944	France
Pvt. Joseph Veenstra -	June 6, 1944	France
T/Sgt. August Olsen -	June 7, 1944	Germany
Pfc. Arnold Deahn -	June 29, 1944	Europe
Albert W. Wahlgren -	July 10, 1944	Fort Jackson, S. C.
Russell Horgesheimer -	July 24, 1944	At Sea
Pfc. Milton Gaihter -	July 30, 1944	France
Cpl. Joseph Pallay -	August 7, 1944	France
Lt. J. Kenneth Howmiller -	August 19, 1944	Willow Run, Mich.
Pfc. Jacob John Koenes -	October 8, 1944	France
Sgt. LeRoy Holbrook -	November 17, 1944	Germany
Lt. Louis Hoekstra -	December 1, 1944	Bakersfield, Calif.
Pvt. William Miller -	January 15, 1945	Luzon
Pfc. Leader Thaldorf -	January 18, 1945	Luxenburg
Pvt. John Ridder -	January 22, 1945	Luxenburg
Sgt. Richard Murphy -	February 19, 1945	Iow Jima
Pvt. Henry Walters -	February 20, 1945	Luzon
Pvt. John Wall -	February 23, 1945	Germany
Pvt. Floyd Dust	May 1, 1945	Germany
Lt. Glenn Sidney Eby -		Austria
Herman DeBus		
Erwin H. Diekelman		

American Legion

This program from the 150th anniversary of American Legion Post 697 includes the names of those veterans of Lansing who were killed during service in World War II. The commander of the post was William George. (Courtesy of the Lansing Historical Society.

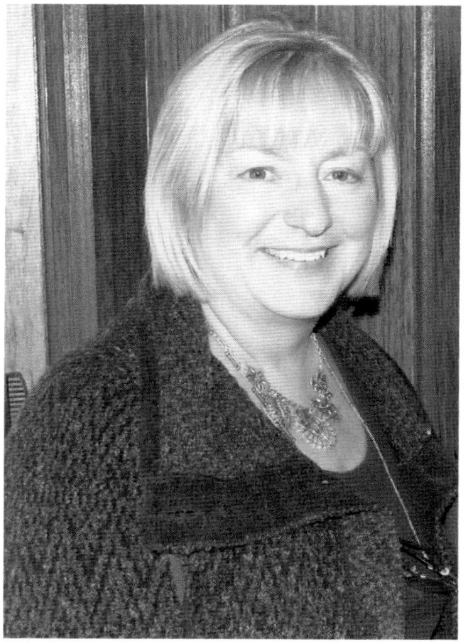

Debbie Bach

As a member of the General Federation of Woman's Clubs since 1976, Debbie Bach has served as president, co-president, vice president, and secretary of the Lansing Junior Woman's Club and is current president of the Lansing Woman's Club as well as serving on many committees and officer posts on the regional, state, and national level. She has been a "Junior of the Year" recipient and won a Lansing Special Volunteer Award. As a member, she supported Prevent Child Abuse Illinois and joined the board in 2005 and serves as the present board president. She has held several other positions within the organization over the years. She and her husband, Don, owned the Cam Golf store on Torrence Avenue until it was sold in 1991. They continue to run a wholesale division in Lynwood. They have three children and one grandchild. She has also been a member of the Lansing Business Woman's Association, Lansing Chamber of Commerce, PTA, Sports Booster Club, and Girl Scouts. (Carrie Steinweg.)

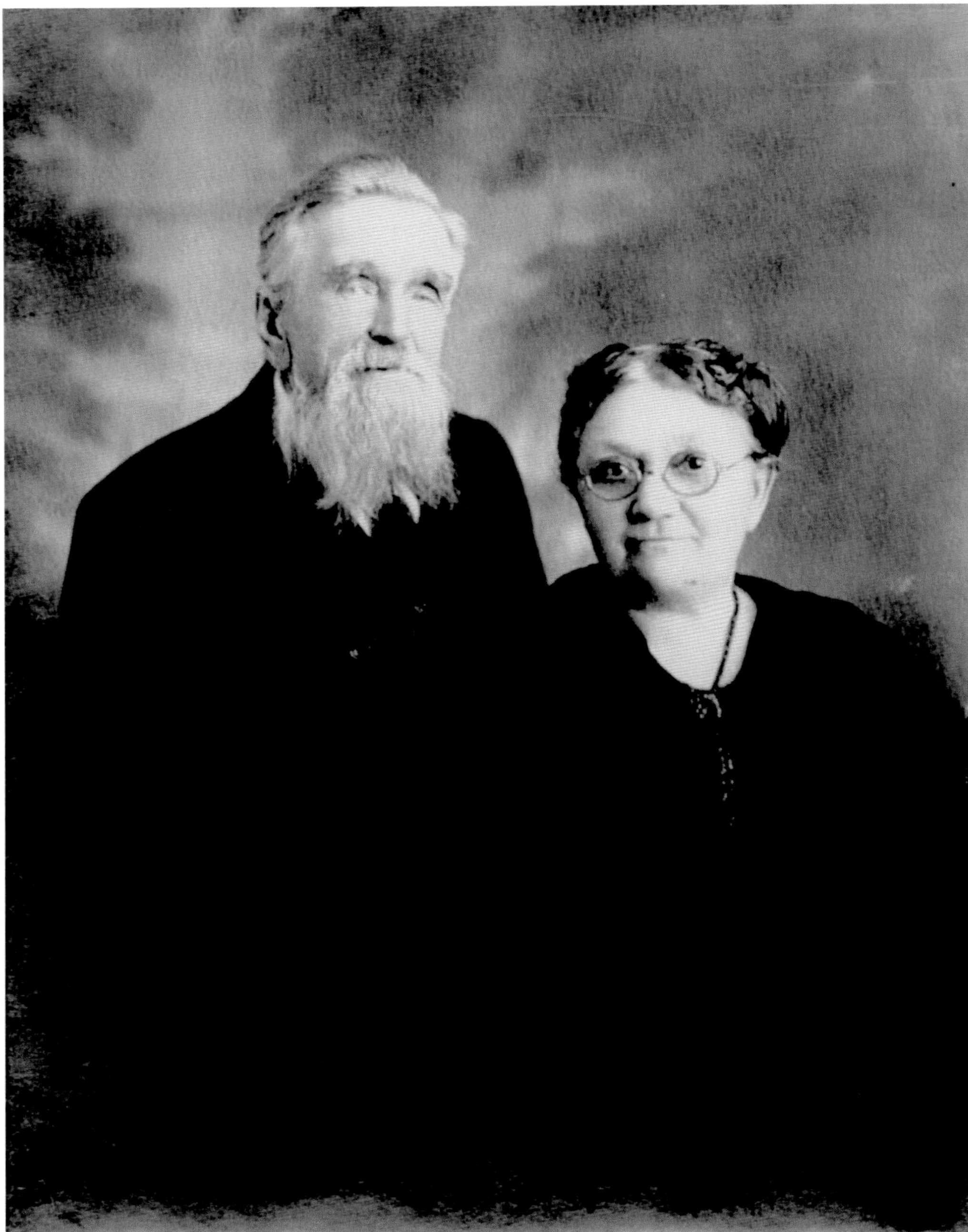

Henry Hildebrandt

Henry Hildebrandt was the son of August and Christine Hildebrandt, the first permanent German settlers to come to the Lansing area. In October 1862, Henry became one of five Lansing men to serve in the Union army during the Civil War. He served in Tennessee. Henry donated land for the building of Trinity Lutheran Church. He was first married to Emma and had two children. He and his second wife, Mary Gertz, had 11 children, five of whom died at birth. (Courtesy of the Lansing Historical Society.)

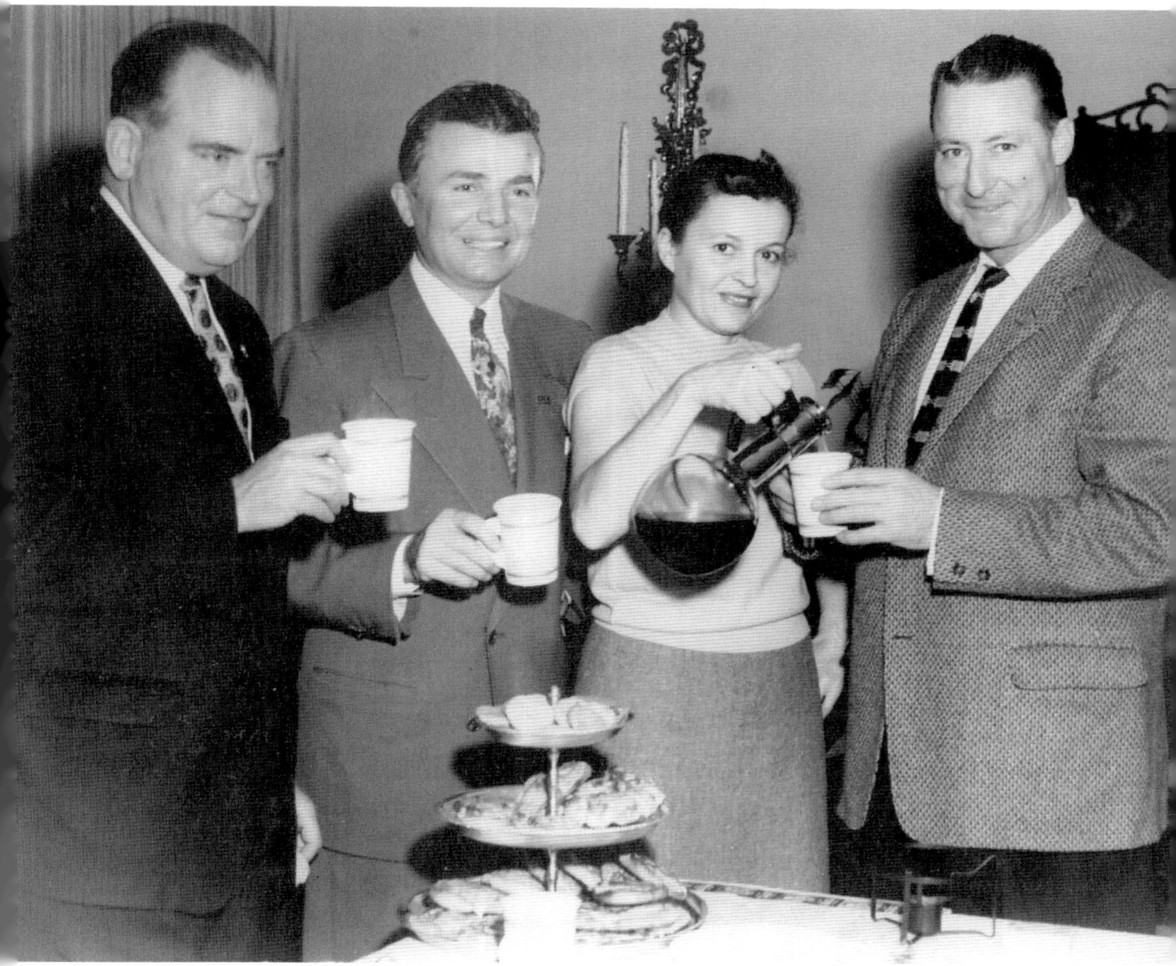

Jack Walker
Jack Walker (far right) was an attorney for the village of Lansing and the school board. He was a state senator, a state representative, and speaker of the house from 1969 to 1971. He is pictured with (from left to right) Hayes Robertson, who was an Illinois state senator from Flossmoor and a descendant of Pres. Rutherford B. Hayes; Maurino Richton, who was mayor of Chicago Heights and an Illinois state representative; and his wife, Pearl Walker. Jack's daughter Karen Walker-Kehl said that he had been orphaned as a child and was a big advocate of education. After his death, she learned that he had personally offered financial assistance to several local people to help them through college. "He was a great father and loved kids," said Walker-Kehl. "He taught us to play every sport and he was a lot of fun."

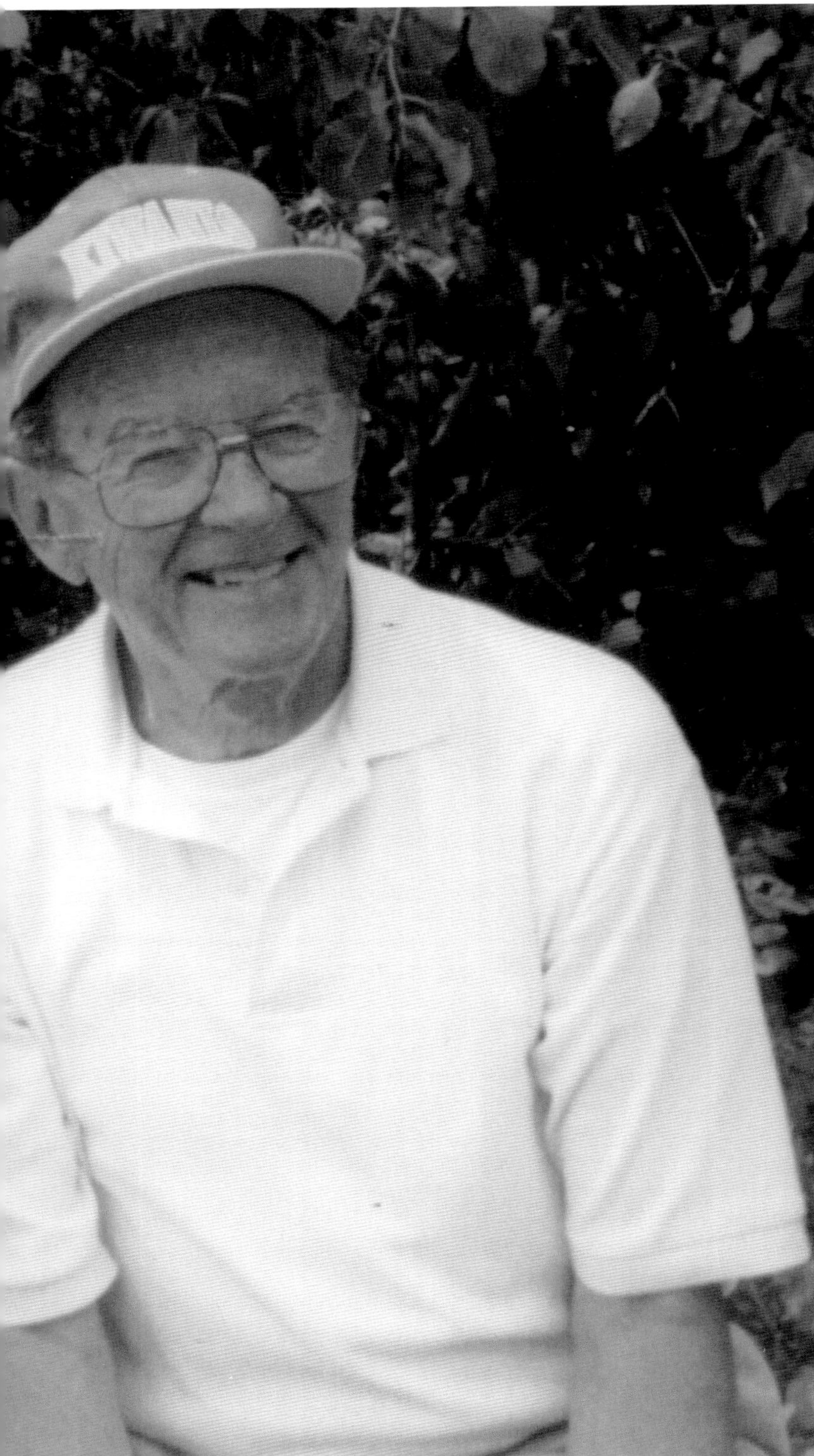

Tom Gavin
Raymond "Tom" Gavin was born in Maywood, Illinois, in 1923 and played baseball and basketball at Proviso East High School. He attended Illinois Institute of Technology, majoring in chemical engineering. He also attended Great Lakes Naval Center and was honorably discharged as a second lieutenant. He was hired by Swift & Company to do adhesive research, and he acquired numerous patents in his 40-plus years in the field. In 1948, he married Reinelda "Honey" Backes and they had three children. In 1958, Tom began coaching little league when his son Mike was eight years old. For 52 years, he continued his involvement with the Lansing Old Timers organization until he suffered a stroke at the Lansing Little League Complex, where he spent so much of his time, in 2010. His coaching highlights include more than 580 wins in more than 1,000 games. He coaches 400 kids and was able to coach his grandson, who was awarded a baseball scholarship to Eastern Illinois University. In 2011, a ceremony was held naming a field at Lions Stadium "Tom Gavin Field" in his honor. (Courtesy of Pat Gavin.)

CHAPTER SEVEN

Success Stories

Every town has its stories of success, of those ordinary children who grew up to do extraordinary things or have amazing success in their fields. Lansing has produced a number of individuals who have gone on to play professional sports, made it onto big stages and screens, and made those of us who still call Lansing home very proud.

Pierre Thomas

Charles Pierre Thomas grew up in Lynwood playing baseball and it was not until just before high school that he began to play football for the Lansing Lions. Pierre led Thornton Fractional South High School to the state semifinals as a senior and set a school career record of 88 touchdowns and 5,522 rushing yards that also ranked in the top 10 in Illinois state history. He was recruited by the University of Illinois and ranked sixth in the school's history with 2,545 rushing yards. He set a school record with 1,494 kickoff return yards. He is second in school history with 4,451 all-purpose yards. Pierre currently plays in the NFL for the New Orleans Saints, who in 2009 defeated the Indiana Colts in Super Bowl XLIV. Thomas carried the ball nine times for 30 yards and caught six passes for 55 yards with a 16-yard touchdown on a screen pass in the third quarter to give the Saints their first ever Super Bowl touchdown. Pierre has returned to Lansing to talk to youths in the Lansing Lions football program. (Courtesy of Chris Mahoney)

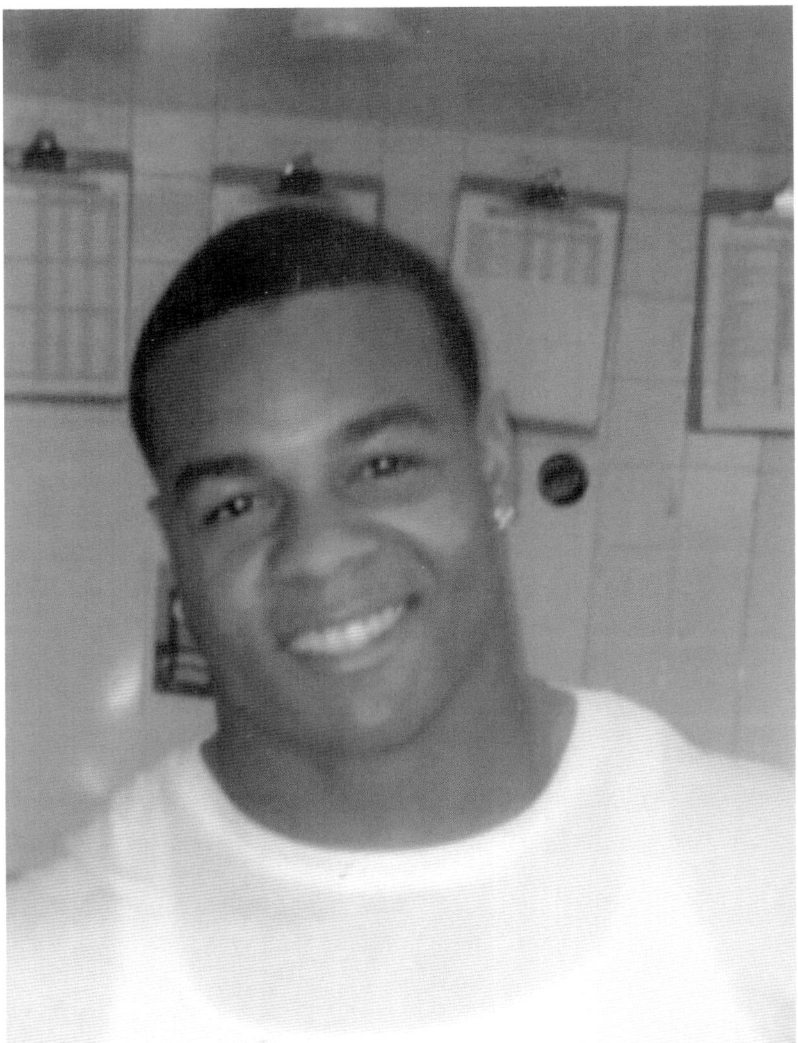

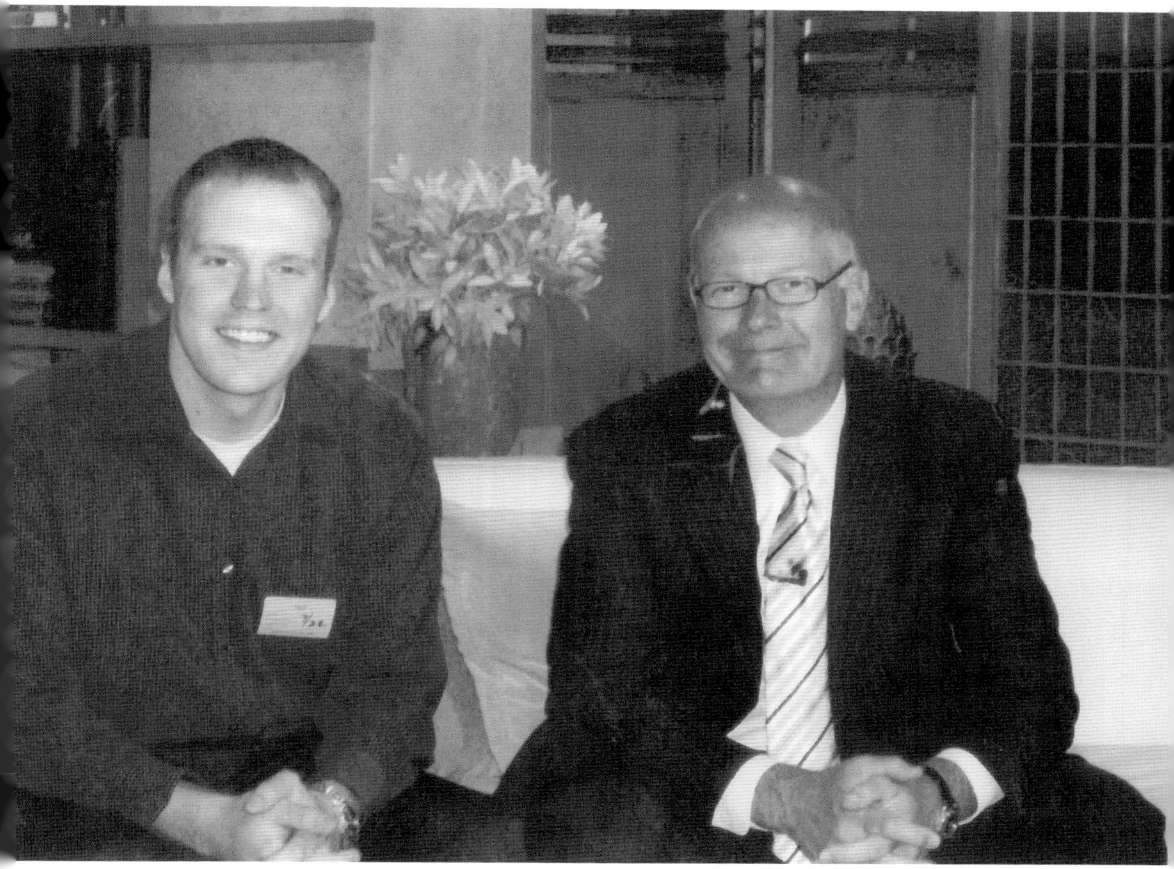

Harry Smith

Television journalist Harry Smith (right) is one of the most nationally recognized figures to have been raised in Lansing. Smith graduated from Thornton Fractional South in 1969. In 2008, CBS News did a segment on his high school career that was transmitted via satellite to him in the studio. He lettered in football, basketball, and track. He was football all-conference and was a *Hammond Times* All-Star. He was in the Letterman's Club, newspaper staff, school bands, Russian Club, a cappella choir, National Forensic League, and speech club. His nephew is currently a teacher at the school. Smith graduated from Central College in Pella, Iowa, with a bachelor of arts degree in communications and theater. His broadcasting career began in radio in the early 1980s. In a long career with CBS, he was a contributor to the *CBS Evening News with Dan Rather*, *48 Hours*, and CBS News documentaries. He also was coanchor of *This Morning* and *The Early Show*. He lives in New York with his wife, sportscaster Andrea Joyce, and their two sons. (Courtesy of Doug Smith.)

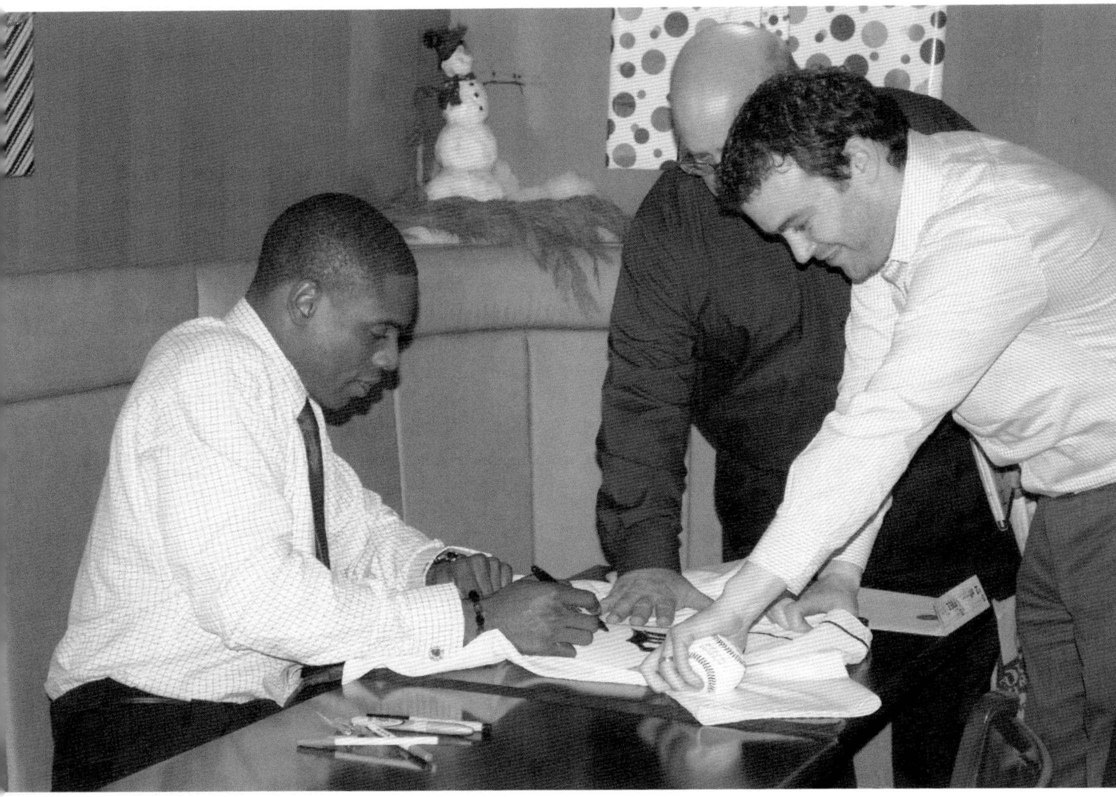

Curtis Granderson

Born to two Chicago schoolteachers, Curtis Granderson was raised in Lynwood and played Little League in Lansing in his early years. He played baseball and basketball at Thornton Fractional South High School, graduating in 2000. He played baseball at the University of Illinois, Chicago. He played minor league ball for the Detroit Tigers organization before making his major league debut in September 2004. In 2006, he became the starting center fielder for the Tigers. In 2007 and 2008, he led the American League in triples and following both seasons, he worked as a TBS commentator during the playoffs. In 2009, he played in his first all-star game. Granderson is one of only four major league players in the elite 20-20-20-20 club, alongside Willie Mays, Frank Schuelte, and Jimmy Rollins, hitting that milestone in 2007. In 2009, he released the book *All You Can Be: Dream It, Draw It, Become It*. Following the 2009 season, Curtis was acquired by the Yankees. He hit a home run on his very first at-bat with the Yankees on April 4, 2010. On August 2011, Curtis and Mark Teixeira became the first Yankees teammates to hit 30 home runs in 115 games since Roger Maris and Mickey Mantle in 1961. In 2011, he hit a career-high 31 home runs. In 2011, he was again voted to the all-star team, led the American League in RBIs, and received the Silver Slugger Award. In August 2011, he was named Major League Baseball Player of the Month. Curtis resides in Chicago in the off-season and in December 2011, returned to Lansing for an assembly at Thornton Fractional South High School where his jersey number was retired. He also took time to attend a fundraising event for the Babe Ruth league and is pictured there signing autographs. (Above, author's collection; both at right, courtesy of Damian Rico.)

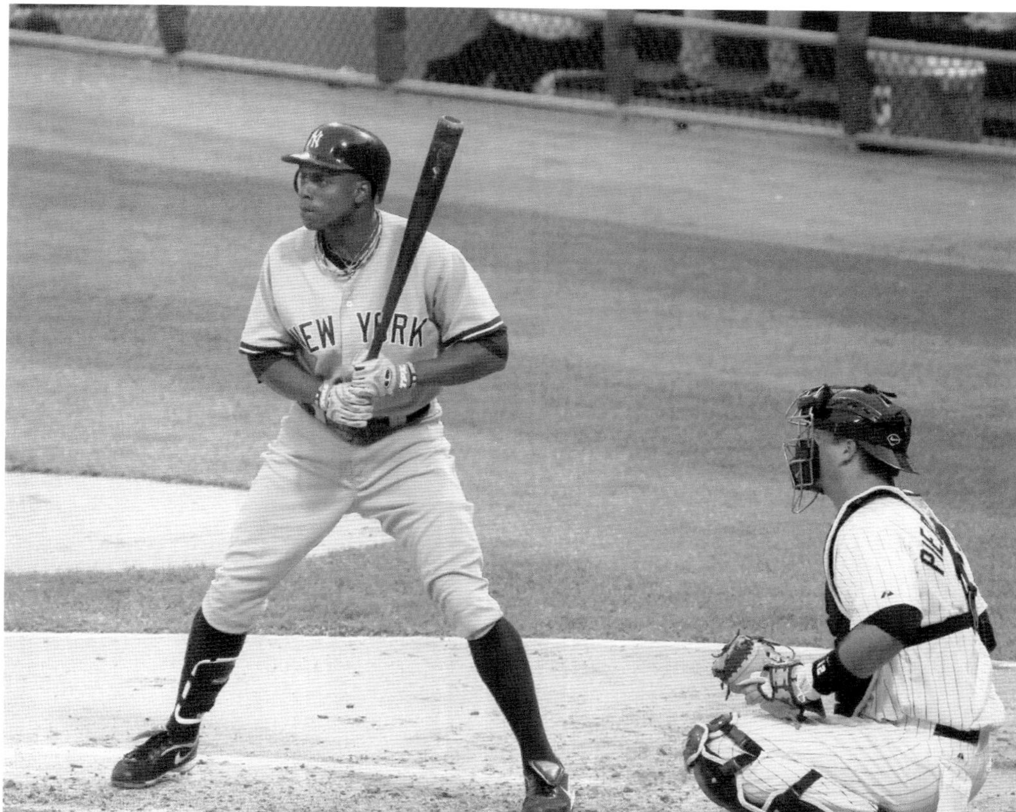

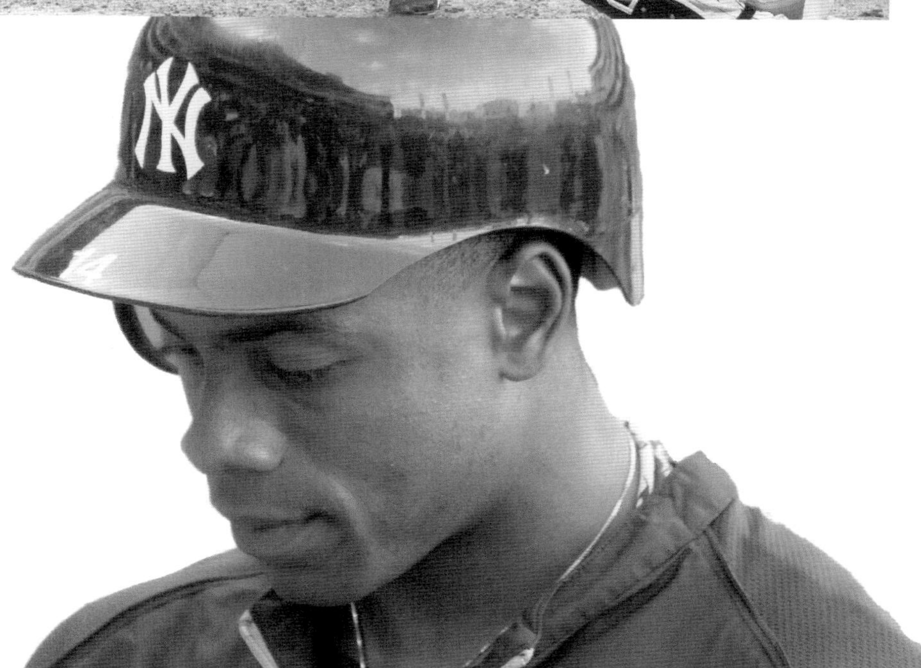

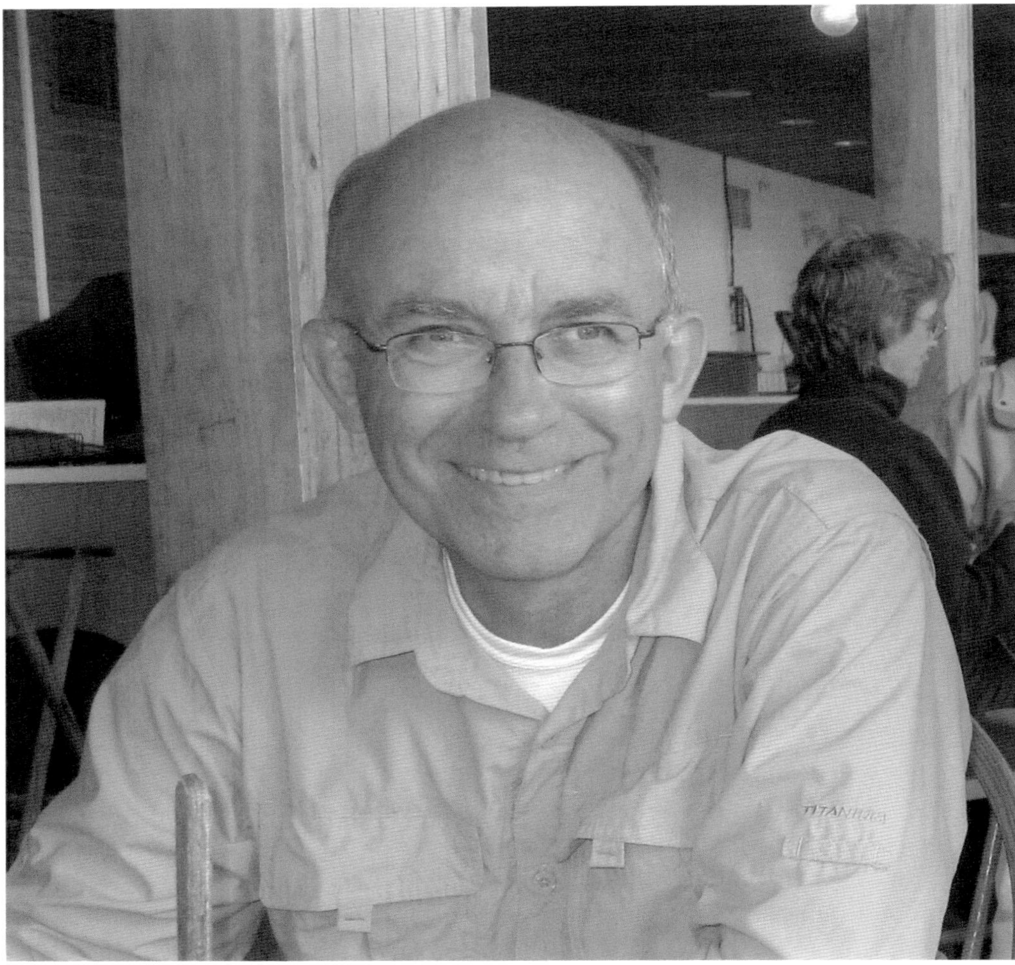

Tom Dorsch

A 1965 graduate of Thornton Fractional South High School, Tom Dorsch went on to medical school at Loyola University's Stritch School of Medicine, graduating in 1973. He completed his residency at the Edward Hines Jr. VA Hospital in Hines, Illinois, in 1977. He is currently an endocrinologist in Peoria, Illinois, and has been involved in diabetes research. (Courtesy of Tom Dorsch.)

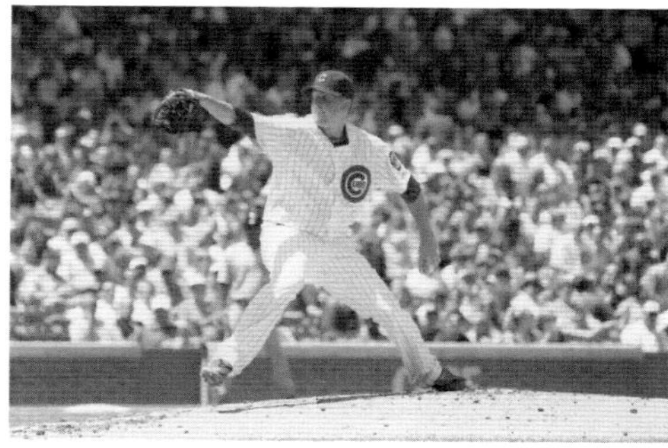

Tom Gorzelanny
Tom Gorzelanny grew up in Lansing, attending Marist High School. He was drafted out of high school by the Chicago White Sox, but chose to play college baseball rather than going right into professional baseball. He played two seasons with the Pittsburgh Pirates in 2007 and 2008. In 2009, he was traded to the Chicago Cubs and pitched two seasons with the team before being acquired by the Washington Nationals in 2011. (Courtesy of the Chicago Cubs.)

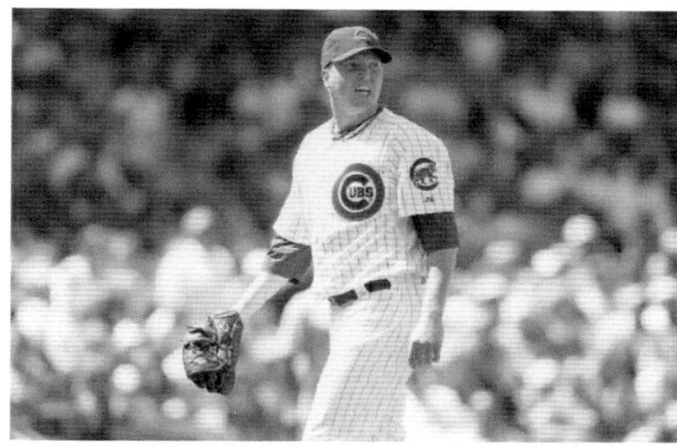

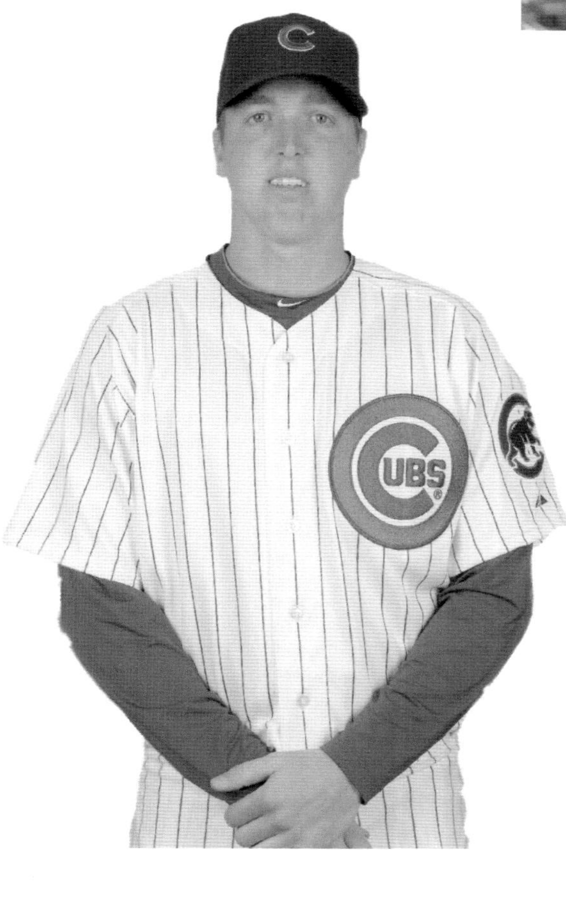

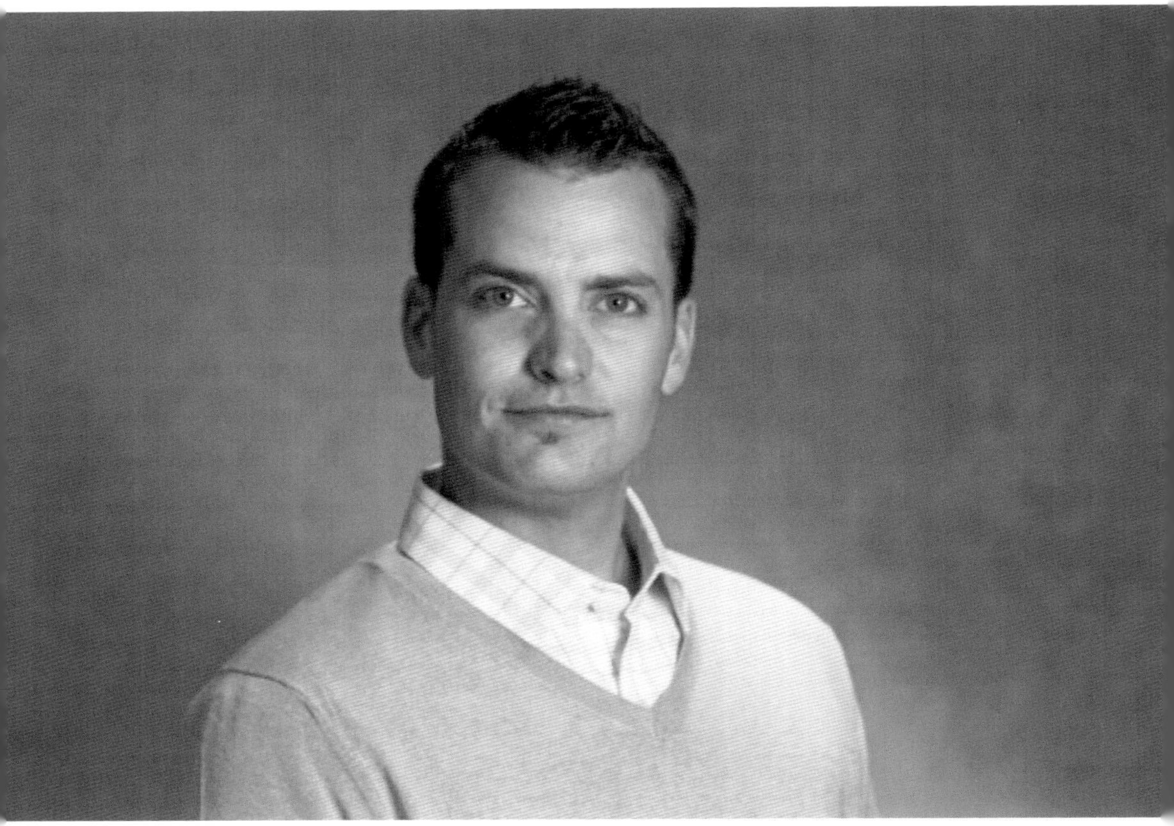

Louis Boyd

A graduate of Thornton Fractional South High School, Boyd was active in the school's drama department. He acted in school productions and also learned his way around behind the scenes. He attended Milliken University and graduated with a degree in theater and acting. His first job after heading to the West Coast was as a production assistant for an ABC reality show. He has been a coordinating producer for two seasons on the Food Network and worked as a producer and director on a Style Network show that earned him a Daytime Emmy nomination. In 2010, he was named vice president of alternative programming at CBS, overseeing the production of such shows as *Survivor, Undercover Boss, Amazing Race,* and *Big Brother.* (Courtesy of Louis Boyd.)

ABOUT THE LANSING HISTORICAL SOCIETY

The Lansing Historical Society was established in 1976 to preserve the past of the Village of Lansing through collections of records and artifacts on display at the Lansing Historical Museum in the lower level of the Lansing Public Library. Meetings of the Lansing Historical Society are held the fourth Monday of each month (except for January, July, August, and December.) Museum hours are Monday from 6:00 to 8:00 p.m., Wednesday from 3:00 to 5:00 p.m., and Saturday from 10:00 a.m. until noon. Hours are extended from late November through the end of the year for the viewing of the annual Festival of Lights exhibit. (Author's collection.)

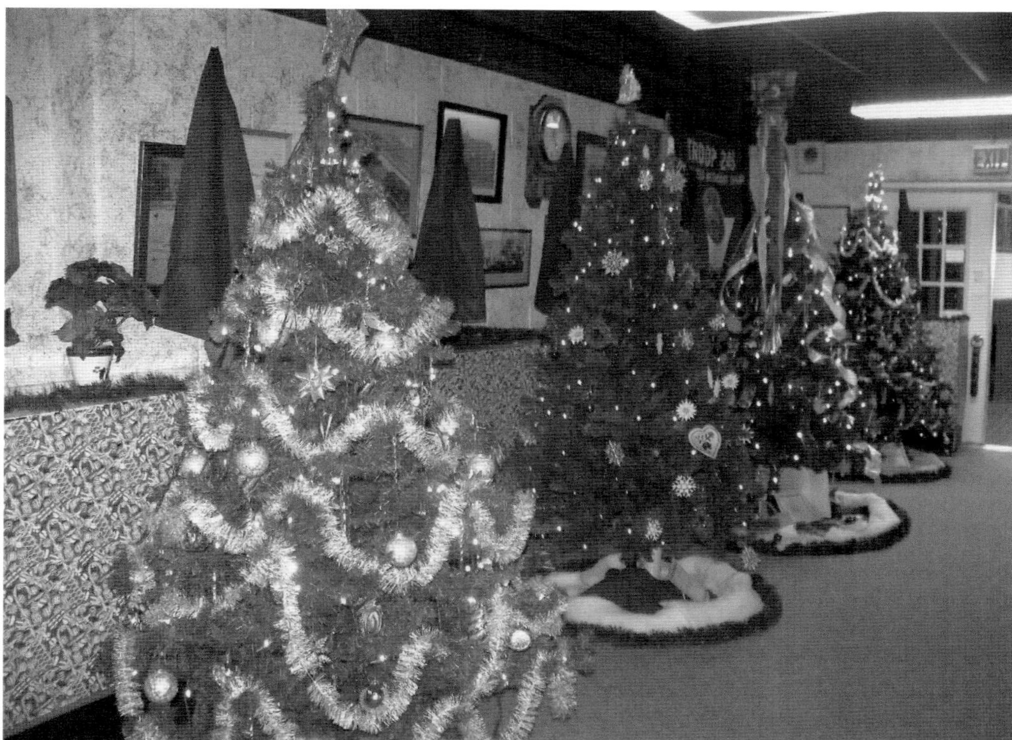

The Festival of Lights is an annual exhibit at the Lansing Historical Society. (Author's collection.)

INDEX